4 515185

THE ECONOMICS
OF THE SPECIAL TAXATION
OF CHAIN STORES

This is a volume in the
Arno Press Collection

SMALL BUSINESS ENTERPRISE IN AMERICA

Advisory Editors
Stuart Bruchey
Vincent P. Carosso

Research Associate
Eleanor Bruchey

See last pages of this volume
for a complete list of titles.

THE ECONOMICS
OF THE SPECIAL TAXATION
OF CHAIN STORES

Bruce Robert Morris

ARNO PRESS
A New York Times Company
New York • 1979

336.27
M 870

Editorial Supervision: RITA LAWN

———•———

First publication 1979 by Arno Press Inc.

Copyright © 1979 by Bruce Robert Morris

SMALL BUSINESS ENTERPRISE IN AMERICA
ISBN for complete set: 0-405-11457-5
See last pages of this volume for titles.

Manufactured in the United States of America

———•———

Library of Congress Cataloging in Publication Data

Morris, Bruce Robert, 1909–
    The economics of the special taxation of chain stores.

    (Small business enterprise in America)
    Originally presented as the author's thesis, University
of Illinois, 1937.
    Bibliography: p.
    1. Chain stores--Taxation--United States. I. Title.
II. Series.
HF5468.M6 1979   336.2'7   78-18971
ISBN 0-405-11474-5

THE ECONOMICS OF THE SPECIAL TAXATION
OF CHAIN STORES

BY

BRUCE ROBERT MORRIS
A.B., Western Reserve University, 1931
M.A., Ohio State University, 1932

THESIS

SUBMITTED IN PARTIAL FULFILLMENT OF THE REQUIREMENTS FOR THE
DEGREE OF DOCTOR OF PHILOSOPHY IN ECONOMICS IN THE
GRADUATE SCHOOL OF THE UNIVERSITY
OF ILLINOIS, 1937

URBANA, ILLINOIS

PREFACE

The object of this study is to determine whether special taxes on chain stores can be justified under any, or all of three motives; first, to regulate the chain stores; second, to equalize the burden of taxes of chain stores and independent stores under existing tax laws; and, third, to raise revenue.

Few matters have been as clouded with propaganda and sentiment as has that of the operations and policies of chain stores. The present study has been undertaken in the hope that it may present one phase of the chain-store question in an impartial light. An effort has been made to be as objective as possible and to point out both sides of the question and all limitations upon the data used.

The writer appreciates the helpful suggestions and advice given him by Professor M. H. Hunter, under whose supervision the thesis was prepared.

TABLE OF CONTENTS

LIST OF TABLES

CHAPTER I
INTRODUCTION

Chain stores are being subjected to taxation which does not apply to stores individually owned. Chain stores, as well as other stores, pay many different kinds of taxes. This study is concerned only with one type, the taxes which are imposed exclusively on chain stores. The object of this study is to determine the desirability of such taxes.

There could be two general approaches to this problem – the legal and the economic. The courts have reviewed a considerable number of cases which involve such special taxation of chain stores but this phase of the problem will not be touched, except briefly to point out the power of the states to levy such taxes. The economic validity of such taxation is the sole question to be considered here; the purpose is to attempt to find what is right from the economic standpoint rather than what is legal.

What is a chain of stores? There are many definitions of a chain system. In various definitions the following attributes have been said to characterize the chain-store organization:

> A group of stores;
> Decentralized location;
> Sales at retail;
> Central management;
> Central merchandising;
> Central ownership.

Not all writers would agree that all of the above factors are necessary to constitute a chain system. There is, first of all, considerable controversy as to how many stores it takes to make a chain. Many hold that as soon as a merchant opens his second store he must be considered as the operator of a chain. In an early case which dealt with the legality of the classification of chain stores for purposes of taxation[1], the Supreme Court of the United States declared that chains were distinct from other types of stores because of quantity buying, central warehousing, abundant supply of capital, unified advertising, specialized management, etc. If such factors were made the determining factors in the decision as to the number of stores necessary to constitute a chain it would require a considerable number of stores before a chain would be formed, just how many, no one knows. The Bureau of Census, faced with this problem, arbitrarily chose four stores as the minimum number necessary to form a chain. Since the most reliable data is from this source, this number of stores will be used in this study.

Not everyone agrees as to what constitutes a store. Gasoline stations and milk routes have tried to avoid the payment of special chain-store taxes on the ground that they are not stores. The Supreme Court has apparently settled the question in respect to gasoline stations by a decision that they are stores within the meaning of the law[2]. A store will be considered as any organization which sells goods or services at retail at a fixed place of business.

The outstanding characteristics of the chain, aside from the ownership of multiple outlets, are central ownership, central merchandising, and central management. It is the usual practice of chains to hire specialists to operate the business from central headquarters, who specify, in more or less detail, the methods of

1. State Board of Tax Commissioners of Indiana vs. Jackson, 283 U.S. 534-535 (1931).
2. Fox vs. Standard Oil Company of New Jersey, 294 U.S. 95 (1935).

the operation of the store, the merchandise to be carried, etc.
Most chains are centrally owned but many writers insist that mere
ownership does not make a chain. Many department stores are centrally owned but can not be considered chains because there is no
central determination of policy. A chain system, in the true sense
of the word, exists only when the merchandising, buying, and operating policies, or a good share of them, are centralized outside the
retail stores. The manner of operation, as well as the ownership
or number of units, is important to a distinction between chain and
other types of stores. The recognized chains differ in respect to
the extent of central operation but all have some part of their
policies determined centrally. The so-called voluntary chains,
which are not subject to the special chain-store taxes, are aggre-
gations of individual merchants, grouped together for cooperative
purchasing and for mutual aid in solving their management problems.
The extent of cooperation and mutual aid vary within wide limits.
The voluntary chains differ from chains in that no central organization can compel adherence to policies which might be determined
upon. If such organizations should develop a system of rigid central control, they probably would be classed as chains, even if
they were not centrally owned. As an example of this, gasoline
chains have been unable to avoid special taxation by the device of
a sale of their stores to the managers and a system of leases which
gave the central organization virtually the same control as before
over operating policies.

Centralized merchandising and operation makes for standardized goods and policies. Hence, each unit of a chain will be
found to carry substantially similar lines or classes of merchandise

and to operate by about the same methods.

Thus, a chain-store system can be defined as a group of four or more retail stores, which sells, under central ownership, management and merchandising policies, substantially similar lines of merchandise. Throughout this study this type of organization will be compared constantly to the so-called independent or individual store and contrasted with it. An independent store is one which is individually owned and whose policies are determined independently by the owner, subject to the command of no superior organization.

Some men, in an effort to reach out for more customers, have multiplied the number of their stores and formed a chain, rather than to follow the practice of others who have enlarged a single store and extended delivery service and remained independent. Chain systems may operate over a narrow or wide area. Those which operate solely in a narrow region are called local chains; those which operate in one part of the country, sectional chains; and those which operate over a considerable part of the country, national chains. There is considerable difference in the operating methods and policies of these three different types of chains, and it is important that such a distinction be kept in mind. Special chain-store taxes catch all three types, but with a different degree of severity. They fall most heavily on the concentrated local chain (for such taxes are usually imposed according to the number of units which are operated within a state). Moreover, the charges often made against chains do not apply with equal force to all types. A governmental policy which seems just as

applied to one may not be just when applied to another. As far as
the community is concerned, the local chain may be considered as an
independent.

A few warnings and qualifications must be made before the
nature of the problem involved can be clearly understood. There
are important limitations to this study which should be noted.

The problem is a difficult one to face impartially because of the publicity it has been accorded. There are many people
who have very decided views as to the policy which they think governments should take toward the chains. This is reflected in the
literature, much of which is obviously prejudiced and biassed. A
good deal of the argument has been based on sentimental grounds.
This is an economic and social problem and the matter should be
settled on such grounds.

Quantitative proof of the various contentions is practically impossible. The only substantial amount of quantitative
data which can be accepted as being true is contained in an investigation of chain stores made by the Federal Trade Commission
(1928-1933), the three census of retail business conducted by the
United States Bureau of Census (1929, 1933, 1935), the trial census of American business taken in 1927 by the Bureau of Census and
the United States Chamber of Commerce, and in isolated studies of
a particular problem in limited regions. None include data on all
the problems which are to be considered. None are free of faults.
In the Federal Trade Commission study a sample of one-half the
chain units was taken. This is a sufficient number for a sample
but it did not prove to be truly representative of conditions. The
Commission restricted its investigation to twenty-six lines of

business. In their study reports of one-half of the stores and over one-third of the sales of chains were of the grocery and meat business, a situation which gives undue weight to conditions in this line of activity. The study by the Commission also included a greater proportion of the larger chains than of the smaller[3] and was made in response to a request from the United States Senate that the Commission see if the chain stores were tending toward a monopoly. The purpose was to see if the chain store were harmful, and not to bring out its advantages. Any use of data except for its original purpose is fraught with danger.

The census enumerations for the three different years are not in all cases exactly comparable. Only rough comparisons can be made, so that no significance can be put on slight differences. Some things were enumerated in one year and not in another.

The trial census of 1927 was not representative and merely portrays conditions as they existed in the eleven cities for which the census was taken. The same defect of lack of representativeness must be charged to the individual studies that have been made. They only prove a point for a particular instance. Care must be taken against the formation of general conclusions from particular instances.

The fact that few writers can agree exactly as to what constitutes a chain store makes available data of little value for purposes of comparison. The enumerators often have not made it perfectly clear just what was to be counted as a chain.

3. For the Federal Trade Commission's own description of the limitations of its data see its "Letter of Submittal" to Volume I of its Chain Store Inquiry, Senate Document #31, 72d Congress, 1st session, pp. vii, viii, ix. 1932 Government Printing Office, Washington, D. C.

It is impossible to make an original statistical survey of the various problems which must be considered. Retailing, in 1929, was approximately a fifty billion dollar business and was carried on by over a million stores, including almost 150,000 chain stores, operated by over seven thousand chain systems. To get a statistical sample that would be adequate and representative would require the resources of the government.

Such data as has been assembled generally has been presented in the form of averages of mass figures. Comparison on the basis of averages is misleading, for an average gives no indication of how wide the extremes may be in the individual figures. The wider the extremes, the less valuable is the average. A few abnormal figures may make an average worthless. Particularly is this difficulty enhanced when it is remembered that the data on chain stores are not truly representative and when the average often includes figures from a large number of different lines of business; from all different sizes of enterprises; from all kinds of stores; from stores with different locations, both downtown and neighborhood; from stores in different towns each with a different cost of doing business, a different cost of living, etc.; and from stores of all types of price policy. Averages are always misleading, but when two or more different things are averaged, no valid comparison can be made. With these limitations upon the available data, the use of quantitative material must play a less important part in this study than is desired. Where allowances can be made for defects in the data, such material will be given; otherwise indirect evidence will be presented on each problem that arises.

The literature on the subject is full of the fallacy of

a condemnation of all chains because one particular chain was found wanting in some respect. One must distinguish between "all" and "some", that is, between statements which refer to all in a group or only some part of a group. There also is the danger of trying to prove a case by isolated instances. One probably can find cases where all the evils that have been charged to chains have occurred, but one could also find cases where just the opposite could be said. The interest of this study is not to see if certain evils do exist in isolated cases but to see if such evils are the usual practice of chains or, if they are so inherent in the chain form of organization that the only possible remedy is the elimination of multiple ownership and operation. The chains can not be praised or condemned in general terms, some chains may deserve extinction, others may enjoy the utmost respect. To classify all in the same category and to discuss them in general terms is unsatisfactory and unfair. The purpose of this thesis will be to examine the validity of the chain idea and not that of any and every particular chain.

The word, "chain", is often used synonomously with "cash-and-carry". The chains have usually adopted a policy of limited service, whereas the majority of independents have adopted a full-service policy. Some of the agitation against chains has been due to this confusion of terms. Some chains give service and some independents eliminate all services. This study is interested primarily in multiple ownership and not in the services offered (but both will have to be discussed since the words are closely tied in the public's mind). The problem to be considered is whether multiple ownership brings evils.

There is also a similar confusion in the terms, "multiple-ownership" and "absentee-ownership". The former usually involves the latter although not always, as in the case of a local chain. Moreover, absentee-ownership may be true of the independent store.

One must also guard against thinking of the chain problem in terms of the "A & P", "Woolworth", "J. C. Penney", etc., for these are only a part of the picture. There are many small chains which are affected by anti-chain taxes.

The chain problem centers around a few fields, particularly the grocery and drug business. Most of the literature deals with these fields and the discussion will be largely confined to them. Chains are strong in other fields, particularly in the variety and gasoline fields, yet there is apparently little opposition there. The same objections are not made to chains in these fields and yet chain tax laws hit them. The fact that some types are singled out for attack shows that the problem lies in particular methods rather than in the chain idea itself. This situation proposes another question: "Can one justify special chain taxes on all types of chains?"

There is a four-fold justification for studying the economics of special chain-store taxation: first, much of the literature on the subject is obviously unscientific and of a prejudiced character; second, the chain-store system is an important part of our retailing mechanism; third, the cost of the distribution of goods usually is looked upon as excessive; and fourth, special chain-store taxation has assumed considerable proportions.

Much of the opposition to the chain stores is honest and dignified, but much of it is unscrupulous. Many of the charges made against the chains are, no doubt, based on fact, but all too many of them are wild assertions based on no actual circumstance. These latter are born of prejudice. Unfortunately, all persons do not discriminate between legitimate statements and unfounded charges. The problem involved is to separate out the solid charges from the empty.

The people who oppose the chains are the individual merchants who are the competitors of the chains, middlemen of all types and those who depend upon them, politicians who aspire to office, and professional agitators, or as they prefer to be called, friends of the individual merchant.

A favorite device of chain opponents is to use words in connection with chains which are designed to connect the chain in the public's mind with undesirable evils, whether the chain has any such connection or not. Some of such stories deal with monopoly, Wall Street, destruction of equal opportunity and individual initiative, a system of slavery, "as bad as Sovietism in Russia", high finance, "other people's money". Much dust is raised around the issue by the inclusion into a discussion of chains of a statement of all the ills of the country with an indirect indication that the chains are responsible for such ills, although no direct charges are made[4]. A brief example of this is a statement by H. W. Huber, lieutenant-governor of Wisconsin in 1931: "Coincident with the chain-store invasion in the last few years (1929-1931) the resources of the state banks of Wisconsin have fallen off more

---

4. Outstanding examples of this are Givins, R. H., Jr., Outlawry of Chain Stores, 2nd edition. 1936, Better Business Publishing Company, Tampa, Florida; and Davis, T. C., Chain Stores vs. Farm Problem. 1933, George W. King Printing Company, Baltimore.

than $45,000,000. Before then they were increasing and in 1927
the increase was $22,000,000 . . ."[5] It would not take much thought
to deduce that chains were not the only factors which caused such a
decline, but the impression given is that chains are solely responsible. A number of changes have occurred in the last decade or so
when chains have seen their greatest growth and some of these changes have been for the worse. It is doubtful, however, that the
chains have been responsible for all of them. Something causes
such things and when people attach a blame it is only natural for
them to pick out something they do not like. For this reason the
opponents of the chains often single out the chains and blame them.

Many of the anti-chain statements are designed to appeal
to sentiment rather than to reason. Much is made of the hard-
heartedness of the chain in demanding cash, "even though the man
has a sick child at home who needs the food or medicine and has
not the ready cash with which to purchase them". Much is made of
the "menace to the community's prosperity", "the fly-by-night
peddler of bargains", "a soul-less and conscienceless machine",
"robots of distribution", "feudal, foreign-owned and operated system". More is made of the opposing virtues of independents.

> "He has been a good friend, a good Samaritan, a good
> citizen. He has contributed liberally to social, religious,
> and civic causes. He owned his home, his place of business,
> and perhaps a farm. He was a big taxpayer, interested in all
> politics , quick to fight corruption or dishonesty. He was
> proud of his town, because there he was born, married, raised
> his family, and at the end it was there he would be buried.
> It was a part of him and he loved it."[6]

5. Commercial Law Journal, Vol. XXXVI, (March, 1936), p. 151.
6. Fiske, R. T., "Retail Development", Proceedings of the National
Association of Commercial Organization Secretaries, 1933, p. 99.

This is a description which the individual merchant scarcely would apply to himself.

The worst of the anti-chain propaganda comes from those who wish to make political capital of the anti-chain movement or to commercialize on the prejudices of the persons whose interests are tied up with those of the so-called independent.

The anti-chain movement furnishes excellent campaign material and enables politicians to wax eloquent against Wall Street, predatory interests, and in behalf of the farmer, the home, the independent dealer, etc. To attack the chain is an excellent way to get votes for several reasons: the independents and their families far outnumber the chain employees; there is always an element which favors any bill aimed at "big business"; and since the movement is often clothed in revenue terms, many support it because they feel that they thereby escape taxes. The worst offenders are the local politicians, but M. M. Zimmerman has stated[7] that in 1931 twelve United States senators, seven United States congressmen, and seven state governors had spoken against chains. Most of the men in the latter groups are probably sincere in their belief that chains are harmful to the country but some of their statements smack of passion and prejudice[8].

7. The Challenge of Chain-Store Distribution, p. 5, 1931, Harper and Brothers, New York.
8. Wright Patman, congressman from Texas, - "So the point is whether or not you are going to give the people who built this country in times of peace and helped to save it in times of war an opportunity to get some of the benefits of it; or whether or not you are going to have absentee ownership from New York City control all the business of this Nation." Hearings Before the Committee on Judiciary, House of Representatives, 74th Congress, 1st session, "To Amend the Clayton Act," Part I, p. 194. (continued on next page)

Many men, who profess to help the independent out of
sympathy for him, oppose chains for their own profit. Many accuse
W. K. Henderson of Shreveport, Louisiana of such a motive. One
evening Henderson made a chance remark against chain stores over
his radio station. Congratulatory letters poured in and at once
Henderson recognized the possibilities of exploitation. He col-
lected large sums from contributions to his program, from the organization of a Merchants' Minute Men Association (getting about
10,000 members with twelve dollars dues, all of which went to Henderson to pay the overhead of the organization and the radio station), and from the sale of coffee at one dollar a pound (admit-
tedly more than it was worth). It is estimated that he made a
half-million dollars from his anti-chain campaign[9]. His popularity
passed when he tried to sell too many articles and so led the
people to believe that the whole thing was a scheme to make money
for Henderson. For a short period many imitators sprang up; for
example, Zimmerman[10] says that in 1931 there were twelve anti-
chain radio stations and twenty-four anti-chain publications. <u>Busi-
ness Week</u>[11] claims that, in 1930, 260 anti-chain associations

8. (cont'd) Governor F. D. Sampson of Kentucky, - "Many, if not all,
of these concerns are owned by foreign capital, are operated from
foreign offices, pay little or no taxes, deposit their moneys only
temporarily in our banks and move it on to headquarters through the
next mail, pay low salaries, sell inferior goods, give short weight
and measure, fight our local business people, invest in no property
and prey upon the public in divers and sundry ways, all to their
great profit and to the hurt of our people who pay the taxes."
<u>The Interstate Grocer</u>, St. Louis, Missouri, January 18, 1930, p. 1.
    Senator Royal S. Copeland of New York on July 17, 1930, -
"When a chain store enters a city block ten other stores close up.
In smaller cities and towns the chain-store contributes nothing to
the community. Chains are parasites. I think they undermine the
foundations of the country." <u>Chain Store Age</u>, August, 1930, p. 20.
9. Hardy, F. K., <u>The Special Taxation of Chain Stores</u>, p. 112,
Ph.D. thesis, University of Wisconsin, 1934.
10. <u>Op. cit.</u>, p. 5.   11. April 9, 1930, p. 22.

existed in thirty-five states. Independent merchants joined these associations in such great numbers that the National Association of Retail Grocers was forced to warn its members against the racketeering possibilities.

The chains have not been free of such practices themselves. The Patman hearings[12] brought out clearly that chains have extensive organizations to issue propaganda and have hired men to work in other organizations in their behalf. They have, at times, controlled statements which seem to come from an unprejudiced source. But chains are "on the spot" and have to be more careful than independents in what they say. Hence, their statements are more cautious and are restricted to an emphasis of low prices, increased value of property, steady employment, higher rents, etc.

Such literature tends to becloud the issue and make it difficult for the public to decide on an attitude toward chains. The type of discussion on this problem that has been general signifies nothing so far as the real merits of the case go, but tends to raise doubts in the minds of the people and thus accomplishes its purpose almost as well as would direct proof. Such statements win over many unthinking persons who base their actions on emotion and sentiment. There has been too much emotional misrepresentation and it is time that the problem was considered on the facts. That little attention has been accorded the problem can be seen from the fact that only one recent textbook on public finance devotes as

12. Hearings Before the Special Committee to Investigate the American Retail Federation, 74th Congress, 1st session, 1935, Government Printing Office, Washington, D. C.

much as two pages to chain-store taxation.

The chain system of merchandising is an important feature of our system of retail distribution. Anything that affects so important an agency deserves serious consideration.

Although the chain is usually thought of as a product of the last few decades, its origins are lost in antiquity. The first recorded chain is that established by On Lo Kass, a Chinese merchant who established a chain of a large number of stores in China as far back as 200 B.C. There are records which indicate central management and ownership of retail shops in Greece and Rome; for example, an inscription on a wall in Pompeii offered a five-year lease on some property which included nine hundred retail shops.[13] In the fifteenth century the famous Fuggers family of Augsburg, Germany established a chain of wholesale and resale houses. In the seventeenth century English foreign trade was carried on by monopolistic corporations which maintained chains of trading posts in the territories abroad and bought and sold under central control and management. In 1693 the Mitsui of Japan started a chain of apothecary shops which exists to this day.

The oldest chain on the American continent is the Hudson's Bay Company, established in 1670 as a string of trading posts and which still exists as a chain of ten department stores and 250 trading posts. The chain movement in the United States is supposed to have started with the establishment of The Great Atlantic and

13. Nystrom, P. H., "Retail Trade", Encyclopedia of the Social Sciences, (1934), Vol. XIII, p. 351.

Pacific Tea Company in 1858 but chains of stores were not unknown before that time[14]. Soon after the "A & P" (as everyone calls The Great Atlantic and Pacific Tea Company) was organized, several other chains started, mainly in the variety (five-and-ten) and grocery fields, but the hardships were many and expansion slow. Nearly all of the early chains developed from a single store and expansion came from reinvested capital. The chain period really belongs to the period which followed the World War, when expansion was so great as to amount almost to a revolution. Census figures show the number of units in chains of four or more units to have been 159,638 in 1929, 152,308 in 1933, and 127,483 in 1935. The sales in the latter three years were found to be: $10,740,385,205; $6,767,766,000; and $7,550,186,000. Estimates of the percentage of total retail sales made by chains show more clearly the expansion of chains: J. P. Nichols[15] quotes estimates of four per cent for 1921, six per cent for 1923, eight per cent for 1926 and twelve per cent for 1927. A further estimate from the same source places the chain proportion at 14.8 per cent for 1928. The government census show the ratios to be 19.2 per cent in 1929, 25.2 per cent in 1933, and 22.8 per cent in 1935.

When one looks at the total number of chain stores and

14. Jones, F. M., "Retail Sales in the United States, 1800-1860", Journal of Marketing, Vol. I, (Oct., 1936), p. 139 states that Andrew Jackson, in 1803, operated three or more stores in different parts of Tennessee and that, in 1811, the Worthington Mfg. Co., of Worthington, Ohio operated nine stores and manufactured woolen cloth, hats, caps, etc. Several other instances are also recorded. Benjamin Franklin operated a chain of seven printing shops with a separate partner for each, a form of organization which the present J. C. Penney Company formerly used with modifications.
15. Chain Store Manual, 1932 edition, p. 11, 1932, National Chain-Store Association, New York.

the sales volume of chains, the total looks impressive because the average reader has little idea of the magnitude of retailing. When one compares the business done by chains to that done by indepen- dents the picture is less impressive for the greatest percentage of the total retail trade ever done by chains in any one year amounted only to about twenty-five per cent.

Total figures, however, do not show the true importance of chains. The strength of chains in various lines of business, in different areas of the country, in different sized towns, and the proportion of business done by large and small chains, nation- al and local chains, are of more significance.

Chains handle almost every kind of portable standardized commodity, but are partial to the fields of foods, drugs, notions, dry goods, tobacco, shoes, restaurants, variety stores, and gaso- line filling stations. Chains are least effective in the fields of sporting goods, dairy products, paints and wall paper, electrical appliances, flowers, jewelry, hardware, gift and art goods, and luggage. Table I shows the proportions of business done by chains in a few fields.

It is significant that chains show their greatest develop- ment in the same fields in both the United States and Canada, as Table II shows. This indicates that there are products more sus- ceptible than others to the chain system of merchandising.

More significant is the proportion of business which chains do in certain lines of business in the large centers of popu- lation. Although anti-chain agitation is essentially a small-town movement, in no place does the chain have a stronger hold than in the large cities. The strength of the chains in certain lines of

business in the cities of the United States with a population of
500,000 and over is shown in Table III. The true chain problem
in these cities could be obtained only by an analysis of the extent of inter-chain competition in the various fields. The percentage done by the chains in the various lines is misleading, however, because the same product may be handled in several different
classes of stores; for example, the proportion of grocery store
sales made by chains is not the same as the proportion of grocery
sales made by chains because many types of stores other than grocery stores handle such products. The lines between the different
types of retail stores are growing hazier in almost every field.
On the other hand, in the fields in which chains operate they do
not handle all quality lines but operate mainly in the lower and
medium quality lines. Hence, the chain ratio in the items which
they do handle would probably be greater than an average of the
total business would show. These two complications can not be
accounted for from our present statistics so that the picture of
the chains' part in the retail world must necessarily be a rough
sketch. But it is sufficient to indicate the importance of the
chains.

Chain stores are of various sizes and range from the
large national chains to the four-store local chains. For all
practical purposes the operation of the local chains and their
economic effect is no different than that of the so-called independent store. To get a more accurate picture of the chains' part
in the retail trade the proportion of the business done by the
strictly local chain ought to be deducted.

In 1914 most of the chains were small. In a short while

Table I

CHAIN-STORE SALES: PERCENTAGE OF THE BUSINESS IN VARIOUS FIELDS
DONE BY CHAINS FOR SELECTED YEARS

Line of Business	Percentage of Business Done in Each Year		
	1929[a]	1933[a]	1935[b]
Accessories-Tires-Batteries	x[c]	x	23.8
Cigar Stores and Stands	25.1	33.9	35.8
(groceries and meats) Combination Stores	32.2	43.7	39.1
Department Stores	16.7	23.9	26.7
Drugs	18.5	25.1	28.8;15.4[d]
Family Clothing	27.3	20.3	20.6
Filling Stations	33.8	35.5	21.5
Furniture	14.2	14.2	13.5
Groceries	45.7	45.0	38.2
Hardware	x	4.1	4.3
Lumber and Building Material Dealers	x	x	23.8
Men's Stores	21.2	22.0	21.0
Radio Stores	19.1	15.6	23.1
Restaurants and Eating Places . . .	13.6	14.9	14.5
Shoe Stores	38.0	46.2	50.0
Women's Apparel	22.7	23.4	25.2
Variety	89.2	91.2	90.8

[a] Bureau of Census, Census of American Business, 1933, "Chains and Independents", p. 2-A. 1935, Government Printing Office, Washington, D. C.

[b] Bureau of Census, Census of Business, 1935, Vol. IV, "Retail Distribution", "Types of Operation", p. 9. 1937, Government Printing Office, Washington, D. C.

[c] The symbol, "x", is used when the figures do not permit of comparison.

[d] Drug stores with fountains and drug stores without fountains.

---

several veritable giants appeared, such as the "A & P" with over

fifteen thousand stores and a sales volume of one billion dollars

a year in 1929; "Woolworth", with almost two thousand stores and

one-quarter billion of sales; and J. C. Penney & Company, with al-

most 1,500 stores and $225,000,000 in sales. Particularly in 1926,

a year in which there were many mergers and consolidations, did the

Table II

CHAIN-STORE SALES: RANK OF LINES OF BUSINESS IN THE UNITED STATES
AND CANADA, ACCORDING TO VOLUME OF SALES DONE BY CHAINS IN 1933

Line of Business	Rank in United States	Rank in Canada
Grocery and Meat	1	1
Variety	2	2
Filling Station	3	3
Drug	4	4
Restaurant	5	6
Shoe	6	7
Women's Apparel	7	13
Motor Dealer	8	5
Men and Boy's Apparel	9	10
Furniture	10	12
Cigars and Tobacco Stands	11	9
Household Appliances	12	11

Source:
Phillips, C. F., "The Chain Store in the United States and
Canada", American Economic Review, Vol. XXVII, (March, 1937),
p. 90.

---

average size of the chain systems increase. When one thinks of a
chain store, he usually thinks of a unit of some nation-wide chain,
such as "A & P", "Woolworth", "Walgreen", or "Penney". The typical
chain organization is not the huge, national chain but the small
local chain.

A better picture, however, of the importance of the big
chains is shown by a list of the number of stores operated by chains
in different-sized groups in each field of business. Table IV
summarizes this data. In only relatively few fields do the large
chains dominate, such as in tobacco, groceries and meats, dry goods
and apparel, variety stores, and drugs. The smaller chains dominate such fields as unlimited-price variety stores, men's ready-to-
wear, men's furnishings, women's accessories, dry goods, furniture,

Table IV

SIZE OF CHAIN STORES: PERCENTAGE DISTRIBUTION OF THE NUMBER OF CHAIN STORES OPERATED IN VARIOUS LINES OF BUSINESS BY CHAINS OF VARIOUS SIZE FOR 1727 CHAINS WHICH MADE RETURNS TO THE FEDERAL TRADE COMMISSION, 1928

Line of Business	Percentage of Chain-Store Units Operated by Chains of Different Numbers of Stores							
	2-5	6-10	11-25	26-50	51-100	101-500	501-1000	Over 1000
Grocery	1.5	1.9	4.0	6.8	6.9	34.1	24.1	20.0
Grocery and Meat	.6	.7	1.3	1.6	3.3	12.6	3.9	76.0
Meat	10.1	12.9	16.0	25.3	13.8	21.9		
Confectionery	7.6	7.2	22.6	24.5	19.8	18.3		
Drug	20.9	7.9	11.9	4.5	17.0	11.8	26.0	
Tobacco	.7	1.8	5.2	.8	2.5	8.3		80.7
Variety ($1 limit)	2.7	4.0	2.4	6.5	3.4	29.0	11.8	40.2
Variety ($5 limit)	27.2	21.5	32.8	18.5				
Variety (unlimited)	25.9	31.8	42.3					
Men's Ready-To-Wear	25.5	29.8	26.5	18.2				
Women's Ready-To-Wear	25.4	19.1	23.9					
Men's and Women's Ready-To-Wear	20.0	16.2	15.4	41.2	31.6			
Men's Furnishings	36.2	16.5	34.8	12.5	7.2			
Women's Accessories	12.6	8.4	45.5	33.5				
Hats and Caps	7.4	1.9	10.8	24.9	32.6	22.4		
Millinery	5.7	9.8	23.4	16.9	22.6	21.6		
Men's Shoes	2.8	4.6	6.1	15.0	50.2	21.3		
Women's Shoes	13.3	7.9	25.1	32.3	21.4			
Men's and Women's Shoes	11.1	8.7	17.8	7.8	17.4	37.2		
Dry Goods	76.4	13.6	10.0					
Dry Goods and Apparel	15.6	12.0	7.1	5.8	2.8			56.7
Department Store	11.8	6.7	7.8	4.6		69.1		
General Merchandise	27.4	32.6	15.6		24.4			
Furniture	54.5	9.1	16.4	20.0				
Musical Instruments	24.6	23.2	32.6	19.6				
Hardware	45.5	26.8	9.9	17.8				

Source:
Federal Trade Commission; Chain Stores, Scope of the Chain-Store Inquiry, p. 18. Senate Document # 31, 72d Congress, 1st Session. 1932, Government Printing Office, Washington, D. C.

musical instruments, and hardware. A good deal of the chain volume
in certain lines is handled by essentially local stores.

In only one census, that of 1929, did the Bureau of Census record the proportion of business done by local, sectional, and national chains. Table V shows the proportion of business done in certain fields by single-store independents, two- and three-store independents, local, sectional, and national chains. The so-called chain problem exists in the business done by the sectional and national chains. Only in the variety, grocery, combination grocery and meat, shoe, and filling-station fields did the sectional and national chains do as much as one-fifth of the total business in 1929.

The percentage done by sectional and national chains varies by states. To avoid too burdensome a table the percentages of the total business done in each group of states, rather than the data for each separate state, is given in Table VI. With the percentage done by local chains counted as business done by independents the chains do not seem to dominate the business of any section of the country. The largest percentage done in any one state by sectional and national chains combined was in Massachusetts where they did 16.36 per cent of the total business.

There is evidence of concentration of the chains in certain sections of the country, particularly the sections east of the Mississippi River and north of the Ohio, and on the Pacific Coast. Table VII shows the ratio of business done by all chains in every state for the three years in which a business census was taken. It will be noted that the states in which chains do the greatest

Table V

CHAIN-STORE SALES: PERCENTAGE OF BUSINESS DONE IN THE UNITED STATES
BY TYPES OF OPERATION IN SEVENTEEN KINDS OF BUSINESS, 1929

Line of Business	Type of Operation						
	Single Stores	Two- and three-store Independent Branches	Local Chains	Total Independent	Sectional Chains	National Chains	Total Chain
Department Stores	60.79	11.51	2.57	74.87	2.03	11.96	13.99
Variety	8.12	1.65	2.67	12.44	5.67	81.78	87.45
Men's and Boys' Clothing and Furnishings	66.57	11.35	8.45	86.37	6.53	6.18	12.71
Family Clothing	56.76	14.70	7.69	79.15	11.60	8.00	19.60
Women's Ready-To-Wear	58.27	16.00	4.08	78.35	10.12	8.51	18.63
Shoe	42.51	11.01	11.04	64.56	8.58	18.33	26.91
Furniture	68.28	15.65	8.74	92.67	5.00	.42	5.42
Radio and Music	66.59	12.44	11.34	90.37	4.10	3.66	7.76
Grocery	46.07	2.49	10.66	59.22	10.48	24.56	35.04
Combination (grocery and meat)	57.35	5.75	8.80	71.90	5.62	17.80	23.42
Restaurants	78.34	7.74	6.72	92.80	3.85	3.06	6.91
Cigar	67.23	6.25	5.34	78.82	.60	19.18	19.78
Filling Stations	55.09	7.18	9.64	71.91	17.16	7.06	24.22
Coal, Wood, Ice	71.42	8.63	11.50	91.55	6.82		6.82
Drug	71.59	9.57	7.84	89.00	2.72	7.93	10.65
Hardware	87.76	6.83	2.30	96.89	.08	.61	1.41
Jewelry	78.16	14.81	3.80	96.77	1.52	1.07	2.59
Total	64.11	8.84	6.71	79.66	4.46	8.06	12.52

Source:
   Bureau of the Census, Fifteenth Census of the United States, Distribution, Vol. I, Part I, "Retail Distribution",
   P. 71. 1932, Government Printing Office, Washington, D. C. (Figures for all other types omitted.)

Table VI

CHAIN-STORE SALES: PERCENTAGE OF THE TOTAL BUSINESS DONE IN VARIOUS SECTIONS
OF THE COUNTRY IN 1929 BY TYPES OF OPERATION

Section of the Country	Type of Operation						
	Single Stores	Two- and three-store Independent Branches	Local Chains	Total Independent	Sectional Chains	National Chains	Total Chain
United States Total	64.11	8.84	6.71	79.66	4.46	8.06	12.52
New England	64.46	11.28	5.80	81.54	6.54	8.52	15.06
Middle Atlantic	64.46	9.33	7.79	81.58	5.69	8.23	13.92
East North Central	63.89	8.29	7.42	79.60	3.59	9.99	13.58
West North Central	62.32	7.17	4.47	73.96	3.88	6.43	10.31
South Atlantic	66.35	6.88	4.36	77.59	4.49	8.20	12.69
East South Central	62.64	6.83	3.17	72.64	2.37	7.44	9.81
West South Central	64.04	8.18	6.89	79.11	2.70	5.71	8.41
Mountain	67.44	8.87	4.85	81.16	4.50	6.92	11.42
Pacific	62.93	12.05	9.68	84.66	4.55	6.81	11.36

Source:
Bureau of the Census, Fifteenth Census of United States, Distribution, Vol. I, Part II, "Retail
Distribution", pp. 36-37. 1932, Government Printing Office, Washington, D. C. (Figures for
all other types omitted.)

Table VII

CHAIN-STORE SALES: PERCENTAGE OF THE TOTAL RETAIL BUSINESS DONE BY ALL CHAINS
IN EACH STATE OF THE UNITED STATES IN 1929, 1933, 1935

State	Percentage of Business Done By All Chains		
	1929	1933	1935
Connecticut	21.1	27.5	24.5
Maine	13.7	18.5	19.6
Massachusetts	23.8	30.8	28.9
New Hampshire	16.1	22.3	20.6
Rhode Island	24.2	29.5	26.2
Vermont	10.5	17.6	18.3
New Jersey	22.5	27.3	25.1
New York	23.9	27.8	25.0
Pennsylvania	21.2	29.0	24.9
Illinois	23.6	30.6	29.3
Indiana	19.0	27.0	24.3
Michigan	23.5	30.0	25.3
Ohio	21.7	28.1	24.0
Wisconsin	16.5	19.5	17.6
Iowa	15.0	20.8	17.7
Kansas	15.9	21.3	17.8
Minnesota	13.5	17.8	15.1
Missouri	18.0	22.3	20.4
Nebraska	13.0	17.9	16.5
North Dakota	13.1	18.2	15.9
South Dakota	13.9	21.4	18.1
Delaware	16.5	23.9	19.9
District of Columbia	26.3	28.4	29.7
Florida	17.5	24.9	22.2
Georgia	17.0	21.3	18.7
Maryland	18.8	20.4	19.2
North Carolina	16.1	22.0	19.8
South Carolina	13.1	17.6	16.2
Virginia	16.4	20.6	19.2
West Virginia	17.4	21.9	21.3
Alabama	14.5	17.9	16.7
Kentucky	15.2	22.1	19.5
Mississippi	7.5	12.3	11.1
Tennessee	14.8	19.5	17.9
Arkansas	11.5	14.1	12.3
Louisiana	13.2	18.5	17.8
Oklahoma	18.2	22.4	21.4
Texas	16.4	19.2	18.0
Arizona	21.6	27.2	22.2
Colorado	15.9	19.6	22.3
Idaho	20.7	23.1	19.9
Montana	15.1	16.9	14.8
Nevada	10.3	19.0	15.2
New Mexico	13.6	16.1	15.9
Utah	17.5	24.5	22.2
Wyoming	12.2	15.4	14.7
California	23.1	27.7	25.7
Oregon	16.5	19.3	17.7
Washington	18.4	21.3	18.7

Source: Bureau of Census, Census of Business, 1935, op. cit., p. 43 ff.

percentage of business are almost without exception the industrial
states. Chains tend to do a large percentage of the business where
there are the greatest number of inhabitants per square mile or
where a few large cities contain the bulk of the population. It is
significant, too, that in ranking the states according to the number of chains per 100,000 population the Federal Trade Commission
found an unmistakable correlation with the ranking of states according to the proportion of individuals who filed federal income-
tax returns.[16]

Almost two-fifths (39.8 per cent) of the business done
by chains in 1933 was done in the five states of New York, Pennsylvania, Ohio, Illinois, and Massachusetts while another twenty
per cent (20.3 per cent) was added in New Jersey, California, Michigan, Indiana, and Missouri. Although these are also among the most
populous states, the percentage of total population found in these
states is 50.6 per cent for the ten states (as against 60.1 per
cent of the chain business), and 30.3 per cent for the five states
with the most chains (as against 39.8 per cent of the chain business). Hence there is an unmistakable tendency for chains to concentrate more than population. Similarly, the twelve states with
the lowest proportion of chain business (Nevada, New Mexico, Wyo-
ming, Delaware, Vermont, Idaho, Utah, Arizona, New Hampshire, North
Dakota, South Dakota, and Montana) are the least populous states.
These states contain 4.9 per cent of the total population and
do 4.0 per cent of the chain business. In practically all of

16. Federal Trade Commission, Chain Stores, State Distribution of
Chain Stores, p. 19. Senate Document #130, 73d Congress, 2nd session. 1934, Government Printing Office, Washington, D. C.

these latter states, however, the local chains do a large share of
the business.   There seems to have been a tendency for chains to locate in the more populous areas and gradually to work out to the less
populous and less densely settled areas and to the smaller communities.

The chain store is essentially an urban institution and
concentrates in the large towns, or in groups of small towns located fairly close together.   This tendency is affected by such
things as the closeness of other large towns, the average income of
the people, the strength of independent competition, etc.   Table III
shows clearly how the chains dominate the trade in certain lines of
business in the larger cities.   Table VIII shows the percentage of
business done by chains in different-sized cities in relation to the
proportion of population contained in those cities.   The chains do
a larger proportion of the total business in cities than in smaller
towns.   Not only is the chain an urban institution but it also tends
to operate more in the central sections of cities than in the out-
lying districts.

The high cost of living is a vital problem.   High prices
have brought the question as to whether the distributive system is
as efficient as it might be.   Consumers see that the cost of production has decreased and that the cost of marketing has increased.
So pronounced are these trends that marketing costs are often looked
upon as one of the greatest sore spots of our economic system.   Increased efficiency in the distributive system is being demanded today as never before, and every part of the mechanism is being tested
to cut down the total cost of selling.

Studies show that marketing takes one-half of what the
consumer pays for many goods.   It was estimated in 1929 that the

Table VIII

CHAIN-STORE SALES: PERCENTAGE OF RETAIL BUSINESS DONE
BY CHAINS, AND PERCENTAGE OF TOTAL POPULATION
IN DIFFERENT-SIZED CITIES, 1933

City-Size Groups	Percentage of Total Population	Percentage of Sales Made by Chains
500,000 or more	17.0	26.0
250,000 to 500,000	6.5	11.0
100,000 to 250,000	6.1	9.0
All over 100,000	29.6	46.0
75,000 to 100,000	1.8	3.0
50,000 to 75,000	3.5	5.0
30,000 to 50,000	3.9	5.0
20,000 to 30,000	3.2	4.0
10,000 to 20,000	5.6	7.0
5,000 to 10,000	4.8	7.0
2,500 to 5,000	3.8	5.0
All Cities 2,500 to 100,000	26.6	36.0
All Other Areas	43.8	18.0

Source:
Bureau of the Census, Census of American Business, 1933, op. cit.,
"Stores and Sales by Size of City", p. 1.

total marketing costs amounted to $39,423,000,000 and production

costs to $36,169,000,000 or that marketing costs accounted for 52.2

per cent of the total price of goods.[17] Distribution costs run as

high as two-thirds of the total selling price of some products. Re-

tailing is the most expensive step in the distributive set-up. Mar-

keting, and retailing in particular, is one of the last remaining

fields where the value of the dollar may be increased. Anything which

helps to cut down this cost deserves serious attention. Anything

which affects the cost of distribution is vitally important to the

consumer - and also to the producer, for every dollar saved in dis-

17. Converse, P. D., The Elements of Marketing, Revised Edition,
p. 10; 1935, Prentice-Hall, Inc., New York.

tribution means a possible lowering of the selling price of the good and an increase in the demand for it. Mass production can be maintained only by the maintenance of a low selling price. The progress in production has made a study of distribution necessary.

It can not be inferred that all the cost of marketing is wasted. The consumers are demanding more and more things of the distributive system, things that cost money, such as an increased variety of goods, more style and fad merchandise, sales in smaller quantities and in packages, and more service. Expenditure on functions that are demanded can not be classed as waste. There is waste only when the function could be performed at a lower cost. Then, too, the machine age has dropped many new problems on the door step of distribution. Increased specialization and localization of production has increased marketing costs, particularly transportation and demand creation, but the consumer is not necessarily injured, for while such new production techniques may necessitate increased marketing costs, they may so decrease production costs as actually to result in a saving.

We can not escape the just cost of distribution but the last word in distributive efficiency has not been said. Considerable waste does exist. Dr. Julius Klein, of the Department of Commerce, is quoted as saying that a conservative estimate of the waste in distribution would be fifteen per cent.[18] On the 1929 basis of the total cost of distribution this would mean a waste of about six billion dollars annually, an amount which could well be used in purchasing additional automobiles, radios, etc., to say

18. Ibid., p. 24.

nothing of needed food and clothing. The National Business Survey Conference[19] estimated marketing wastes of eight billions of dollars. It often has been said that, with all the study that has been devoted to production production methods in the United States are scarcely fifty per cent efficient. If this is true of production, what must be the case in marketing to which little attention has been given until the last two decades!

Although on every hand cries arise to ask for lower costs of distribution and for more efficient merchandising, special taxes are being placed on an important agency of retailing with no great evidence that the effects of such taxes on the cost of living and the cost of distribution have even been given a thought. The chain is an example of a new device to attack distribution costs. Whether the chain is the key to the problem is not settled, but the chain has contributed much and deserves consideration. No organization which affords a real service to the public ought to be penalized by adverse legislation. If the chains are doing a good job of marketing, it is time that the subject of their taxation be investigated. One of the objects of this study will be to see if the chain-store system leads to more orderly and less wasteful marketing. The problem is to see if the public would lose if the chain form of organization should be eliminated or seriously handicapped.

The chains are subjected to a considerable number of special taxes. Twenty-two states[20] (the laws of three states, Del-

19. Quoted by Lyons, R. W., "Chain-Store Laws Valid - What Then?" Chain Store Progress, Vol. III, (July, 1931), p. 1.
20. See Appendix A for a list of the provisions of these taxes. In addition to the twenty-two laws now in existence Maine repealed her law in the summer of 1937 and Wisconsin allowed hers to expire by limitation in July, 1937.

aware, Virginia, and Tennessee are, however, sometimes not classified as anti-chain taxes) and a number of localities have such
taxes. The number has been increasing steadily. Eight laws were
passed in 1935, some of which, however, merely amended or repealed
older laws. There was little activity along such lines in 1936,
which was an off-year for most state legislatures. In the list of
states which have special chain-store taxes several facts stand
out: first, with only a few exceptions, the states where the chains
do the largest percentage of business do not have special chain
taxes; second, the greatest anti-chain movement appears to be in
the South, the northern states of the North Central group, and in
the Mountain group of states, regions where chains are in the minority (and were when the laws were passed); third, there is an aston-
ishing diversity in such laws and no two states have the same schedule of rates; and fourth, the rates of such taxes are increasing
constantly.

Two general methods are used to tax chains, a graduated
license tax based on the number of stores and a graduated gross
sales tax, (the Delaware tax on foreign corporations which operate
stores within the state and the Virginia tax on wholesale houses
which supply their own stores are exceptions and often are not
looked upon as chain-store taxes). The graduated gross sales tax
is of doubtful constitutionality so that a graduated license tax is
the most popular form. The graduated sales taxes that still exist
will probably be stricken from the books by the courts.

No uniformity exists in the tax laws. Of the present
license laws, seven exempt the first store while thirteen require a
small payment, which ranges from one to ten dollars. The maximum

rate varies from ten dollars (plus a gross sales tax) in South Dakota to $750 in Texas. The minimum number of stores required to
give the maximum rate varies from eleven in South Dakota and Montana to 501 in Pennsylvania (501 in Louisiana also, but the basis
of the tax is the number of stores in the chain rather than the
number which are operated in the state). Table IX shows how the
amount charged for different numbers of stores varies from state to
state. The tax on two stores varies from three dollars in Mississippi to one hundred dollars in Florida; on five stores, from twenty
dollars in Minnesota to $500 in Florida; on ten stores, from forty-
five dollars in Minnesota to $2,000 in Florida and Idaho; on twen-
ty-five stores, from $198 in South Dakota to $12,500 in Idaho; on
fifty stores, from $446 in South Dakota to $25,000 in Idaho; and on
200 stores, from $1,946 in South Dakota to $125,582 in Texas.

Just as much variation exists in the exemptions granted.
Twelve of the twenty states with so-called anti-chain taxes exempt
stores which deal mainly in petroleum products; two states (Alabama and Iowa) exempt ice plants; Minnesota exempts stores ninety-
five per cent of whose sales are fuel, lumber, building materials,
or grains; North Carolina exempts whoesale dealers in motor vehicles
and automobile equipment and supply dealers who sell at wholesale;
Texas exempts the building material business, oil and gas well sup-
pliers, and manufacturer-owned outlets; Mississippi exempts gas
and electrical appliance stores maintained by utilities; Iowa and
Wisconsin exempt a large number of fields.

The states in which chain taxes are most severe, Colorado,
Florida, Idaho, Michigan, Mississippi, and Texas, were all passed
too late (excepting Colorado and Idaho) to afford a picture of the

Table IX

CHAIN-STORE TAXES: TOTAL TAX BILL IN THE STATES
UNDER SPECIAL CHAIN-STORE TAX LAWS FOR SELECTED NUMBERS OF STORES

State	Number of Stores						
	1	2	5	10	25	50	200
Alabama	$ 1.00	$ 16.00	$ 61.00	$ 173.50	$ 1,050.00	$ 3,862.50	$ 20,737.50
Colorado	2.00	12.00	82.00	532.00	3,382.00	10,882.00	55,882.00
Florida[a]	10.00	100.00	500.00	2000.00	10,000.00	20,000.00	80,000.00
Idaho	5.00	20.00	275.00	2000.00	12,500.00	25,000.00	100,000.00
Indiana	3.00	13.00	43.00	143.00	1,193.00	7,943.00	30,143.00
Iowa[b]	x	10.00	25.00	50.00	375.00	2,250.00	25,500.00
Kentucky	2.00	22.00	82.00	182.00	932.00	3,432.00	25,932.00
Louisiana[c]	10.00	20.00	50.00	100.00	325.00	775.00	5,900.00
Maine	1.00	6.00	21.00	61.00	386.00	1,636.00	9,136.00
Maryland	x	5.00	20.00	120.00	1,870.00	5,620.00	28,120.00
Michigan	x	10.00	70.00	320.00	2,570.00	8,820.00	46,320.00
Minnesota[d]	x	5.00	20.00	45.00	370.00	2,245.00	25,495.00
Mississippi	x	3.00	33.00	93.00	698.00	6,323.00	51,323.00
Montana	2.50	5.00	55.00	175.00	625.00	1,375.00	5,875.00
North Carolina	x	50.00	200.00	560.00	2,060.00	6,410.00	34,785.00
Pennsylvania	1.00	6.00	21.00	71.00	571.00	2,821.00	49,071.00
South Carolina	5.00	15.00	75.00	275.00	1,725.00	5,425.00	28,925.00
South Dakota	1.00	6.00	21.00	46.00	196.00	446.00	1,946.00
Texas	1.00	7.00	82.00	332.00	3,082.00	13,082.00	125,582.00
West Virginia	2.00	7.00	22.00	72.00	497.00	2,672.00	34,250.00
Wisconsin	x	25.00	100.00	350.00	2,600.00	8,850.00	46,350.00

a Plus a gross receipts tax for each store of one-half of one per cent of sales (originally made graduated).
b Originally a gross sales tax, also, but this part was declared unconstitutional.
c The rate is based on the number of stores wherever located.
d Plus a gross sales tax.

effect of such taxes on the census figures. In Idaho the percentage of business done by chains dropped from 23.1 per cent in 1933 to 19.9 per cent in 1935; in Colorado the chain proportion rose from 19.6 per cent to 22.3 per cent in the same years; Florida has had a succession of increasingly severe taxes, yet the chains' ratio has tended to fluctuate almost exactly with that of the national average; Indiana made her tax much more drastic in 1933 than in 1929 yet the chain ratio was seemingly little affected.

If chain tax laws are not sufficiently drastic to hamper the chains, it has not been through the fault of the sponsors of such laws; for example, a bill was introduced in Illinois which provided for a tax of $1000 a store on all stores over ten, and a city ordinance of Hamtramck, Michigan placed a tax of $1000 a store on all stores over four. Probably well over five hundred anti-chain tax bills have been introduced into the various legislatures since the first one in 1925. Forty-nine have been passed and twenty-two remain in operation. The others have been superseded by new laws, repealed, or declared unconstitutional.

Anti-chain taxes exist in a number of cities, the most significant of which are those in Bainbridge, Ga., Charleston, W. Va., Clarksburg, W. Va., Durham, N. C., Fredericksburg, Va., Little Rock, Ark., Portland, Ore., Spartanburg, S. C., and Wheeling, W. Va. The maximum rates for these cities are presented in Table X. Ordinances have also been enacted in St. Louis, Mo., Knoxville, Tenn., Maplewood, Mo., Red Bank, N. J., Hamtramck, Mich., Charlotte, N. C., Aberdeen, Wash., and Capital Heights, Md., but most of these have been voided or repealed. One man estimated that in 1932 some three thousand cities were preparing chain-tax bills.[21]

21. MacDonald, G., "Chain Tax Bills Now in Almost Every Legislature", Progressive Grocer, September, 1932, p. 24.

Table X

CHAIN-STORE TAXES: MAXIMUM RATE OF CHAIN-STORE TAXES
IN VARIOUS CITIES

City	Maximum Rate	Minimum Number of Stores Where Maximum Rate Applies
Bainbridge, Ga.	a	a
Charleston, W. Va.	$250	76
Clarksburg, W. Va.	200	21
Durham, N. C.	50	2
Fredericksburg, W. Va.	250	2
Little Rock, Ark.	125	13
Portland, Ore.	50	21
Wheeling, W. Va.	300	21

a A gross sales tax with a maximum rate of five per cent to
apply on sales above $70,000.

Source:
Nichols, J. P., Retailers' Manual of Taxes and Regulations,
p. 78 ff. 1935, Institute of Distribution, Inc., New York.

The anti-chain movement has taken numerous directions
and special taxation is only one phase of the campaign against
chains. The most important of these are resale price maintenance
laws, or the so-called "Fair Trade Acts", the purpose of which is
to stop price-cutting by allowing the manufacturer to set the retail price of his product. Such laws have been enacted in many
states. Numerous unsuccessful attempts have been made to get such
laws enacted into federal law. Somewhat similar laws in California,
Nevada, and North Carolina prevent the location of a store next to
another established store and the quotation of prices below the
legitimate cost of doing business. The California law prevents
price discrimination in different parts of the state unless based
on the quality of the goods, the quantity sold, or the cost of
transportation.

Several proposals have been made in the federal and state

legislatures to take away the chains' buying advantages. Some propose to prevent manufacturers from selling directly to retailers,
some would take away all quantity discounts, some would give the
wholesaler a functional discount, etc. The Robinson-Patman Act,
which was enacted into national law in 1936, prevents excessive
quantity discounts, and forbids advertising allowances except where
earned, and brokerage allowances altogether.

Some bills have tried to eliminate certain chains entirely; for example, a Pennsylvania statute confined the ownership
of drug stores to licensed pharmacists and provided that in case of
corporate ownership every stockholder must be a registered pharma-
cist (declared unconstitutional); Maryland in 1927 made it unlawful
for anyone to own or operate more than five stores in Allegheny
Company (voided by courts); a bill was introduced in Iowa to eliminate all corporations which sold at retail; a bill was considered
in Florida to prevent the ownership by one person of more than one
store which sold a similar line of goods. A Colorado law, aimed
primarily at drug stores, prevents the operation of a restaurant
in connection with any other business. In 1928 Cedar Rapids, Iowa
passed an ordinance which forbade chain stores to sell cigarettes.

The chains have carried nearly every such law to the
courts so that a body of opinions which concern such taxes has
grown up. The following is a brief account of the law on the subject as it appears to one not trained in the law.

As far as the courts are concerned, chain-store tax laws
must stand or fall on their legality as revenue measures for they
are written ostensibly for such a purpose. The courts have re-
peatedly said that they would not question the motives of the leg-

islature but would accept such laws at their avowed purpose.[22] All
attempts to bring the laws into question under the police power have
failed. Accordingly, the states do not have to prove the necessity for the regulation of chains but only have to justify the classification of chains for purposes of taxation. The courts do not
have to decide whether chains are beneficial to the public; the
question is whether chain stores may be lawfully taxed. Whether
the courts would uphold a chain tax passed avowedly as a police
measure is a matter of doubt. A sufficient social interest would
have to be found but it is possible that the courts would permit
the legislatures to be the judge of the social interest or policy
involved. It is unfortunate that the anti-chain tax laws could not
have been tested on such grounds. The courts act on the assumption
that the legislature had a proper motive and that, if the legislature acts within the power conferred, no court can declare such a
law invalid merely because it appears to the court unwise or unjust.
The courts will inquire, not into the motive, but into the results
of such actions to hamper the chains.[23] If the Federal Government
should pass such a tax, it would have to be a true fiscal measure
unless it should fall within the sphere of the other federal powers.
If it were not a true tax, it would be treated as an improper attempt to extend the federal sphere.[24] States, with their residual
powers, do not have to meet this requirement .

These special taxes are contested usually on the ground
that they deny equal protection of the law in that one form of

22. Fox vs. Standard Oil of New Jersey, 294 U.S. 101 (1935).
23. See C. F. Smith Co. vs. Fitzgerald et al, 270 Mich. 259, (1935).
24. Mount, K. L., "Chain-Store Taxation Before the Courts", George Washington Law Review, Vol. IV, (March, 1936), p. 346.

business is taxed more than its competitor. The courts uniformly hold that the equal protection clause was not intended to force the states to adopt an iron rule of equal taxation. It does not prevent the classification of subjects for taxation and a heavier tax on one class than another, provided only that that classification be reasonable and not arbitrary, that the classification apply alike to all under the same circumstances and subjects no one to an arbitrary exercise of power, and that the classification has a relation to the purpose of the legislature. Thus, if the distinctions between two groups are genuine, the courts will permit classification for purposes of taxation.[25] It is necessary only that the class taxed actually be a "class" and include all persons similarly situated, although there must be some "real and substantial difference" to constitute a "class". If this is satisfied, the courts will not inquire into the propriety or justness of the tax. The problem is to define a "real and substantial difference". However, the courts have been liberal in their interpretations.

In the application of these principles to the taxation of chain stores, the courts have seen a sufficient distinction between the chain-store method of doing business and the independent method to render classification lawful. In the early cases[26] which did not get to the United States Supreme Court, the state courts declared such classification unconstitutional, largely because the tax was made to apply to chains of six stores (or some like number) or more. The courts were unable to see a difference between a

25. See Louis K. Liggett et al. vs. Amos et al., 104 Fla. 609,(1932)
26. See F. W. Woolworth Co. et al. vs. Harrison et al., 42 Ga. 432 (1931). Great Atlantic and Pacific Tea Co. vs. Doughton, 196 N.C. 145 (1928).

chain of six stores and one of five stores except that of the number of stores, a basis insufficient to uphold a classification.
The Supreme Court of North Carolina in Great Atlantic and Pacific
Tea Company vs. Doughton (1928)[27] made such a holding but the same
court in 1930[28] upheld a tax on chains of two or more stores and
apparently saw a real and substantial difference between merchants
who operated two or more stores and those who operated only one
store.

The first case to appear before the United States Supreme
Court was State Board of Tax Commissioners of Indiana vs. Jackson[29]
which has become the controlling case in chain-store taxation. The
district court[30] had held the Indiana law (a progressive license
tax graduated on the number of stores) unconstitutional on the
grounds that the tax was determined solely by the number of stores
and that the differences said to exist between chains and independents (lack of interest of chains in the community, failure of
chains to encourage their employees to maintain homes in the community, taking money out of town, etc.), although they might be
true of some chains, were not true of all chains. On appeal to the
Supreme Court, the decision was reversed on a five-to-four decision. Justice Roberts, in the majority opinion, found many points
of difference between chains and independents.[31] He conceded that
some of these characteristics might also be found in large independents but that all combined existed only in chains. He pointed out
that others had found these differences to be so great that they

27. Op. cit.
28. Great Atlantic and Pacific Tea Co. vs. Maxwell, 199 N. C. 433,
(1930).
29. 283 U. S. 527 (1931). 30. District Court, Southern District of
Indiana, 38 Fed. (2nd) 652 (1930). 31. See page two.

had found it desirable to operate under chain methods. If such differences exist in men's practices, the difference between chains and independents must be so substantial as to form a legitimate basis for government action. Succeeding cases have followed this decision.[32] There is no doubt that differences do exist and that the federal constitution will not prevent the imposition of graduated license taxes on chain stores, graduation being permitted on the grounds that if two stores exhibit the peculiar characteristics, a greater number of stores will possess these same characteristics in greater degree.[33] Whether such laws contravene the state constitution must be determined in the state courts as the law is passed. The state courts have uniformly upheld such laws.

Graduated gross receipts taxes have not met such a kind fate at the hands of the courts. The controlling case is Stewart Dry Goods Company vs. Lewis et al.[34] in which a Kentucky law was held invalid. After the district court had upheld a classification based on gross sales,[35] the United States Supreme Court reversed the decision. Justice Roberts again delivered the majority opinion. He argued that gross sales bear no relation to profits and that there was no proof that the graduation was adjusted to net earnings (on the face of the measure the thing taxed) and that "It exacts

---

32. Great Atlantic and Pacific Tea Company vs. Maxwell, op. cit.
    Fox vs. Standard Oil of New Jersey, 294 U. S. 87 (1935).
    Louis K. Liggett et al. vs. Lee et al. 288 U.S. 517 (1933).
33. Columbia Law Review, January, 1931, "Chain-Store Taxation Constitutional Question", p. 153.
34. 294 U.S. 550 (1935).
35. Moore et al. vs. State Board of Charities and Corrections, Court of Appeals of Kentucky, June 19, 1931, 40 S.W. (2nd), 349 (1931).

from two persons different amounts for the privilege of doing exactly similar acts because one has performed the act oftener than the other." A classification based on the number of sales was held, therefore, to be an unreasonable classification. The precedent was followed in a case which involved the graduated gross sales feature of the Iowa anti-chain tax bill.[36]

The courts have indicated also that once states obtain the right to tax there is no limitation to the extent to which they might go in exercising such power. The court said in Fox vs. Standard Oil of New Jersey (1935),[37] "When the power to tax exists, the extent of the burden is a matter for the discretion of the lawmakers . . . . Even if the tax should destroy a business, it would not be made invalid or require compensation upon that ground alone." Where classification is reasonable, the state may burden any business which it wishes to discourage; the power to tax involves the power to destroy.[38]

Although the power to impose license taxes has been upheld, some peculiarities of such laws have been questioned. The right to exempt certain classes of chain operators has been upheld if such exemption is reasonable.[39] Gasoline stations are stores within the meaning of the law unless specifically exempt.[40] An

36. Valentine vs. Great Atlantic and Pacific Tea Co., 299 U.S. 32, (1936). 37. Op. cit., pp. 99-100.
38. Quoting Justice Roberts in Stewart Dry Goods vs. Lewis, op.cit., p. 563, (1935), "Once the lawfulness of the method of levying the tax is affirmed the judicial function ceases. He deludes himself by a false hope who supposes that if this court shall at some future time conclude the burden of the taxation has become inordinately oppressive, it can interdict the tax."
39. Gasoline stations can be exempted on the grounds that they are subject to other special taxes. See J. C. Penney Co. vs. Diefendorf, 54 Idaho 374 (1934) and C. F. Smith Co. vs. Fitzgerald, op. cit.
40. Fox vs. Standard Oil of New Jersey, op. cit., p. 95.

extra tax imposed on chains which operate in more than one county (a Florida law) is an unlawful classification.[41] An Idaho law, which classified chains according to the number of stores in each chain and taxed every store in the chain (instead of the number added in each group) at the highest rate was upheld.[42] In the same case a property tax off-set clause was upheld. A Louisiana law, which based the classification for fixing the rate on the number of stores wherever located, although the tax is imposed only on the number within the state, was upheld.[43] A Virginia law, which placed special taxes on distributing houses which supplied goods to their own stores, was upheld.[44] The power of municipalities to impose special taxes upon chain stores depends on the authority granted by the state to levy such taxes.[45]

The opponents of the chains make much of the fact that the Supreme Court of the United States has upheld such laws and assert that it proves the wisdom of such taxes. Such a belief is not justified for the courts have been careful to point out that they are not passing on the desirability of such taxes.[46] The existing court decisions can not be used as anti-chain arguments.

The power of the states to levy license taxes is so well settled that the only recourse of the chains against such taxes is to the people. As was pointed out in one case,[47] the laws could

41. Louis K. Liggett et al. vs. Lee et al., 288 U.S. 517 (1933).
42. J. C. Penney Co. vs. Diefendorf et al., op. cit.
43. Great Atlantic and Pacific Tea Co. vs. Grosjean, 57 Sup. Ct., 772 (1937).   44. Great Atlantic and Pacific Tea Co. vs. Morrissett et al., op. cit.   45. Great Atlantic and Pacific Tea Co. vs. City of Spartanburg, 170 S. C. 262 (1933).
46. In Fox vs. Standard Oil of New Jersey, op. cit., 101, "We have no thought in anything we have written to declare it (such a law) expedient or even just, or for that matter to declare the contrary." In State Board of Tax Commissioners of Indiana vs. Jackson, op. cit., p. 537, "It is not the function of this court in cases like the present to consider the propriety or justness of the tax . . ."
47. C. F. Smith Co. vs. Fitzgerald et al., op. cit., p. 358-359.

possibly have been more just and more wise from an economic point of view but that is a question that concerns the legislatures. The legislature, however, must give an account of its stewardship to the people. If chains are to have relief from such taxes, they must persuade the people of the unsoundness of the legislation and not the courts. The same competitive advantages which the courts found sufficient to justify classification might, moreover, be made into very persuasive arguments to present to the voters. The purpose of the succeeding chapters will be to see what the legislatures should do about taxing chains.

CHAPTER II

THE CHAIN STORE AND THE CONSUMER

There are three motives for the levy of special taxes on chain stores: to discriminate against them or to regulate them, (depending on whether it is the chains' or their opponents' viewpoint that is being considered), to raise revenue, and to equalize existing tax burdens.

Although some revenue is raised from chain taxes, the main purpose is not revenue. As a general rule this legislation has been introduced under the guise of revenue measures but in most cases it has been designed to place an extra burden on the chains so that either they would be forced from business or would lose most of their competitive advantages. Most chain opponents deny that regulation or discrimination has been their objective but a few have admitted the regulatory motive.[1] Charles A. Beard has expressed his opinion of chain-store tax laws in the following words:

> "All this is being done under the guise of taxation. The purpose is not revenue but the destruction of multiple retail establishments. It is not claimed that they are monopolies to be dissolved as contrary to public policy. They are not denounced as insanitary and subject to the police power. They are declared to be enemies of the public -- especially local retail merchants - and are to be destroyed by heavy taxation."[2]

---

1. The Kentucky gross sales tax was first introduced under the title: "An Act to restrain the unfair competition of chain stores and in aid of individual merchants of the commonwealth." Before it was passed it was changed to read: "An Act relating to revenue and taxation imposing an excise tax. . . ."
2. "Planning and Chain Stores", New Republic, Vol. LXXIII, (Nov.30, 1932), p. 67.

The Wisconsin tax was passed to equalize the burden of existing taxes on chain and independent stores. It was felt that the existing taxes, especially the general property tax, were falling more heavily on the independents. Under this motive the special taxes were designed to make the chains pay their fair share of taxes.

The plan of this study will be to see whether special chain-store taxes can be justified under any of these three motives. Chapters Two through Five will deal with the regulatory motive, and Chapter Six with the other two. Certain charges are made against chains as the basis for the need of regulation. These charges will be taken up one by one to see what truth there is in them.

Opposition to the chains comes largely from their competitors and is based on fear of their large size, their financial support, their scientific methods, and sometimes their unfair tactics. The charges made against the chains take various forms, from inefficiency in the performance of the retail function to unfair competition and unwanted social and economic evils.

It is charged that the chain store does not perform the economic functions of retailing as well as does the independent and that the chains exploit the public. The supposed low prices of the chains are said to be only imaginary, considering quality and service, that chain prices are lower than independents' prices on goods which can be readily compared, but that, on unidentified brands chain prices are higher than those found in individual stores. It is claimed that the chain store sells goods that are inferior in quality and that they take every opportunity to short-

change or short-weight their customers. The chains are said to sell
smaller packages of many products than do the independents. The
chains do not give all the services that a customer needs and wants;
the customers are forced to go to the store and pick out their own
goods; they cannot get the things they need unless they pay cash
for them, and they must carry their purchases home no matter what
the weather conditions may be. Moreover, the chain limits the
variety of products available to the customer and offers only standardized goods.

It is also claimed that the chains are disturbing the
existing channels of trade, and are crowding out the independent
retailer, the wholesaler, and the salesman. Supposedly, these
classes render a high service to the community and are indispen-
sable to it and should be preserved, even if at heavy cost. Bad
as it is to eliminate these classes, it is even worse if done by
unfair methods of competition. It is charged that the chains are
not driving out their competitors because of superior efficiency
but because of unfair methods of competition, particularly local
price-cutting and the loss leader policy.

The ability of the chains to undersell the independents
is said to be due, not to efficiency, but to the ability of the
chains, by reason of their large size and ready cash, to beat down
the prices of the things they buy. The biggest advantage of the
chains is their ability to buy their merchandise at very low prices,
lower than cash and quantity discounts would warrant. They supposedly do this by the lure of large orders and when finally they
are purchasing a large share of the manufacturers' output, they refuse to renew their purchases except on their own terms. It is

charged that the chains force their employees to work long hours at a driving pace and for low wages, and thus gain a competitive advantage which the independent is too considerate to meet. The chains are said to make full use of banking service and do not maintain a very large balance, or make use of the loan service. Nor do they pay a fee large enough to recompense the bank. By the use of the same pressure the chains supposedly can obtain their advertising, and their insurance and can rent their buildings on better terms than can the independents.

The chains are said to have bad economic and social effects. Inasmuch as they are absentee-owned, they have no interest in the local community and do nothing to build it up. In fact they actually tend to destroy it since they take money out of the community, hire outside help, do not buy locally, do not own any local property, refuse to cooperate in local charities and activities, and take so much of their employees' time that the employees are unable to participate in normal home, religious, and community life. The chain stores are supposed to be tending to create great monopolies in retailing, a situation that would give a few corporations centralized power over the lives of the people and would concentrate the wealth of the nation in a few Wall Street hands. Chains also are said to restrict individual opportunity, to prevent the individual from setting up in business for himself, and to leave open only one opportunity, that of being an employee of an impersonal corporation. The greater sales of the chains per employee, moreover, tend to bring about technological unemployment.

From the point of view of the consumer the test to be applied to the chain store is whether the chain supplies the public's needs efficiently and economically. The only justification any organization of any kind can have for continued existence is that it do a job well. The ideal distributive system would be the one that would bridge the gap between producer and consumer at the least possible cost. Success in retailing should depend upon a performance of the retail functions better than anyone else could do. The consuming public wants the organization that can best meet its needs.

The retailer has two main functions; to act as a purchasing agent for the consumer and a selling agent for the producer. He also has a secondary function of participation in community activities. From the consumers' viewpoint the function of a retail establishment is to anticipate the public needs, assemble the goods, and store them until the customer wants them. In other words, the retailer is the purchasing agent for the American household. Perhaps the most difficult retail function is the purchase of goods that the consumer will want. The retailer must estimate the consumers' demands in advance, must know the sources of a great variety of goods, quantities, sizes, etc. He must decide on only a relatively small number of the products and qualities and sizes available and pick those that will please the customers best. He must then furnish such goods, plus whatever services are demanded, at a convenient place, in convenient quantities, at the right time, and at the least possible cost.

It must be emphasized that there are different grades of customers, that not everyone wants the same products, the same brands, the same qualities, the same services. It is the job of the retailer to meet the needs and wishes of the class of people to whom he caters.

Regardless of who performs these duties of the retailer
they must be performed. The one who renders these functions satisfactorily earns what the public pays him. If the chains do a good
job of retailing, they deserve consideration; if they do not, there
is no harm involved in their extinction. They can justify their
existence only by the fulfillment of a need. So, also, with the
independent.

What does the public look for in a retail store? The
consumer usually looks for the following: low prices, plainly
marked, for the grade of merchandise bought; good qualities of the
grade bought; an efficient performance of the services desired; convenient location; a complete stock of fresh, clean goods; a variety
of selection in the stock; courtesy and friendliness in dealing;
honesty and reliability of the dealer; a clean and sanitary, neat
and orderly store, well-ventilated and lighted, with neat and
pleasing clerks and attractive displays. The prices, stock, and
services must be adjusted to the clientele for there is considerable
variation in the quality of merchandise and amount of service demanded, and in the price which people at different income levels
are willing to pay. The retailer must first determine just whom he
wishes to serve and cater to him in these respects.

Two questions must be answered before anything else is
discussed. Does the chain store perform its functions well? Does
it give the public what it wants? The things that must be considered are price, quality of goods, services given, convenience of
location, completeness and variety of stocks, anticipation of demand, honesty, cleanliness, etc.

Chains compete largely on the basis of price and claim to

sell their goods more cheaply than do the independents. Numerous
studies, as indicated in Table XI, seem to show that the chains afford a saving of approximately ten per cent. All of these studies
were made in single localities, and practically all were limited to
a small number of nationally advertised products (in order to obtain
prices on identical things). The independents object that the use
of branded products in such studies gives an unfair advantage to the
chains for these are the very products which the chain uses as foot-
balls in their price wars. Chains are said to use nationally advertised goods as loss leaders and to make up for this loss by higher
prices on items which can not readily be identified.[3] Chains, of
course, deny this charge and counter with the statement that it is
on these items that the independent makes the greatest effort to
meet the chains' prices. The effect of quality studies on the values
received at chains and independent stores will be discussed below.
Another limitation of these studies involves the validity of average
prices. The chain is given a different price advantage if different
types of averages are used and if different weights are assigned the
commodities studied. Also, the investigators have averaged the
prices of stores of different sizes, of different locations, and of
different service policies. There have been no studies made of the
prices of chains and independents which are located next to each
other and which perform the same services.

The studies are correct only for a limited purpose, that
of a comparison of prices on a small number of branded items, but
the unanimity shown is indicative that the chains are somewhat underselling the independents. Experience and the independents' own fears
tend to back up this conclusion. If the chains did not sell more

3. See Chapter III for a discussion of this point.

cheaply than the independent, at least on some articles, it could
not hold its trade.[4] It must offer a price advantage to induce customers to go without the services which the independent has to offer.
The chain seems to retain its customers. Surveys of the reasons why
customers patronize chain stores show that the great majority do so
because they feel they get a saving in price.[5] The independents'
own insistence that anti-chain tax laws be passed "to equalize competition" tacitly admits such a differential.

The method followed in the various studies differed little
in most cases. Those of R. S. Vaile,[6] R. S. Alexander,[7] the Federal
Trade Commission,[8] E. Bjorklund and J. L. Palmer,[9] C. F. Phillips,[10]

---

4. The Federal Trade Commission, in its final report ("Final Report
on the Chain Store Inquiry", 74th Congress, 1st session, Sen. Doc.
No. 4. 1935, Government Printing Office, Washington, D. C., p.66)
concluded, "The economic advantage of chain stores in the way of
lower selling prices is illustrated by the fact that in the smaller
towns, at least, people of lower incomes patronize chain stores to
a greater extent than do those with larger incomes. . . . The most
frequently stated reason for patronizing chain stores is lower prices and no other one reason for buying from chains approaches it in
importance."
5. R. S. Vaile, "Grocery Retailing", University of Minnesota Studies
in Economics and Business, No. 1, 1932, University of Minnesota
Press, Minneapolis, reports that price as a patronage motive is mentioned almost exclusively in connection with chain stores.
    In Trade Information Bulletin, No. 575, of the Bureau of For-
eign and Domestic Commerce, 1928, Government Printing Office, Washington, D. C., ninety-four per cent of the people who replied said
chain prices were lower.
    In a study by P. D. Converse, Bulletin of the National Associa-
tion of Teachers of Marketing and Advertising, (Oct. 1931) p. 19,
55.4 per cent of the customers who patronized national or sectional
chains did so predominantly because of price.
6. "Grocery Retailing", op. cit.
7. "A Study in Retail Grocery Prices", 1929, New York Journal of
Commerce, New York.
8. Chain Store Inquiry, Vol. IV, "Prices, Margins, Etc. of Chain and
Independent Distributors", 1933, Government Printing Office, Washington, D. C.   9. "A Study of the Prices of Chain and Independent Grocers in Chicago", School of Commerce and Administration Studies, Vol. I, No. 4. 1930, University of Chicago Press, Chicago.
10. "Chain, Voluntary Chain, and Independent Grocery Store Prices,
1930 and 1934". Journal of Business, Vol. VIII. (1935), pp. 143-149.

M. D. Taylor,[11], R. L. Furst,[12] D. Dowe,[13], M. Rush,[14], M. R. Brewster,[15], P. D. Converse,[16], all dealt only with nationally advertised products. In practically every case the articles selected were not representative either of the stock carried by the usual grocer or of the weekly food budget of the individual. Commodities were selected which were standardized and which were carried in a large number of stores. A few studies were representative of only a limited section of the city studied. R. S. Alexander limited his survey to poor and Jewish neighborhoods; D. Dowe to wealthy neighborhoods and residential districts; and P. D. Converse eliminated most of the small neighborhood stores. In the rest, either the entire city or a supposedly representative sample was taken. Different types of averages and different weights applied to the commodities produced only minor changes in the final result.

Several studies on branded drugs bring out the same results. In February, 1934, J. H. Cover[17] found a price differential in favor of chains over cash-and-carry independents on forty-two

11. "Prices in Chain and Independent Grocery Stores in Durham, North Carolina". Harvard Business Review, Vol. VIII, (1930), pp. 413-424. "Prices of Branded Grocery Commodities During the Depression", Harvard Business Review, Vol. XII, (1934), pp.437-449.
12. "Grocery Chains in Fort Wayne, Indiana", M. A. Thesis, School of Commerce and Administration, 1931, U. of Chicago, Chicago.
13. "A Comparison of Independent and Chain Store Prices", Journal of Business, U. of Chicago, Vol. V, (1932), pp. 130-144.
14. "Consumers Save Ten Per Cent in Albuquerque Stores", Chain Store Progress, Vol. III, (Nov. 1931), p. 4.
15. "Chain and Independent Store Prices in Atlanta", Georgia Business Review, January 31, 1931, pp. 9-10.
16. "Prices and Services of Chain and Independent Stores in Champaign-Urbana, Illinois." Bulletin of the National Association of Teachers of Marketing and Advertising, October, 1931.
17. "Retail Price Behavior", Studies in Business Administration, Vol. V, No. 2. School of Business, University of Chicago, 1935, U. of Chicago Press, Chicago.

drug products, including prescriptions, proprietaries, toiletries, and sundries, of six per cent in Atlanta and fifteen per cent in Washington, D. C. The Federal Trade Commission[18] found chain prices to be lower than the prices of independents by 22.72 per cent on 226 branded drug items in Washington, D. C., by 20.35 per cent on 268 items in Cincinnati, by 20.69 per cent on 212 items in Memphis, and 17.48 per cent on 256 items in Detroit.

E. Z. Palmer[19] and S. A. Larsen[20] tried to select a more representative list of goods, using personal judgment as a test of quality. The studies of E. G. Ernst and E. M. Hartl[21] and of J. H. Cover[22] included a large number of items, many of them unstandardized, and made no attempt to correct for possible quality differences. R. S. Vaile and A. M. Child[23] selected all non-standardized items and corrected the actual prices for quality differences.

In collecting the individual prices the investigators found a wide range in the extent to which chains were underselling the average independent on individual items. In some cases the average independent was equalling or bettering the chain price; in others, the independent sold as high as twenty per cent above the chains. The chains also differed among themselves. Although the average prices in each of the large chains was usually about the

18. Chain Store Inquiry, Vol. IV, "Prices, Margins, Etc. of Chain and Independent Distributors", 1933, Government Printing Office, Washington, D. C.
19. "E. Z. Palmer Finds Chains in Lexington 14.3 Per Cent Below Independents". Chain Store Progress, Vol. II, Sept. 1930, p. 4, ff. Also letter from E. Z. Palmer.
20. "Present Status of Chain Retailing". Quarterly Journal, N. Dak. University, Vol. XXIII, Winter 1932, pp. 109-124.
21. "Chains versus Independents", Nation, Vol.CXXXI, Nov. 12, 1930, pp. 517-519.
22. Op. cit.
23. "Grocery Qualities and Prices", U. of Minnesota Studies in Economics and Business, No. 7, 1933, U. of Minnesota Press, Minneapolis.

same, some would be much lower on a few items than the others. In
a comparison of chain prices with the average prices of certain independents it was found that the more efficient independents were
not being undersold (making due allowance for the cost of the services). Some independents probably sell as high as twenty per cent
above the chains, whereas some cash-and-carry independents, especially if they belong to a voluntary chains, may sell below the
chain. The Federal Trade Commission concluded that chain prices
were lower.

> "The Commission's study tends to establish the fact that
> on the average, chain stores can and do sell at prices which
> are somewhat lower than the prices charged by independent re-
> tailers or even cooperative chains. . . . On the basis of
> these studies, it may be definitely stated that chain-store
> prices on comparable standard-brand merchandise average sub-
> stantially lower than those of independent retailers."[24]

These studies prove, at the very least, that if the housewife is willing to shop to find the chain store which is quoting
the lowest price on each article and if she is willing to do without certain services, she can save a large amount on her food bill,
especially on the staple items. Moreover, by a careful selection
of specials she can make a surprisingly large further saving. It
is on the fast-selling items of large demand that the chains make
their greatest deductions.[25]

A comparison of chain and independent prices does not
tell the entire saving which the chain brings on standardized items.
There is no way to tell whether independent prices would be higher
if chain competition did not force down prices. On the other hand,

24. Chain Store Inquiry, "Final Report on the Chain Store Investigation", op. cit., pp. 28-29.
25. P. D. Converse, The Elements of Marketing, Revised edition,
p. 416, 1935, Prentice-Hall Inc., N. Y.

it is also possible that the chains have not lowered prices as much
as they are able, especially where severe inter-chain competition
does not exist. There is, of course, no evidence of this beyond the
large profits of chains.

The above studies offer little evidence as to whether the
independents are lessening the price differential between them and
the chain. It is generally felt that they are doing a somewhat better job in respect to price than five or ten years ago. The average
prices do not show this but the apparent contradiction is due to the
fact that a large number of small grocery stores have been opened
during the depression years. Each year sees more independents,
however, able to meet chain competition in price.

Only in the grocery and drug fields can price comparisons
be made. In the other retail lines products are so unstandardized
that comparisons are impossible. But the studies in the grocery
and drug fields do show that multiple ownership can bring certain
types of products to the consumer at a saving.

The price controversy, however, centers around the showing which the chain makes on unstandardized goods. The independent
sympathizers claim that here the chains make up for losses which
they incur on nationally advertised products which are said to be
sold below cost. The chains insist that they offer an even better
saving on their non-standardized products.

Only one study[26] has made an attempt to measure the difference in value of the products bought at chain and independent
stores. Here, non-identical but comparable canned goods were used.
Both a price index and a quality index were made and the two were

---

26. R. S. Vaile and A. M. Child, op. cit.

finally combined into a value index. Three tests of quality were
made; first, fifty homemakers were asked to rate the goods; second,
a group of expert buyers for wholesale houses and large institutions did the same; and third, a small committee of experts, with
some laboratory assistance, ranked the goods. Probably the most
outstanding feature of the study was that the homemakers ranked the
products almost exactly the same as did the experts, which shows
that consumers can protect themselves in respect to quality if they
will occasionally try competing brands and act on their own judgment. The study concluded that the chains showed a saving on this
type of good.

> "The prices charged in ownership chains are markedly
> lower, grade for grade, than the prices in other types of re-
> tail outlets. The average price of grade A products is 16
> per cent lower in ownership chains than in all the stores com-
> bined. Ownership chain store prices of grade B and grade C
> goods are, respectively, 10 and 20 per cent lower than the
> corresponding prices in all stores. These lower prices are
> offset in part by poorer quality. Ownership chain value,
> based on a combination of price and quality figures, is 14
> per cent higher for grade A products and nearly 10 per cent
> higher for all grades combined than the corresponding values
> in all outlets. . . . This finding with respect to price har-
> monizes rather closely with the studies of prices of identical
> goods and strengthens the conclusion that consumers may save
> about 10 per cent on their staple grocery expenditures by
> patronizing the cash and carry ownership chain stores."[27]

Chains do concentrate on the lower grades of merchandise,
largely because there is a greater volume of demand for such goods
than for the de luxe qualities. However, where there is a sufficiently large demand the chains will carry the higher grades of
goods. In the grades the chains do handle, however, they carry a
high quality of merchandise. Many persons can not afford to pay
the extra premium necessary to buy the finest quality products. It
would be a good thing if they could, but many families must be con-

---

27. Ibid., p. 13, 14.

tent with a lower standard of living and certain grades of goods are
put out to meet their needs. In most canned products definite grades
are established and a minimum quality required for each grade. Government machinery would keep chain products above this minimum. The
chain, however, has not been satisfied with the mere minimum, but
has gone on and required higher standards.

The quality question centers largely around the private
brands of the chains. It is contended that the chains induce people
into their stores by the use of loss leaders on nationally-known
merchandise and then persuade the customer to take the chains' own
brands, on which there is a liberal markup. There is no doubt that
the chains have a higher profit margin on their own goods than on
those of the national advertiser. Professor P. D. Converse reports[28]
the average percentage of gross margin on private brands in the grocery field (analysis of thirty-four commodities and 249 price comparisons) to be 23.1 per cent and the highest and lowest margins on
standard brands to be 19.0 per cent and 17.8 per cent respectively.
Similar figures in the drug field were: private brand average, 62.0
per cent, highest and lowest for standard brands, 33.6 per cent and
23.3 per cent; on toilet articles, 63.2 per cent, 38.9 per cent and
21.9 per cent. On the other hand, the private brands undersold the
standard brands in these fields by 12.3, 15.7, and 26.5 per cent
respectively. Assuming, for the moment, that the loss leader and
substitution policy is followed, is the consumer necessarily hurt
thereby? On the average, would the consumer lose by the use of the
private brands of the chain as over against the nationally advertised product at the prices charged by the average independent?

28. Marketing Notes, p. 66. 1933, Daniels and Shoaff, Champaign,Ill.

The chains can not afford to guess at quality. There has been so much agitation against them, and they are so much in the public eye, that any departure from this policy would immediately result in the loss of customer goodwill. The Kroger Grocery and Baking Company has set up the Kroger Food Foundation with an endowment of one million dollars to further research in the qualities of foodstuffs. The chains apply rigorous tests to all products which they buy; the manufacturers have found no buyer more insistent than the chains that quality be high; in fact, they often complain of the pressure the chains put on them.[29] The variety stores, which certainly give quality for the prices they receive, are constantly engaged in a study of how higher-priced merchandise can be made to sell at variety-store prices. The quality may not be as good, but many articles are made available to people who could not enjoy them before in any form. Chain buying specifications are extensive and constant checks are made on quality. In no other product is this shown more than in the case of butter. Poor butter will drive a customer away from a store quicker than almost any other factor. The chains have taken the lead in a demand that butter qualities be raised. One writer in a dairy paper says,

"My observations are that the chains are not only out to buy the best butter they can get but are ready to encourage any movement which will improve quality. Their consistent demands for quality stock have encouraged the creameries to improve the quality of their make more than any other single factor during the past few years. Without their big demands for quality butter there would have been far less incentive to supply top-notch goods."[30]

It costs money to get customers into a store for the first time.

---

29. See Chapter III.
30. The Dairy Record, (St. Paul, Minneapolis, March 13, 1929), Reprint from column, "The Market Viewpoint".

To keep them coming back the store must satisfy them, not only in price, but in service and other things as well. The fact that chain-store sales are not dropping off markedly indicates that the quality offered, in relation to the price, is satisfactory.

The Federal Trade Commission studied the quality of chain-canned fruits and vegetables.[31] They purchased a number of items in Des Moines, Memphis, and Detroit and had them graded. On vegetables the chains were only slightly below the nationally advertising manufacturers in the proportion of their cans grading "fancy", "extra-standard", and "standard". The chains showed a lower proportion of "fancy" fruits but a larger proportion of "choice". In both fruits and vegetables in the two highest grades the national advertisers had 79.1 per cent of their products, the wholesalers 75.1 per cent, the chains 74.5 per cent, and the cooperatives 73.3 per cent,[32] a fact which shows that the chains do not concentrate entirely on the lower grades. All the cans bought were scored and the averages recorded. Table XII shows the results of this scoring. From these average scores it seems that the average quality of the private brands of the chain stores compares favorably with those of other types of distributors. The chains' products showed less variation in quality than did those of the other brand-owners, that is, a consumer who buys a chain-store brand is more likely to obtain the quality specified on the label than if she bought a product with any other brand. Table XIII shows the percentage of cans which showed variations in grades. Professor N. H. Comish, a professor

31. Federal Trade Commission, Chain Store Inquiry, Vol. IV, "Quality of Canned Fruits and Vegetables", 72d Congress, 2d Session, Sen. Doc. #170, 1933, Government Printing Office, Washington, D. C.
32. Ibid., p. 10.

at the University of Oregon, says that the charge of inferior quality is of doubtful value.

"Indeed, several investigations conducted by the author
lead to the conclusion that on an average the chain handles
equally as high quality goods as comparable independents."[33]

It can not be assumed that the nationally advertised product is always a good bargain. The consumer may be paying too much
for reputation and a standardized product. In many cases she can
do as well or better in a chain brand. She can get a product which
is just as standardized from just as reputable a dealer. Mrs. I.
H. Engel, representing Consumer's Research, Inc., in a hearing before the United States Senate,[34] hit at the supposed superiority
of the nationally advertised product. She insisted that the general belief in the superiority of trade-marked and nationally advertised articles was quite unfounded as demonstrated by numerous
tests which were filed in the records. Also, such products sold
all out of proportion to the cost of the product or the reputation
of the manufacturer and were not always of standard quality. It
was also pointed out that large quantity buyers (supposedly the ones
able to conduct extensive tests) generally buy, not the heavily advertised brand, but a much lower-priced brand "which is essentially
the same product without the expensively-established name". Her
conclusion was that trade-marking was a great asset to the consumer
but that there was no excuse for a glorification of it. In several

33. N. H. Comish, Marketing of Manufactured Goods, p. 126, 1935, The
Stratford Company, Boston.

34. Hearings Before the Committee on Interstate Commerce, U. S. Sen-
ate, 72d Congress, 1st Session. On S. 97, Capper-Kelly Fair Trade
Bill, February 29, March 1, 2, 1932, pp. 174-183. 1932, Government
Printing Office, Washington, D. C.

hearings[35] representatives of R. H. Macy and Company, New York brought samples of nationally advertised goods and Macy's private brands, certified to be of similar quality, and showed that the latter possessed a great advantage in price. They admitted that they made a large profit on their private brands but denied that the consumer was being injured, especially in view of the high prices charged for nationally advertised products.

The above discussion is not expected to prove that all chain brands are superior to all manufacturers' brands. It shows that the quality of the products handled by chains is comparable to that handled by the independent stores and that the price differential between the two can not be explained on such a basis. In some products the chain, with its private brand, will have the advantage; in others, the independent, with a wholesaler's private brand, will have the advantage; in both, the nationally advertised product may be bought. It behooves the consumer to compare the different brands so as to find the one which gives the best value. By a proper distribution of her patronage she can make her dollar buy better goods.

Consumers, moreover, can protect themselves, as is shown by the Minneapolis study.[36] The fact that consumers buy chain goods to the extent of about ten billions of dollars a year indicates that the quality is satisfactory. The chain could not survive on inferior quality. The public will "take care" of any store which

35. Hearings Before Committee on Interstate and Foreign Commerce, House of Representatives, 64th Congress, 2nd session, On HR 13,568, Regulation of Prices, January 5-11, 1917, p. 124. 1917, Government Printing Office, Washington, D. C. Hearings Before the Committee on Interstate and Foreign Commerce, House of Representatives, 69th Congress, 1st session, On HR #11, Price Regulation for Trade-Marked Articles. Apr.22,23,1936, p.289ff;1926, Gov't Ptg. Off.,Wash.,D.C.
36. See page 56.

sells inferior goods. If a store grows in sales it is as a result of a growth in public confidence, and confidence is not built on poor values. Not all consumers can judge quality but the great majority of them can. To assume that chain success is based upon selling unknowing consumers low-grade merchandise would be the same as to say that most buyers do not know even approximately the value of merchandise. Most housewives could make a fairly accurate estimate in the case of goods they use constantly and it is in these lines that the chain concentrates. Hence, if people in large numbers buy chain brands, it can be assumed that they think they get as much for their money as they would if they bought competitive products. Tastes differ and no quality ratings can ever hope to decide what it is best for all consumers to buy. Some consumers will always decide against the quality tests. If a store can satisfy individual preferences, it meets an economic need.

Studies of patronage motives show that consumers have no objection to the quality of goods found in chain stores. A study by the Bureau of Foreign and Domestic Commerce[37] showed that five per cent of the people who patronized chain stores felt that the quality was higher, seventy-nine per cent said it was the same, and thirteen per cent said it was inferior. In various studies of patronage motives "quality of products" was not rated very high, which suggests that the quality offered by the different outlets was sufficiently similar that the consumers did not condemn one store and choose another on that basis.[38]

---

37. Op. cit., p. 24.
38. R. S. Vaile, "Grocery Retailing", op. cit., p. 48, reports only 25 per cent of the housewives gave quality as a reason for trading at neighborhood stores. R. Cassady and M. J. Ostlund, "The Re-
(Continued on next page)

Table XII

QUALITY OF CHAIN-STORE PRODUCTS: AVERAGE SCORES,
BY GRADES OF CANNED VEGETABLES AND CANNED FRUITS,
FOR SPECIFIC BRAND-OWNING GROUPS

Grades	Manufac-turers	Distributors		
		Wholesalers	Chain Stores	Cooperatives
Canned Vegetables				
Fancy	91.1	91.3	91.4	93.0
Extra Standard	82.9	83.5	82.3	81.2
Standard	72.2	74.3	70.9	73.0
3 Combined	79.1	79.7	79.6	80.0
Canned Fruits				
Fancy	91.1	91.7	91.2	91.5
Choice	85.5	85.6	86.7	85.6
Standard	76.4	74.3	75.5	75.1
3 Combined	84.7	85.6	86.6	84.2

Source: Federal Trade Commission, Chain Store Inquiry, Vol. III,
"Quality of Canned Fruits and Vegetables", 72d Congress, 2d Session,
Sen. Doc. No. 170, p. 12. 1933, Government Printing Office, Wash-
ington, D. C.

Table XIII

QUALITY OF CHAIN-STORE PRODUCTS: PERCENTAGE OF CANS
WHICH VARY FROM PRINTED LABEL, BY TYPE OF DISTRIBUTOR

Distributor	Vegetables	Fruits
Manufacturers	46.8	59.6
Wholesalers	36.9	50.0
Chains	29.2	25.9
Cooperatives	38.5	37.5
All	41.2	51.9

Source: Federal Trade Commission, Chain Store Inquiry, Vol. III,
Sen. Doc. No. 170, op. cit., pp. 15, 16.

Price, in relation to quality, is only one part of value.
When a consumer buys a product, she buys more than the physical
commodity. She buys also service, convenience, honest dealing,
cleanliness, adequacy of stocks, etc. All of these must be taken
into consideration in a determination of the value of a product
from different sources. It must be remembered that all people do
not want the same thing in a retail store. People differ as to the
amount of service, convenience, and variety of products which they
desire. Every store must adjust itself to a definite type of want
and can not meet the desires of all people. The question is not
whether the independent has more to offer than the chain but whether
many people want what each has to offer. In respect to service the
independent store and chain store are usually run on opposite principles. Is there a demand for each type of operation? If so,
does each type carry out its intended function properly?

Chains usually operate on a limited-service plan. The
Federal Trade Commission[39] found that approximately ninety per cent
of the business of chains was done for cash, 88.8 per cent was on
a no-free-delivery basis, and that 51.2 per cent of the chains accepted no telephone orders. Some chains do give full-service and
are apparently successful at it, as in the furniture business, but
for the most part limited-service is characteristic of the chain

---

38. (cont'd) tail Distribution Structure of the Small City", _Uni-
versity_ _of_ _Minnesota_ _Studies_ _in_ _Economics_ _and_ _Business_, No. 12,
1935, University of Minnesota Press, Minneapolis, found that in a
small town the residents ranked quality fifth in groceries and
fourth in drugs, whereas they ranked it first in ten of the others
and second in the remaining two. This indicates that grocery and
drug qualities must be so near alike in chains and independents that
it does not influence the purchaser one way or the other.
39. _Chain_ _Store_ _Inquiry_, Vol. II, "Service Features in Chain Stores",
73d Congress, 2d Session, Sen. Doc. No. 91. 1934, Government
Printing Office, Washington, D. C.

system.

A product which the consumer goes to the store to purchase, pays cash for, and carries home is a different commodity than one for which the order is taken by telephone, sold on a credit basis, and delivered to the customer's home. It takes money to perform such services and the customer is expected to pay for them. It is only natural that service stores should sell for somewhat more than do the non-service stores. How much this differential should be is a matter of controversy but liberal estimates place the cost of credit and delivery at about four per cent of sales.[40] This accounts for some, but not all of the price differential between chains and independents. It represents the consumers' wage for financing himself and for being his own delivery boy.

Although the service store is justified in adding such a charge, it is no criticism of the chain that it does not make such services available. Some people are willing to forego the enjoyment of such services if they are thereby able to save on the purchase price of the goods. For some people it would not be a saving to perform these marketing functions themselves, but some can well afford to go to the store and carry their own goods home. If the consumer feels that he can do these things cheaper than the retailer can do them, he should have an opportunity to do so. The ideal of the distributing system should be to get the marketing functions done as cheaply as possible. If the customer can do part of the functions more efficiently than the retailer, it is an economic practice for him to do so. The time of many people is so valuable that they can afford to pay the retailer to give them these extra

40. McNair, M. P., "Trends in Large-Scale Retailing", Harvard Business Review, Vol. X, (October, 1931), p. 287.

services. But it is not fair that all pay just so a few might enjoy such services. With the establishment of widespread organizations which sell on a non-service policy the consumer now has a
choice in the matter. She can select a store which renders any
type of service she desires. The fact that the different types are
well patronized indicates that different buyers do want different
amounts of service.

Although the chains eliminate many services, they perform the others efficiently. They make a special effort to wait
on customers promptly and courteously and to have the stocks arranged in a convenient manner. All chain units do not measure up
to a high standard in these matters, but only until the supervisor
can correct the situation.

It is charged that the chains obtain some of their advantage by giving short weights and by short-changing their customers. In choosing a store the customer wants honest dealing as
well as good merchandise. No store could exist long unless it
treated its customers fairly. The success of the chains has been
too sustained to support such a charge. Chain progress has been
too rapid to be based on deception.

No chain store organization would condone such a practice
on the part of its employees. They would realize that any manager
clever enough and crooked enough to steal from the public would
steal twice as often from his own organization. What the chain
would gain from the public would be more than lost in the necessity
for an increase in the checks on their managers. The chain store
has too much at stake to try to put one over on the customer. Its
success depends on goodwill. No chain would jeopardize this by the

adoption of a policy of cheating. The chains carefully watch for all cases of dishonesty.

Although the chains forbid such practices and make the employees responsible for their actions, it is often said that they force their managers to be dishonest by making them responsible for all shrinkage. On all commodities delivered to the stores in bulk the manager is expected to return an amount equal to the full weight times the price per pound. This does not allow for loss of weight due to evaporation of the moisture content or for slight overweights which are normally to be expected. Rather than be short and so have his wages reduced the manager is said to make it up on his customers.

Chain practice differs in this respect. Most chains permit a slight shrinkage of bulk items. Others allow no definite shrinkage but overlook all slight amounts.[41] They claim that if the manager uses reasonable care he need not come out short. It is only the inefficient manager who exceeds his shrinkage allowance. Moreover, the manager has legitimate ways of making an overage. Some goods gain in weight during storage, and goods sold in combinations or in pairs (for example, two for a quarter) are often sold singly at a fraction-of-a-cent higher price. These are billed to the manager at the paired-price. This problem does not arise in some fields where chains are strong; for example, in the drug field where there are ordinarily no bulk products sold except prescriptions, a phase of the business in which chains apparently take little interest.

It is also claimed that manufacturers sell the chains

41. Chain Store Inquiry, Vol. III, "Short Weighing and Overweighing in Chain and Independent Grocery Stores", 72d Congress, 2d Session, Sen. Doc. No. 153. 1933, Government Printing Office, Washington, D. C.

smaller-weight packages than they do the independents although the packages are the same size and shape so as to fool the public. Manufacturers emphatically deny this. The chains have encouraged the sale of products in smaller packages but these smaller sizes have also been available to the independent. The chain, due to its rapid turnover, usually gets such products first, but does not have the exclusive right to them. In his price study E. Z. Palmer[42] took especial note of the sizes of standard goods sold in chains and independents. In only one case did the chains appear to have a special size and here they sold a ten-ounce package for the same as the independents sold an eight-ounce package. The Federal Government requires that the contents of all packages be plainly marked so that a careful buyer would not lose by such a practice if it did exist.

Chain managers are occasionally convicted of short-weighting but a recital of isolated cases proves nothing. This does not prove that chains are more guilty than independents for court records will show that independents also are frequently found guilty of the same practice.

The Federal Trade Commission[43] found nothing on which to condemn the chains more than the independents in this respect. They found that both were guilty of the practice to about the same degree, and that there was considerable room for improvement in both. They purchased five bulk items in four cities in a total of 1,691 stores; 50.3 per cent of the purchases in chains and 47.8 per cent in inde-

42. "E. Z. Palmer Finds Chains in Lexington 14.3 Per Cent Below Independents", Chain Store Progress, Vol. II, (Sept. 1930), p. 5.
43. Chain Store Inquiry, Vol. III, "Shortweighing and Overweighing in Chain and Independent Grocery Stores", op. cit.

pendent stores were short; the chains gave overweight on 34.1 per cent of the purchases and the independents on 43.8 per cent. The total shortweight amounted to 0.987 of one per cent in the chains and 1.265 per cent in the independents. The total net shortage (deducting overages) was 0.321 of one per cent in chains and 0.143 of one per cent in independents, a slight advantage in favor of the independent. This was not found to be true of all four cities for in one the chains gave less total shortweight than did the independents, which indicates that it is possible that a larger sample would show the two types of stores about equal in this respect. Of fourteen chain groups three gave net overages. It is on pre-weighed items that chains are said to practice short-weighting most often. The Commission found that short weights occurred more frequently on these items but that the chains had a smaller proportion than did the independents. The net shortage of the chains was 0.719 of one per cent as against 1.005 per cent for the independents.

At the same time the Commission studied shortchanging and overchanging. The results showed remarkably few cases of either. Eight chain units out of 702 shopped gave short change to the amount of twenty-nine cents and two gave too much change to the amount of six cents. Two out of 320 cooperatives were short sixteen cents and eight gave a total of twenty-three cents too much. Twelve independents out of 669 cases gave forty-three cents shortchange and eleven gave twenty-three cents too much.

The conclusion to be reached from this study is that shortweighting and shortchanging are the result of carelessness rather than conspiracy. Weighing goods in a hurry during rush hours or failing to make proper allowance for shrinkage of preweighed items probably accounts for most cases. Of course, there are bound to be a few dishonest managers and a few dishonest storeowners.

Several smaller studies have been made of the same problem and tend to bear out the above conclusions. E. Heyman[44] wrote to thirty-two county clerks in Michigan in the counties which contained the larger cities and received replies from thirty. In only two had chain stores been convicted of this practice. In 1930 in Detroit in the grocery business fourteen chains and twenty-eight independents were convicted and in Kalamazoo eleven chains and nine independents. Detroit has 17,000 chain stores which do sixty per cent of the grocery business, but only fourteen chain managers were found guilty. In Kalamazoo the chains had less convictions than independents in proportion to numbers.

Prof. M. D. Taylor of North Carolina University[45] made a study based on 177 purchases of items selected by conference with anti-chain and independent store organizations. He shopped eleven chains and ten independents. No cases of shortchanging or incorrect additions were reported. Several of the independents appeared to be giving dishonest weights or had inaccurate scales or the clerks were careless for they gave a good deal of short weight, a fact which puts the figures for independents in a bad light. The chains were short on eighteen per cent of the purchases and independents on forty-four per cent. The average shortage was 0.67 of an ounce for chains, and 0.70 of an ounce for independents. Independents gave overweight more often. Professor Taylor's conclusion was

44. "Charges of Short Weight Practices Unfounded", Chain Store Progress, Vol. III, (March 1931), p. 4.
45. "A Study of Weights in Chain and Independent Grocery Stores in Durham, North Carolina", Harvard Business Review, Vol. IX, (July 1931), pp. 443-455.

that the chains gave more accurate weights but that there was room
for improvement in both. There was no evidence that chains sold
smaller packages of branded commodities than did independents.

Professor R. S. Vaile of the University of Minnesota and
Miss A. M. Child checked convictions for violations of food laws
(short weights, etc.) in Minneapolis for one year. They found nine
convictions for chains and twenty-six for independents. Their conclusion was that, "In neither case does the number of convictions
indicate a serious situation or one that would strongly influence
consumers to favor either group of stores."[46]

Professor P. D. Converse of the University of Illinois[47]
found, in 154 purchases in twelve chain and ten independent stores,
that independents gave the correct charge on 66.0 per cent of the
purchases, an overcharge on 18.5 per cent, and an undercharge on
15.5 per cent. The corresponding percentages for chains were 68.6,
11.8, and 19.6, which shows a decided advantage for the chain. If
the independent with the worst record were excluded the independent
stores had the following percentages, 75.0, 7.5, and 17.5, an advantage in favor of the independents. Most of the over and under-
charges were for such small amounts that Professor Converse concluded that they were probably due to mistakes rather than to attempts to cheat.

In the other characteristics wanted in a retail store the
chain does not lag behind the independent. Most chains are as conveniently located and some are even more accessible due to the fact

46. R. S. Vaile and A. M. Child, op. cit., p. 17.
47. "Prices and Services of Chain and Independent Stores in Champaign-Urbana, Illinois", op. cit., p. 26.

that the chains hire experts on location and are able and willing to pay more for desirable locations. Of course, chains are not ordinarily located in neighborhoods but seek the down-town locations where the volume of business is greatest. But the fact that volume is the greatest there shows that people like to trade in a shopping center.

Chains have been leaders in the maintenance of clean, well-lighted, and well-ventilated stores; in the brightness of the exterior of the store; in the convenient arrangement of their stocks; in the conspicuous marking of the prices of their goods.

The chains usually carry a more complete line of staple products, especially nationally advertised articles, and are less frequently out of them. However, they carry a smaller assortment of all types of products, for they limit their stocks to only a few of the most rapidly moving items in each type of good. The independent more often caters to individual desires and carries a wide range of products and brands. Part of his higher prices are due to this factor.

Allowing for the extra services of the independent, for the greater variety of goods, etc., the average chain store still undersells the average independent somewhat. Some independents are efficient enough to undersell the chains but they are in the minority. There is nothing inherent in the chain system which permits it to sell below all independents, but the chain organization does offer a means by which all stores in a system may be forced up to the level of the most efficient. This the independents can not do.

The lower prices of the chain may be due to any or all of three things: greater efficiency, a lower average profit, or an

advantage in the purchase of their goods, labor, etc. The independents say that such advantage as may exist is not due to efficiency.

Gross margins and total expenses are two of the most com-
mon measures of the payment society makes for the services of distribution. A comparison of gross margins or total expenses serves
to indicate which units are serving society best. It is not easy
to compare these for different stores because retailing, even in a
single line of business, is carried on under a great many different
conditions. Operating expenses vary with the size of the store,
the size of the city in which the store is located, the location
within the city, the wealth of the community, the section of the
country, and the amount of services rendered. In general, expenses
decline as a store increases in size until a certain size is reached
and then rise again, as Table XIV indicates. Store operating expenses increase with the size of the city. The Bureau of the Census reached the following conclusion:

> "For the same kind and type of business it costs more to
> operate in a large city than in a city of moderate size and
> more in a small city than in a village or country town. . . .
> The general principle that expenses increase with the size of
> city has been definitely established by the Retail Census."[48]

Table XV tends to bear out the same conclusion.

Expenses tend to be higher in central locations and in
high income sections than in the neighborhoods (allowing for the
different services rendered). They are also higher in commercial
and industrial centers.[49] That expenses vary with the section of
the country is shown in Table XVI. The stores in the most densely

48. Bureau of the Census, Fifteenth Census of the United States,
Distribution, Vol. 3, Part I, "Drug Retailing", p. 14. 1933, Government Printing Office, Washington, D. C.
49. Nystrom, P. H., Economics of Retailing, 3d edition, Vol. II,
p. 121. 1930, Ronald Press Company, New York.

Table XIV

RETAIL OPERATING EXPENSES: OPERATING EXPENSES
BY SIZE OF RETAIL SHOPS IN LOUISVILLE IN 1928

| Size of Store | Operating Expenses as a Percentage of Sales | |
	Drug Stores	Grocery Stores
Under 5,000	28.7	15.9
5,000 - 9,999	20.9	11.4
10,000 - 24,999	23.4	10.3
25,000 - 49,999	20.0	11.6
50,000 - 74,999		12.2
75,000 - 99,999	--	13.1
100,000 and over	22.8	15.4

Source:
United States Department of Commerce, Bureau of Foreign and
Domestic Commerce, Louisville Grocery Survey, No. 6, "Census
of Food Distribution". 1930, Government Printing Office, Washington, D. C.

Table XV

RETAIL OPERATING EXPENSES: OPERATING EXPENSES
OF GROCERY STORES BY SIZE OF CITY
IN THE CINCINNATI-LOUISVILLE AREA, IN 1929

Size of City	Operating Expense
Over 100,000	14.59
30,000 - 99,999	13.61
10,000 - 29,999	13.46
5,000 - 9,999	13.91
Under 5,000	13.22

Source:
Fifteenth Census of the United States, Distribution, Vol. III,
Part III, "Food Retailing", p. 18. 1933, Government Printing
Office, Washington, D. C.

settled regions seem to have the highest operating expenses. A
store's expenses will also vary with the extent to which it performs
the wholesale functions and the extent to which it asks the customers
to do part of the retail functions. In judging a store's efficiency
one must determine the number of things performed within the gross
margin. Some stores carry fuller lines than do others and naturally

incur greater expenses in doing so.

A comparison of the average costs of operation in chain and independent stores is, for the above reasons, of rather doubtful validity. In the first place, it involves a comparison of averages. Chain units, in a given line of business, are standardized, and vary within narrower limits than the independents in respect to size, services given, lines of goods carried, etc. An average cost for chain stores would have some significance. But an average for independents has little significance for there are all sorts of independents, efficient and inefficient, large and small, full-service and cash-and-carry. There is an enormous variation among independents in every respect. Similar stores only should be compared but this is not possible. Secondly, there are no complete cost studies available which are strictly comparable so that a patchwork of different studies must be used. The most important of these are the studies made by Harvard University,[50] Nebraska University[51], The Federal Trade Commission,[52] and the United States Census Bureau.[53]

---

50. Bureau of Business Research, Harvard University, Harvard Business Reports.
51. University of Nebraska, Committee on Business Research, College of Business Administration, Nebraska Studies in Business.
52. Federal Trade Commission, Chain Store Inquiry, Vol. V. "Invested Capital and Rates of Return of Retail Chains", 73d Congress, 2d Session, Sen. Doc. No. 87. 1934 Government Printing Office, Washington, D. C. "Sales, Costs, and Profits of Retail Chains", 73d Congress, 1st Session, Sen. Doc. No. 40. 1933 Government Printing Office, Washington, D. C. "Gross Profit and Average Sales Per Store of Retail Chains", 72d Congress, 1st Session, Sen. Doc. No. 178. 1933, Government Printing Office, Washington, D. C.
53. Bureau of Census, Fifteenth Census of United States, 1930, Distribution. 1933, Government Printing Office, Washington, D. C. Census of American Business, Retail Distribution, 1933. 1935, Government Printing Office, Washington, D. C.

With due allowance for the above factors, a rough comparison can be made.

It is difficult to tell from a comparison of the conditions under which chains and independents operate just which one, assuming equal efficiency, would be expected to have the higher operating expense, and by how much. Chains have a better average size than do independents and so would be expected, from this factor, to have somewhat lower expenses. Chains only open units when a careful survey shows that a volume sufficient to permit low operating expenses can be expected. If patronage proves to be such that the volume exceeds that amount which would give the greatest efficiency, a second store is opened in the locality. Independent stores are not all of this optimum size but many are smaller or larger. If the existence of these smaller stores is economically necessary, their higher cost should be allowed for in any comparison of chain and independent prices. If they serve no economic function, no allowance should be made.

A larger proportion of chains than independents are located in the larger cities so that chains might be expected to have a tendency toward higher operating expenses.[54] Chains are also located largely in the down-town districts so that they would have higher expenses on the average than the independents for the same type of store. A larger proportion of the chains than independents are located in the sections of the country where retailing expenses are highest.[55] How much of an advantage in average costs is given to independents by these factors can not be definitely determined

---

54. See Table III.
55. Compare Tables XVI and VI.

but it must amount to at least one per cent of sales. In the Nebraska studies of retail grocery stores in 1929[56] the stores in the two large cities of the state showed operating expenses 1.50 per cent higher than the average for state. The sections of the country in which chains are concentrated have an average operating expense of over two per cent above that of the rest of the country.[57] The Harvard studies found that chain expenses in the New England states were 4.5 per cent higher than those in the West and that total expenses were lower by 4.0 per cent for stores in cities under 50,000 than for those in cities of over 1,000,000 population.[58] The difference in average costs between cities of over 100,000 and cities of 10,000 amounts to one per cent.[59] Not all chains are located in the high expense areas, nor are all independents located in the low expense areas. Allowing for this a one per cent differential does not seem excessive.

Total expenses also vary with the amount of wholesale and retail functions performed by the store. The chains perform more of the wholesale functions but, on the other hand, give fewer retail services. The chains turn over to the customer the functions of credit and delivery, carry restricted lines, do not usually take orders over the telephone, and give less help to the customer in the selection of what she wishes to buy. All these services cost money and allowance should be made for them. Various studies would indicate that the expense of credit and delivery amounts to from two

56. Nebraska Studies in Business, op. cit., No. 27, "Expenses of Retail Grocery Stores, in 1929", page 12. 1930, University of Nebraska Press, Lincoln.
57. See Table XVI.
58. Harvard Studies in Business, op. cit., No. 84, "Expenses and Profits in the Chain Grocery Business in 1929", p. 10, 11. 1931, Murray Printing Company, Cambridge. 59. See Table XV.

to six per cent of sales. A study of all-service stores in Iowa in 1927[60] found that, after arbitrarily allocating all expenses, credit cost 1.54 per cent of sales and delivery 2.90 per cent or a total of approximately 4.44 per cent. The Harvard Studies[61] found credit and delivery expense, on the basis of 1924 figures, to be 3.65 per cent. A study by The Progressive Grocer, a magazine for independents, concluded[62] that credit and delivery in combination grocery and meat stores, when properly and efficiently rendered, need not add more than four per cent to a store's operating costs (in selected efficient stores the difference in cost of service and cash-and-carry stores, although not strictly comparable stores in all other respects, was 2.3 per cent). In twenty-four selected grocery stores fourteen full-service stores had operating expenses only 1.1 per cent higher than ten cash-and-carry stores, which indicates that credit and delivery can be kept low. P. D. Converse[63] estimates that credit and delivery cost from 1.6 per cent to 3.5 per cent of sales in the grocery field, or from two to five per cent if interest on money tied up is included. P. H. Nystrom[64] estimates such expenses in all fields amount to from three to six per cent of sales. In the studies by the Federal Trade Commission the selling prices of a number of goods were totaled in independent stores who gave fifty to one hundred per cent service and in those independents

60. Bristol, W. F., "Operating Costs of Service Grocery Stores in Iowa, 1927", Iowa Studies in Business, No. 6. 1930, College of Commerce, University of Iowa, Iowa City, Iowa.
61. Op. cit., No. 84, "Expenses and Profits in Chain Grocery Business, in 1929", M. P. McNair, p. 19.
62. Progressive Grocer Publications, Operating Expenses of 110 Selected Food Stores, 1935 Butterick Publishing Company, New York.
63. Elements of Marketing, op. cit., p. 405.
64. Economics of Retailing, op. cit., Vol. I, p. 107.

who gave no service. In Washington, D. C.[65] for 261 items the price
at service stores was $53.21 and at no-service stores, $52.27, a
difference of $0.94 and 1.80 per cent of sales. In Cincinnati[66] for
ninety items the corresponding prices were $15.7627 and $15.3210, a
difference of $0.4417 and 2.89 per cent of sales. From these
studies it can be concluded that if the extra services of the independent are rendered efficiently, such services would cost about
four per cent. But not all independents perform full services and
not all chains operate on a no-service basis so that in a comparison
of chain and independent average costs a differential of the full
four per cent should not be allowed the independents. The cost of
delivery, however, is offset to some extent by the fact that no-
delivery stores need a larger proportion of counter clerks.

From this it could be expected that the average costs of
independents in the retail grocery field would be higher than chains
by perhaps two per cent, assuming both to operate with equal efficiency and without wholesale costs. Any appreciably greater difference must be due to less efficiency or to the operation of an
uneconomic size of store. This allowance, of course, does not apply
to any other type of store. What the difference is in other retail
lines is even more of a guess.

Chains vary in the extent to which they perform the wholesale function. The small local chains perform few, if any, while
the large national chains, in some fields, perform most of them. To

65. Chain Store Inquiry, op. cit., Vol. IV., "Prices, Margins, Etc.
of Chain and Independent Distributors", 73d Congress, 1st Session,
Sen. Doc. No. 62, "Groceries, Washington, D. C.", p. 19. 1933, Government Printing Office, Washington, D. C.
66. Ibid., Vol. IV., Sen. Doc. No. 88, "Groceries, Cincinnati", p.19.

make a true comparison of chain and independent costs the whole-saler's costs ought to be added to the independent retailer's costs.

Direct comparisons of chain and independent expenses are limited because of the few studies made of chain expenses. More-over, no exactly comparable studies of independents' expenses were made at the same time. One of the Harvard Business Reports[67] made a study of chain operating results and in 1929, for lack of more comparable data, compared this with operating expenses of retailers in Nebraska and wholesalers in Ohio in 1929. For independents there was a retail gross margin of 18.50 per cent of sales and for whole-salers, 9.70 per cent based on retail sales, or a total of 28.20 per cent. The chain gross margin was 19.40 per cent or a difference of 8.80 per cent in favor of the chains. But this assumes that chains buy no merchandise from wholesalers and that the independents buy all their merchandise through wholesalers. With proper allow-ance for this the difference would be somewhat less. Using the Cen-sus figures for 1929, Professor P. D. Converse[68] found the combined expenses of wholesalers and independent retailers to be 25.30 per cent and that of chains (Federal Trade Commission figures) to be 18.50 per cent. The Census Bureau found that in the same year the expenses of chain grocery stores was 13.84 per cent plus a central office expense of 1.59 per cent or a total of 15.43 per cent,[69] whereas the average grocery store expense was 17.36 per cent[70] and the average general-line wholesaler's expense was 7.5 per cent of his

67. No. 84, op. cit., pp. 14–18.
68. Elements of Marketing, op. cit., page 454.
69. Bureau of the Census, Fifteenth Census of United States, 1930, Distribution, "Retail Chains", p. 21. 1933, Government Printing Office, Washington, D. C.
70. Ibid., Vol. I, Part I, page 51.

Table XVI

RETAIL OPERATING EXPENSES: AVERAGE OPERATING EXPENSES
OF ALL STORES BY SECTIONS OF THE COUNTRY, 1929

Section of the Country	Operating Expenses
New England	25.27
Middle Atlantic	26.34
East North Central	25.34
West North Central	22.74
South Atlantic	23.67
East South Central	21.58
West South Central	22.09
Mountain	23.38
Pacific	26.84
Total United States	24.83

Source:
Bureau of the Census, Fifteenth Census of the United States,
op. cit., Distribution, Vol. I, Part I, p. 54.

---

sales.[71]   Assuming both chain and wholesaler could buy the same product at 84.57 cents the chain price would, according to these figures, be $1.00 and the independent price, $1.10.   Allowing for some
direct buying by independents, the independent price would figure
out somewhat lower than this, although this is partly offset by the
fact that the operating expenses of the chains are figured on a lower
selling price than is that of independents.   Allowing for the fact
that chains buy their merchandise at a somewhat lower price than do
independents,[72] this result checks closely with the results of the
various price studies.   The results of the Federal Trade Commission's
study shows a smaller differential.   It conducted a study[73] in four
cities on a limited number of comparable products, supposedly where
chain gross margins are low.   Using unweighted figures the chain in

---

71. Ibid., Vol. 3, Part 2, "Wholesale Distribution", p. 65.
72. See Chapter III.
73. Chain Store Inquiry, Vol. IV, op. cit.

no place had a gross margin of over three per cent less than the wholesaler-independent system. Weighting the figures by volume of sales the independents made a somewhat poorer showing.

The big saving of the chain in the grocery field seems to be in the wholesale function rather than in the retail function. In a special study of the Cincinnati-Louisville area independent grocery stores were shown to have a lower operating expense than did the chain units. Table XVII summarizes this data. A similar study of drug stores in the Chicago-Milwaukee area (Table XVIII) bears out the same conclusions, namely, that the chain advantage lies in the wholesale part of the business rather than in the retail end. The Federal Trade Commission's study of prices and margins[74] shows that the chain's advantage lies in warehoused goods, which indicates that it can not perform the retail function better than the independent. A summary of this material is presented in Table XIX. On items which came direct from the manufacturer, the independent had a slight advantage in gross margins; on items handled by wholesalers, the percentage markup of the wholesaler-independent system was somewhat higher. In all cases the chain operated on a lower total markup, but inasmuch as their prices were somewhat lower, the percentage of markup was greater.

The 1933 Census figures (Table XX) show the chains to have a slight advantage in the operation of some types of retail stores and to be at a disadvantage in the operation of others. As a whole, the chains seem to have little advantage in the retail end of distribution, excepting in drug stores and cigar stands.

Professor Converse has constructed two tables[75] from

74. Op. cit.
75. Elements of Marketing, op. cit., p. 450 and 454.

Table XVII

RETAIL OPERATING EXPENSES: CHAIN AND INDEPENDENT GROCERY STORE
OPERATING EXPENSES IN THE CINCINNATI-LOUISVILLE AREA,
BY SIZE OF STORE, 1929

			Size of Store			
	Over $100,000	$60,000 to 99,999	$25,000 to 59,999	$10,000 to 24,999	Under $10,000	Total
Number of Chain Units	40	217	319	30	8	614
Store Expense	16.09	13.86	14.18	16.31	24.83	14.36
Number of Independent Units	41	91	650	715	410	1,907
Store Expense	15.59	13.30	12.69	14.47	25.79	14.08

Source:
Bureau of the Census, Fifteenth Census of United States, Distribution, op. cit., Vol. III, Part III, "Food Retailing", p. 81.

Census data, one of which gives the expenses of independent whole-salers and chain warehouses in various retail fields and the other, the combined expenses of the wholesaler and independent retailer and the expenses of the chain system. Tables XXI and XXII contain this material. The great majority of independents buy from service wholesalers so that columns one and three are most properly compared. It will be observed that as a general rule the chains have reached their greatest development in the fields in which they have the greatest advantage in the performance of the wholesaling function. Table XXII overstates the difference between the two systems, inasmuch as the independents do not buy all their goods through the wholesaler nor does the chain buy all its merchandise direct.

The above studies are fragmentary but seem to indicate that the chain system can operate somewhat more efficiently than the wholesaler-independent system. The Federal Trade Commission reached

Table XVIII

RETAIL OPERATING EXPENSES: OPERATING EXPENSES OF RETAIL DRUG STORES IN THE CHICAGO-MILWAUKEE AREA, BY SIZE OF CITY AND TYPE OF OPERATION, 1929

Type of Store	Total for Area		Cities over 150,000		Cities 50,000 to 100,000		25,000 to 49,999		10,000 to 24,999		5,000 to 9,999		Under 5,000	
	Number of Stores	Operating Expenses	Number Stores	Operating Expenses	Number Stores	Operating Expenses	Number Stores	Operating Expenses	Number Stores	Operating Expenses	Number Stores	Operating Expenses	Number Stores	Operating Expenses
Total for Area	3053	28.98	2191	29.81	240	27.06	162	29.00	139	25.88	86	27.40	235	23.61
Independents	2770	29.14	1937	30.28	219	27.36	155	28.68	138	x		x		x
Chains	283	28.60	254	28.97	21	25.92	7	22.44	1	x		x		x
Sales over $100,000	186	27.70	161	28.13	14	24.85	8	23.97	-	-	1	x		
Independents	38	29.02	26	29.67	5	27.36	4	27.55	2	23.17				
Chains	148	27.36	135	27.86	9	23.27	4	21.42	-	-				
Sales $60,000—$99,999	243	29.01	167	29.81	25	29.08	18	27.64	-	-	6	x	4	26.89
Independents	180	27.93	110	28.61	20	28.39	17	x	23	25.18				
Chains	63	31.82	57	31.96	5	31.63	1	x	-	-				
Sales $25,000—$59,999	1204	28.57	842	29.91	112	26.00	62	28.09	68	25.17	44	26.59	76	22.05
Independents	1162	28.33	807	29.65	107	25.63	61	x	67	x				
Chains	42	34.23	35	34.68	5	33.45	1	x	1	x				
Sales $10,000—$24,999	1144	30.40	823	29.45	71	29.48	60	29.88	-	-	32	28.63	118	24.02
Independents	1118	30.19	800	31.17	69	29.57	59	x	40	30.15				
Chains	26	39.34	23	40.88	2	26.56	1	x	-	-				
Under $10,000	276	47.47	198	47.97	18	49.43	14	55.08	6	64.26	3	64.94	37	37.69
Independents	272	47.55	194	48.09	18	49.43	14	55.08	6	64.26				
Chains	4a	36.28	4a	36.28	-	-	-	-	-	-				

a In operation only part of year.

Source: Bureau of the Census Fifteenth Census of United States, Distribution, op. cit., Vol. III, Part I, "Drug Re-tailing", pp. 49-51.

Table XIX

RETAIL MARGINS: GROSS MARGINS AS PERCENTAGE OF SELLING PRICE OF CHAINS AND INDEPENDENT STORES
IN SELECTED CITIES BY TYPE OF COMMODITY

Type of Product	Washington Independent	Washington Chain	Cincinnati Independent	Cincinnati Chain	Memphis Independent	Memphis Chain	Detroit Independent	Detroit Chain
Warehoused items	28.875	24.412	25.426	21.788	29.471	26.097	29.292	26.226
Direct items	20.679	20.760	25.920	24.146	19.810	21.659	26.027	26.340
Semi-direct items	22.475	21.817	---	---	20.649	24.001	26.034	26.650

Source:
Federal Trade Commission, Chain Store Inquiry, Vol. IV, "Prices, Margins, Etc. of Chain
and Independent Distributors", 73d Congress, 1st and 2d Sessions. 1933 and 1934, Government Printing Office, Washington, D. C.

Table XX

RETAIL OPERATING EXPENSES: OPERATING EXPENSES OF CHAIN AND
INDEPENDENT RETAIL STORES IN DIFFERENT RETAIL FIELDS, 1933

Retail Field	Chain Expense, Including Prorated Part of Central Office Expense	Independent Operating Expense, Including Allowance for Proprietor's Services
Grocery	18.70	19.98
Combination (grocery and meat)	18.61	19.87
Variety	28.97	28.89
Drug	28.80[a]; 22.05	30.87
Shoe	31.30	32.40
Filling Station	32.33	27.44
Restaurants, Cafeterias, etc.	57.81	46.24
Hardware	30.13	31.57
Cigar Stands	21.70	27.60
Department	26.61	32.71
General Merchandise and Dry Goods	19.20[b]	
Family Clothing	25.46	26.08
Furniture	38.43	35.16
	43.26	40.70

[a] With and without fountains.
[b] General merchandise and dry goods separate.

Source:
   Bureau of the Census, Census of American Business, 1933, op. cit.,
   "Retail Distribution", Vol. I, p. 30 ff, and Table 1-c, p. A-5.

the following conclusion on this point:

"In general, it was found that the chains were passing
goods into the hands of consumers at a smaller gross margin and
a smaller percentage of the sales price than were either the
independents or the cooperative chains. This was after eliminating special discounts and allowances. This showing is all
the more significant when coupled with the fact that the total
sales price of the chains was less, providing a smaller base
on which to calculate the percentages."[76]

Although the chains exhibit an advantage in total distributive ex-

pense, they do not appear to have much, if any, advantage in the op-

76. Federal Trade Commission, Chain Store Inquiry, "Final Report on
the Chain-Store Investigation", op. cit., p. 67.

Table XXI

WHOLESALE OPERATING EXPENSES: OPERATING EXPENSES OF INDEPENDENT WHOLESALERS AND CHAIN WAREHOUSES

Retail Field	Percentage of Wholesale Selling Price		
	Service Wholesaler	Cash-and-Carry Wholesaler	Chain-Store Warehouses
Drugs, General Line	14.1	13.5	4.1
Drugs, Specialty	26.6	---	9.4
Clothing and Furnishings	14.1	8.2	8.8
Farm Supplies	13.9	7.6	9.7
Confectionery and Soft Drinks	16.3	4.1	15.6
Fruits and Fresh Vegetables	9.0	9.6	7.4
Meats	9.6	10.2	8.1
House Furnishings	16.7	15.8	15.4
Groceries, General Line	9.1	5.5	3.3
Groceries, Specialties	9.9	3.0	2.8
Stationery	23.0	26.2	24.0
Tobacco	7.5	3.4	6.1
Dry Goods and General Line	14.8	---	7.1
Furniture	21.2	---	11.4
Lumber and Building Materials	17.2	---	4.1

Source:
Converse, P. D., _Elements_ _of_ _Marketing_, _op_. _cit_., p. 450.

eration of the retail units. The range of costs in both chains and independents shows it is skill in management, rather than inherent advantages, that gives one retail store an advantage over another. It is not the mechanics of the chain store but the human element in both chain and independent that determines the relative effectiveness of the chain. Both may be operated efficiently and both may be failures, depending largely on the quality of management. The costs of chains and independents, similarly situated and operated successfully, would correspond pretty much to the amount of service rendered. The advantage of the chain lies in being able to enforce

Table XXII

RETAIL AND WHOLESALE OPERATING EXPENSES: COMBINED OPERATING
EXPENSES OF THE WHOLESALER-INDEPENDENT SYSTEM AND THE
CHAIN SYSTEM OF DISTRIBUTION

Retail Field	Combined Expense of Wholesaler and Retailer Census Figures (1929)	Chain Stores, Average for 8 Years, Federal Trade Commission
Shoe	38.0	29.7
Women's Apparel	38.7	29.5
Drug	43.4	32.4
Grocery	25.3	18.5
Meat	26.6	20.0
Hardware	40.2	25.5
Furniture	46.6	37.2
Men's Clothing	39.9	30.4
Men's Furnishings	40.9	36.8

Source:
Converse, P. D., Elements of Marketing, op. cit. p. 454.

minimum standards of efficiency in every one of its stores. There
is no overseer of the average independent to force him to be efficient. Some independents can, and do, exceed the minimum standards
set down by the chain, but a large number do not. The advantage of
the chain lies in offering a uniformly high operating efficiency.

Although the chain seems to have no inherent advantages
in the operation of retail stores, it does have an inherent advantage in the integration of the wholesale and retail functions.
By integration it can eliminate the wholesale selling function, the
expense of the credit department, bad debt losses, interest on outstanding accounts, collections, and the keeping of customers' led-
gers. It usually does not carry as many items, which enables faster stockturn and hence savings on light, taxes, insurance, interest,
and handling. It does not cater to stores by breaking packages; it
can lay out its delivery schedule and route and thus lower delivery

expense; it can choose a location to better advantage. Particularly
does it save on the selling functions. When one realizes that the
"A & P" warehouses can "sell" over 15,000 stores without a salesman (although supervisors are required), whereas an independent
wholesaler must send salesmen to even a larger number of stores to
get the same volume, it is readily apparent where the savings of
the chain system arise. An illustration of this disadvantage of
the independent wholesaler was brought out in the Louisville Survey
of the grocery business. Several whoesalers were competing for the
business of a retailer whose sales averaged ten dollars per day --
and were spending seven-and-a-half dollars a day for the privilege.
A count of callers at one retail store revealed more jobbers' salesmen than customers.[77]

Although chains have an advantage in operating expenses,
that is not to say that they pass the savings on to the public. As
long as there are inefficient independents, the chain need not pass
on as much of these savings as it might otherwise. Competition between the chains themselves is forcing the chains to keep their
prices as close as possible to cost, so that in most cases the public gets the benefit. Due to more rapid turnover than independents,
based on limited lines and scientific merchandising and stock control, the chain can operate on a lower net profit than can the independent. Table XXIII gives the average operating results for the
years 1913 to 1930 of the various types of chains. It will be noted
that some of the chains have made enormous profits on invested capital, although this has been done on a relatively low markup. The

---

77. Quoted by H. S. Hollander, "Chain-Store Invasion Aids Independents", Barrons, Vol. IX, (Oct. 28, 1929), p. 21.

return of the chains has, however, been constantly declining as the independents have improved their efficiency. Chain returns are not as great today as the average for the seventeen years show, years in which average profits were generally high.

Hence, it can be seen that the chains do bring a savings to the public by economies in operation, by curtailed services, and by lower profit per dollar of sales. Two further questions which will be discussed in Chapter Three are whether the chains obtain an advantage by squeezing the employee, the landlord, etc., and how much of the chain advantage in price is due to buying advantages.

Differentials in prices and costs, as now exist between chains and independents, by no means measure the consumer gain from chains. The chains have forced the independent to become more efficient. In the past the inefficiency of distribution has been notorious. The chains have been one of the few to make any breach at all in the spread between the producer's and the consumer's price. The chain has brought stiff competition to the retail field and such rivalry has benefited the consumer. Without the chain the average costs and prices of the independent would probably be higher than they now are. For many years there has been a great cry for lower distribution costs which were to be accomplished at the expense of the middleman, who was decribed as a parasite who preyed on both producer and consumer. The chain has accomplished something toward a reduction in this cost.

Assuming that each competes fairly is there a place in the retail world for both chain and independent? The tendency has been toward chains but will this trend continue and is there a place

Table XXIII

CHAIN-STORE OPERATING RESULTS: AVERAGE OPERATING RESULTS FOR CHAIN STORES, 1913-1930

Retail Field	Business Investment Per Co.	Ave. bus. invest. per store	Return on bus. inves. (Per cent)	Ave. income per store	Return on sales (Per cent)	Stock-turn
Men's Furnishings	$ 92,789	$ 13,367	3.09	$ 414	.75	3.17
Women's Accessories	95,224	9,363	15.95	1,494	2.84	3.91
Millinery	132,178	5,547	27.89	1,547	2.80	21.81
Men's Ready-To-Wear	366,051	66,336	5.61	3,724	2.28	2.61
Women's Ready-To-Wear	490,849	57,022	16.46	9,386	4.90	6.83
Men's and Women's Ready-To-Wear	502,274	44,246	9.71	4,296	4.37	3.40
Dry Goods and Apparel	987,193	42,633	20.35	8,678	6.09	3.66
Dry Goods	261,076	38,044	1.58	602	.76	2.30
Department Store	15,759,113	830,213	9.82	81,546	4.88	4.43
Hats and Caps	371,067	16,323	-0.62	- 101	-.24	3.17
Men's Shoes	206,562	14,454	18.60	2,689	4.80	2.69
Women's Shoes	248,014	19,335	17.75	3,431	3.51	5.32
Men's and Women's Shoes	390,009	22,998	10.15	2,334	3.29	2.61
General Merchandise	235,399	44,802	7.80	3,496	3.60	3.40
Variety (unlimited)	184,890	16,705	.75	125	.30	2.64
Variety ($5 limit)	144,208	13,791	9.40	1,296	2.97	3.42
Variety ($1 limit)	6,216,238	76,547	21.11	16,163	9.42	5.29
Meat	159,013	11,334	16.61	1,882	2.52	29.84
Grocery	861,798	7,930	12.83	1,018	2.24	8.03
Grocery and Meat	2,251,331	7,659	21.56	1,651	2.96	10.61
Drug	649,718	44,565	11.73	5,225	4.44	3.64
Tobacco	1,735,194	23,718	10.20	2,418	3.64	4.72
Hardware	456,670	67,255	3.51	2,361	3.22	1.66
Furniture	1,673,852	315,156	8.02	25,275	8.20	2.80
Confectionery	1,686,740	74,026	10.14	7,508	6.37	7.44
Musical Instruments	1,785,011	187,166	4.98	9,323	4.46	2.96
All Stores	1,503,901	27,157	14.88	4,041	4.62	5.97

Source: Federal Trade Commission, Chain Store Inquiry, op. cit., Senate Document No. 87, "Invested Capital and Rates of Return of Retail Chains," (1934). Turnover figures from Senate Document No. 40, Sales, Costs, and Profits of Retail Chains, (1933), p. 14.

for the independent? Probably both will continue to exist side by side, and each will find its own sphere. Our country is too big for all the business to be done in one way. Just what proportion will be done by each depends upon the consumers' desires and how well each one meets this desire. The world constantly changes and consumers' desires change; businessmen have to keep pace with these changes or lose out. The future of the chain and the independent depends upon the interpretation of these desires and the ability to meet them adequately.

Distribution has known a succession of new types of retailing, from the peddler to the general store, specialty store, mail-order house, department store, house-to-house selling, consumer cooperative, and chain store. Each came in response to the pressure of a large body of consumers who wanted the definite service each had to offer. As each began to grow, it was subjected to condemnation, for each of the existing forms wanted to protect its business from change. It has been the same in all fields. The turnpike opposed the canal; the canal, the railroad; and now the railroad, the motor bus and truck. The independent has in turn opposed the department store, the mail-order house, the house-to-house salesman, and now the chain store. In all previous cases eventually the consuming public made its force felt and institutions which met real needs survived and took their place alongside the older forms. Each grew until the extent of the demand for its peculiar service was reached or until others learned to render the same services better. No distributive device is permanent; it is the distributive functions that are the durable elements.

The chain is now accused of forcing the independent out of

business. If the independent is put out of business, it will be due
to one, or all, of three things: unfair competition on the part of
the chain, the non-existence of a service which the independent can
render, or the failure of the independent to keep up with changing
times and perform a needed service better than any other form of
retailing. There is a place for the independent and many independents will be able to operate efficiently enough to be able to maintain their positions in the face of chain competition. The chain
also will take its place, and, if history repeats itself, both chain
and independent will be fighting some new retail "menace" as yet
unknown.

How much of the total trade the chain will ultimately draw
to itself is not yet known, but many believe it has nearly reached
the extent of its expansion and will continue to exist at about its
present proportions of twenty to twenty-five per cent of the total
business. In the six years 1929 to 1935 the chain absorbed relatively little new business, although this leveling-off may have been
done through fear of expansion during a depression.

In the struggle to serve the consumer the advantage of
the chain lies in specialized management, integration, large-scale
operations, and the elimination of certain functions. The advantages of the independent inhere in personality, flexibility, and
community sympathy.

Chains, as a rule, have greater resources than independents and can hire experts in every phase of the business, whereas
the independent proprietor must do all the work and has no time to
become expert in any one of them. The chains pay huge salaries to
attract men of high calibre, but the amount per store for this ex-

pert management is surprisingly small. As an example, the chains
hire expert buyers. To estimate consumers' desires in advance is
the most difficult retail function. Chain experts, with the help
of past records of the chains, a constant study of market conditions,
and a thorough knowledge of sources of supply can buy to much better advantage than independents. The chains obtain similar advantages from experts on stock control systems, location, display and
stock arrangement, advertising, transportation problems, etc.

As has been indicated, one of the chief advantages of the
chain lies in the fact that minimum standards of efficiency are enforced in every one of their stores through close supervision and
elaborate accounting systems. As a result, the chains are above
the level of the average independent in such things as clean, bright,
and well-lighted places of business; painted and inviting exteriors;
etc. The chains' gains from integration have also been indicated.

The chains gain some advantage from their large size and
widespread operations. Their size and financial strength enable
them to get price concessions, on both their merchandise and supplies.[78] Their size and established reputation enable them to attract trade to a new store immediately and to obtain the trade of
new people who come to a town. Where a number of units are operated under one control, the experience of every unit can be passed
along so that all will profit by each others' mistakes and discoveries. Large size brings efficient use of resources and employees.
The independent and his employees are idle part of the time, or busy
at tasks which could well be done by a low-paid employee, or which
would require little more time with larger volume. Chains can develop research facilities, use private brands, get some gain from

78. See Chapter III.

salvage, and average profits in the various stores. The chains could, and it is charged that they do, reap whatever gains come from unfair practices, such as local price-cutting.

The chains have staked their chances on the existence of customers who are willing to dispense with many services, such as credit, delivery, and telephone orders, services which the independent has found often do not pay for themselves. By the elimination of these the chains can effect operating economies and so reduce selling prices. This policy attracts customers, particularly at periods when there is a need to economize. Not all customers want such services and it is only fair that a place exist where they can buy their merchandise on such terms. The chain has given the consumer a choice as to whether he will pay for services or perform them himself and pocket the savings. The fact that both types of stores are well-patronized indicates that there is room for stores with different service policies. The independent store may still be the most economical place to buy for individuals whose time and energy have a high market value. But a large number of consumers have to stretch their dollar as far as possible and can well afford to spend their time in the performance of some of the marketing functions. A no-service system does not involve the substitution of one type of retailing for another, but provides a supplementary type for which there is a great demand.

The independents have certain advantages which the chains find impossible to duplicate. The independent, with his small overhead, has the advantage of flexibility. He can make the most of changing trade opportunities and of local peculiarities; he has close contact with local market conditions; he can buy as he sees fit and keep open as long as he wants. The operation of a retail store can not be completely standardized. New situations constantly arise that can not be provided for by any system of regulations. The independent can immediately take whatever steps seem necessary, whereas the chain manager is often at a loss how to proceed.

The independent has the advantage of warm and personal contacts with his customers. He probably has been a life-long resident of the town and has many personal friends who buy at his store out of friendship. He knows their special demands and can cater to them with a high brand of selling service. It is in service that the independent finds his greatest competitive weapon. The best service can not be rendered mechanically but takes personal interest and knowledge. In some instances, however, the chain's lack of personality is an advantage. Many people like to shop without being bothered by clerks and without advice and so like the impersonal atmosphere of the chain. In the large town, where customers come and go, the independent has a hard time to apply personal service methods and is at a disadvantage.

The independent has the advantage of community loyalty and sympathy. He can appeal to local pride to patronize him as against the outside-owned and operated chain. He usually gets the major share of the trade, especially in the smaller towns, unless his prices are far out of line.

If expert, the independent can operate more efficiently than can the chain for he has a personal interest in the business and can personally supervise all operations. A man's efficiency is weakened when his orders are passed through too many hands. Each chain unit is a store the same as an independent store. Some of the chain manager's policies are determined at headquarters but in most phases of operation he must face the same problems as the independent. The personal interest of the independent makes him work just a little harder to see that these are solved satisfactorily and that little leaks and losses are eliminated.

Thus, the chain has grown in response to a real need. The chains grew because of the wastefulness of the existing retail organizations and a period of rising costs of living; because of excessive services in which retailers were indulging; and because of the growth of mass production. The chain's most rapid growth came after the World War when our factories were turning out products faster than the small inefficient independents could turn them over to the consumer. The high prices of the independent held back mass consumption. The answer to mass production proved to be mass distribution, with the economies it was able to effect.

At the same time certain facilitating conditions enabled the chain form of distribution to be developed. The chain couldnot exist with slow transportation and small markets. The development of the automobile and hard roads made it possible for a successful merchant to expand because he was now able to make deliveries to each store from a central warehouse and to supervise his scattered stores adequately. The auto also enabled the consumer to pass by his local retailer and to deal with a more distant but more efficient merchant. The consumer could also carry home his goods more conveniently. Our population has become more concentrated so that sufficient demand exists to support a store with a limited stock of goods. The increasing mobility of our population has made personality less of a factor in retailing. Improved accounting and com-

munication have made the operation of wide-flung systems possible.
The increase in the use of standardized, branded, packaged, and advertised goods, for which little selling is required, has permitted
standardized operating policies. Individual purchases have become
so small that it is convenient to carry merchandise home. The growth
of industry with weekly or semi-monthly payment of wages has made
cash sales possible. The abundance of capital in the '20's enabled
the chains to expand more rapidly than ever before.

The chain is best fitted to merchandise goods with the
following characteristics: staples, well-known brands of standard
grades and sizes, price appeal, necessities or semi-necessities (for
the chain must have constant patronage), packaged goods of portable
size, goods with a rapid rate of turnover, and goods which need
little real salesmanship. The independent can not hope to defeat
the chain on a price basis in this class of good. The handling of
this type of merchandise is the chain's place in the retail field.
But the chain seems to be absorbing a share of the sale of other
types of merchandise due to the inefficiency of its competitor. Just
where the chain will stop depends upon the efficiency which the independent obtains.

It is a general rule that the way to meet competition is
to match the efficiency of the competitor or to avoid it by doing
those things he chooses to ignore. These two alternatives are open
to the independent - he can meet the efficiency of the chain or
avoid direct competition by offering a different type of service.

Not all of the advantages attributed to chains are inherent in the chain system. The independents can get many of the
same advantages. In an attempt to compete with the chain the inde-

pendent must do two things: learn to buy cheaply and to operate efficiently. The principles for success are precisely the same for
both types of stores: convenient location, suitable building and
equipment, clean attractive merchandise, services that customers
need and want, etc. The chains have no patents on these but have so
far used them to better advantage. The independent can not hope to
match the chain experts but personal management can make up a good
deal of this loss. In the fields for which the chain is fitted
the individual, except the exceptional one, can not become as efficient, but in the fields where the chain is at a disadvantage the
individual can become expert enough to hold his own. The independent has not been able to match the chain in buying power. The
voluntary chain promises to give some aid in buying and also in
the development of efficient methods, but so far has not been able
to match the chain for it can not control the retail units.

The trouble with the independent has been that he has
stuck to old methods and has placed too much emphasis on fighting
the chain in the legislature rather than on economic grounds. The
greatest difficulty has been to get the wholesaler and independent
to work together. The wholesaler has not acted primarily as a buyer
for the public but as a salesman for the manufacturer and has put
the independent at a disadvantage. Similarly, the independent has
asked too much of the wholesaler and forced him to offer expensive
services to hold his customers. Unless these conditions are over-
come, the independent will have difficulty in meeting chain competition.

There are four major types of competition: competition
in price, quality, service, and terms. No merchant need enter all

four kinds of competition. The chain competes on the basis of
price; the independent must compete on the basis of the other three
factors. The price the independent can charge will be somewhat above
that of the chain but as long as the differential is reasonable,
the independent can maintain himself in his sphere. There are many
things the independent can do better than the chain if he only will.
He can handle the de luxe quality of goods better, for these do not
have a large enough market to give the turnover necessary for chain
success. A parallel can be drawn from the automobile field. All
manufacturers do not try to sell in the same field; if they did,
no one would make any money. Such a policy would be foolish since
there are thousands who are willing to pay extra for the conveniences
and luxuries that come with the higher-priced car.[79] In other products there are consumers who are willing to pay more for better
quality. The independent can also gain an advantage by carrying a
varied stock to meet the personal desires of those who can afford
to pay for this service (but the retailer can not stock too many
slow-moving items). The independent will find that he has an advantage in novelties, fashion goods, unstandardized products, slow-
moving, and high-priced goods. The independent can offer all sorts
of personal services which the chain can not hope to match. He
will take all the convenience neighborhood trade where volume is
too low to justify a chain unit. His personality will permit him
to be dominant in the smaller towns and in neighborhoods where there
is a predominant nationality which prefers to deal with its own
people. In fields where the stock is large and diversified, and

79. Taken from Ohrbach, N. M., Getting Ahead in Retailing, p. 254.
1935, McGraw-Hill Book Company, New York.

the turnover small, as in jewelry and hardware, the chain finds no place. If the independent renders the above services efficiently, no chain can hope to displace him.

The independent must learn that there are some things he can not do. He can not conduct a service and quality business on a price basis. He must learn that there is a decisive line of division between price merchandising and service merchandising. Failure is the fate of the merchant who does not know his own limitations.

There is plenty of evidence that many independents are able to compete today and that more are becoming able to compete each year. The experience of everyone shows that there are independent stores which prosper in the midst of a number of chains. The less efficient independents can not stand such competition, but the alert, efficient independent can, and does. Many independents claim that the best location is next to a chain. Chains are said not to locate near a wideawake independent. The fact that the independents hold on tenaciously shows that they have a place in retailing. The independent as a class is not being eliminated, but is actually increasing in every census count. The independent is doing something and is at least holding his own and may eventually win back some of the business he has lost. The ability of the small merchant to succeed is demonstrated by the growth of chains. Most chains have grown from small unit stores. As an efficient independent drew more trade to him, he expanded and opened a second store and finally a third and fourth. As his superior efficiency enabled him to grow in size, he obtained more and more of the advantages of large size and integration and eventually became a

recognized chain, with all the advantages that go with size added
to his initial advantage of good management. That efficient independents can grow to be chains in the face of chain competition
shows that independents can succeed. The intelligent independents
will take care of themselves and the unintelligent can not be saved
anyway.

Moreover, there are economic limits to the expansion of
the chains besides the competitive efficiency of the independents
and the saturation of the demand for the commodities which the chains
are best fitted to handle. The law of diminishing returns applies
to chains. If a chain gets too large, it becomes unwieldy, its
overhead increases and supervision becomes more difficult. The
chain can expand only within the limits of managerial capacities.
Hired managers lack strong motivation and it is hard to keep all
managers in an extensive system up to a minimum standard. The
limiting factor of the chain is the human element.

CHAPTER III

CHAIN-STORE COMPETITION AND BUYING PRACTICES

Consumers are interested primarily in getting their goods cheaply and, more often than not, overlook the manner in which one competitor treats another competitor or the producers from whom he buys. In the long run, the consumer should be interested in more than cheap prices. He should patronize a store that, besides selling cheaply, competes fairly; pays a fair price for its merchandise, its labor, its banking and other services; builds up the community rather than tears it down; and has no other evil social and economic effects. The objective of any economic institution should be to afford equal opportunity for all and increased comsumption at lower prices, but not at the expense of others.

The chain has reduced the cost of living. The other side of the chain problem is whether it is really a public asset. It may be that the low prices of the chain are costing the nation too much. It is unreasonable to say that the chain should be encouraged merely because it saves a few cents, if it hurts the public in other respects. The consumer can not look on the problem merely as a proposition of cheaper retail service. There are human values and questions of fair play to be considered.

On the other hand, one can not look on the problem solely from the point of view of the existing producer. The fact that hardships are inflicted on others may be the unavoidable price of progress. It is only unreasonable and unfair hardships that are to be condemned. The question now to be considered is whether the chain so conducts its business in respect to others that it is worthy of existence or whether it would be better from the standpoint of the ultimate public interest if the growth of chains were checked.

It is often charged that the chains are driving out the independents, not by means of superior efficiency, but by unfair competition, particularly by local price-cutting and the loss leader policy. Many chains are so far-flung that they can stand financially to cut prices in one locality, even below cost of production, in order to drive out their independent competition. When this is accomplished it is said that they will raise their prices and gain back more than they originally lost. Chains are also accused of offering nationally advertised goods at less than cost, thereby creating an impression of cheapness in all their goods. The consumer thus impressed buys her entire bill of goods at the chain, and pays high prices for the unidentified merchandise. Representative Kelly (Pennsylvania), co-author of the Capper-Kelly price-fixing bill, represents this attitude.

> "I think that fifty per cent of the present chain-store growth is due to this practice of using as bargain bait standard merchandise which is well known nationally at a certain price. They lure the people in by cutting those prices, and then make up their losses on other goods."[1]

As a result of these practices the chain is said to be causing the failure of thousands of independents who otherwise would have survived and taken their place in the community.

There is no doubt that such policies could be practiced by the chain. The "menace" of the chain is this possible abuse of power, and the bigger the chain the more powerful it might possibly

1. Speech before Committee on Rules, House of Representatives, 71st Congress, 2d Session, Hearing on H.R. 11, Capper-Kelly Price-Fixing Bill, May 21, 1930, p. 16. 1930, Government Printing Office, Washington, D.C.

be. Whether this fear actually is realized or is a product of their competitors' imagination is the question to be decided. If the chains are guilty of unfair practices, is their success predicated solely on such methods? If such practices do exist, should the chain be eliminated or does it offer some advantages to the consumer which would justify the existence of chains, shorn of their power to use unfair practices? In other words, could direct legislation solve such a problem without having to go so far as actually to eliminate the chains?

Unfair competition, by whomsoever practiced, is to be condemned.[2] The interests of business men are constantly in conflict, and out of this arises the problem of unfair competition. All competition injures and when one competitor loses, he usually cries, "Foul". Not all competition has been fair. It is easy to find cases of deceit and fraud in business and the deliberate ruining of weak rivals. One needs look only at the history of our great trusts to see how they fed on unscrupulous methods. Such tactics as were used by the trusts tended to make "competition" unendurable and wasteful and resulted in large corporations which could only keep their positions by using their power to eliminate their rivals or to force them to combine with them. If the chains, or anyone else, are engaging in this sort of competition, they are to be condemned. There is no economy in unfair competition. It enables a few to amass a large fortune but, to the many, it spells a large

---

2. It is impossible to give a definition of unfair competition. It usually takes a combination of practices to constitute unfairness. Unfair competition can be considered anything which tends to promote monopoly, to injure the efficient competitor unreasonably, to injure the consumer, to be at the expense of labor or of natural resources, or to be downright dishonest, fraudulent, or coercive.

loss.

A place exists for fair competition. Competition, in a general sense, is rivalry to excel in some activity. The nature and purpose of economic competition is to induce people to produce desirable things and to perform useful services by offering them an opportunity to sell such things for all that other folks are willing and able to pay for them, and at the same insuring that the one who pleases the consumer best will obtain a large share of the business. Unless competition is carried on under rules which assure that the prize will be won by the one who competes efficiently and fairly and honestly, the people in general will be apt to suffer. The ideal of business is a fair field and no favor, that it be required of the victor that he must not actively prevent anyone from competing and that he must not foul, that he win by value rendered and not by trickery. Competition supposedly leads to the survival of the fittest. But the conditions of the competition determine the kind of fitness that will survive -- the survivor of unfair competition will not be the good and efficient producer.

Whether the chain has attained its position by unfair competition and if so, if such practices can be eliminated without the elimination of the advantages of the chain is the matter to be considered. The most frequent charges made against the chains are the loss leader policy and local price-cutting.

The loss leader policy consists of the sale of certain goods, generally nationally advertised goods, at prices lower than usual in order to attract people into the store, in the hope that they will buy enough other merchandise that a profit will be made on the total transaction. There is some controversy as to just what is a "loss leader". Some goods are sold below the net purchase price plus the average cost of doing business; others are sold below the net purchase price. The former are most properly called "leaders"; the latter, "loss leaders". The latter is usually indefensible but the former often can be justified.

From the point of view of the consumer the problem of the loss leader is whether she is deceived by its use. If the consumer is lured to the store and then, under the impression that all other merchandise is equally cheap, is induced to buy non-comparable articles at higher than average prices, there is a different situation than if the other products remain normally-priced or if the consumer buys only the cut-price articles. Also, it is said that the consumer often can not buy the good which is advertised at the cut price. When the customer asks for the article, the clerk is said to try to substitute a private brand upon which there is a high markup. Moreover, competing independents who do not have the resources to carry a large number of loss leaders are found to substitute cheaper brands of poorer quality in order to have a product to sell at the same price as the chains. If these charges are true, the consumer is hurt by the loss leader policy.

On the other hand, the price-cutters insist that they do not sell goods at a low price in order to deceive the public but to get them into the store so that they will buy other merchandise. To get customers into a store costs money. There are two ways to attract them to a store for the first time -- advertising and the loss leaders. Of the two, many seemingly believe that the latter is cheaper and more effective. Once the customer is in the store she sees other merchandise she needs and buys it. If a store sells

one item at a loss and two or three at a normal profit, it may be
better off than if it had sold none at all. Even if a loss is in-
curred on the purchases of a particular customer on one day, if the
store has pleased her, she will return and make numerous other
purchases. Theoretically at least, such a line of reasoning seems
plausible. It is only when the loss leader is used for destructive
purposes that it is to be condemned from the point of view of the
consumer.

Do the chains use loss leaders? There is no doubt but
that they use leaders, in the above sense, and there is some evidence that they use a few loss leaders. Many witnesses in the price
maintenance hearings before Congressional committees have testified
under oath that the chains do resort to such practices. Since such
statements are made under oath, some credence must be given them.
A survey by W. J. Baxter,[3] Director of Research of the Chain Store
Research Bureau, showed that the leading chains were selling fifteen
per cent of their merchandise without profit. E. R. A. Seligman and
R. A. Love,[4] after an extensive study of price-cutting and its problems, came to the conclusion that there was no doubt but that the
leader policy was a widespread feature of chain-store operation.
The Federal Trade Commission reported that "an important aspect of
chain-store price policy is the frequent use of 'leaders' consisting
of specially low-selling prices on particular items".[5] Of 1,458
chains which operated 47,966 stores only 174 chains which operated

3. Chain Store Distribution and Management, p. 17. 1928, Harper and
Brothers, New York.
4. Price-Cutting and Price Maintenance, p. 153. 1932, Harper and
Brothers, New York.
5. Chain Store Inquiry, Vol. V, "Final Report on the Chain-Store Investigation", 74th Congress, 1st Session, Sen. Doc. No. 4, p. 38.
1935, Government Printing Office, Washington, D. C.

8,056 stores admitted that they sold in the last two years of the survey any merchandise at less than net purchase cost. Of 827 chains which operated over 35,000 stores ninety-seven, which operated 12,949 stores admitted that they sold some merchandise on the last week of one year at less than the actual net purchase price plus the average operating expenses for that year. Probably more engaged in this practice than admitted it. The average loss (below net purchase price plus average cost for one week) on leaders reported by grocery and meat chains was about ten per cent and that reported by drug chains about fourteen per cent. The range in loss in grocery and meat stores was 3.3 per cent to 14.6 per cent; in drugs 10.0 per cent to 26.2 per cent.[6] Such a policy was found to be most prevalent in grocery, combination, and drug stores. These also were the only fields in which any chain of over one hundred stores reported such a policy. In the Commission's study of prices and margins[7] further evidence was found that grocery and drug stores used the loss leader policy. In Washington the grocery chains sold 9.5 per cent of the items studied at an average gross profit of less than the average markup of all grocery stores. In Memphis and Detroit the corresponding figures were 5.2 per cent and 8.2 per cent. In drug chains in Washington 38.0 per cent of the items priced were sold at less than 30.0 per cent gross profit, whereas the average gross profit of 118 chain drug companies was 33.28 per cent. The corresponding percentages in Cincinnati, Memphis, and Detroit were 36.6 per cent, 30.7 per cent, and 27.4 per cent. The

6. Federal Trade Commission, Chain Store Inquiry, Vol. III, "Chain-Store Leaders and Loss Leaders", 73d Congress, 1st Session, Sen. Doc. No. 51, p. XI, 1932, Government Printing Office, Washington, D. C.
7. "Final Report of the Chain-Store Inquiry", op. cit., p. 41.

Commission found that none of these were sold at less than net purchase price but that many carried practically no gross profit; for
example, Lavoris averaged only 0.825 of one per cent gross profit
in the Washington stores.

The purposes of such a policy on the part of the chains
is expressed as follows by a chain-store official: "The extent to
which prices are cut depends on competition, the necessity of introducing a commodity, the need for moving a line of goods, and the desire to bring customers into the store."[8] It can thus be seen that
leaders are used for competitive purposes. This study is true only
for 1928. No reliable information can be found to indicate whether
chains still resort to such methods. The opponents say they do;
the chains say they are eliminating leaders. The "A & P" for some
time carried the advertisement, "No More Specials", although this
may not be indicative of their policy. It is generally believed
that the policy of leaders is still followed but there is no proof
that goods are ever sold below the cost to the chain.

The chains did not invent the leader. It has been a feature of retailing as long as there have been regular prices to cut.
Leaders and loss leaders were used before chains ever became an important factor. If there are chains which do not measure up to
exacting standards of competition, there are also a large number of
independents who likewise fall below their own picture of competitive decency. The independents who complain about chain practices
forget the competition that exists in their own ranks and the un-
ethical practices to which they themselves resort. There is no

8. Ibid., p. 39.

correlation between bigness and wickedness -- unfairness seems to exist in small stores just about as frequently as in large ones.[9] Hector Lazo, Washington code advisor for the National Association of Retail Grocers, testified as follows before a Congressional Committee:

> "In this classification, (loss leader selling) as in everything else in the trade, there is no one particular type of distribution which had all the virtues nor any one particular type of distribution which had all the faults."[10]

Dr. Paul Nystrom, expert on retailing at Columbia University writes:

> "It has been frequently remarked among those following price maintenance controversies that breaks or cuts in suggested resale prices during recent years have been more frequently made by independent stores than by either chain stores or department stores."[11]

Hence, it can be seen that the little shopkeepers' morals are no better than the chains'. His opportunities are only more limited.

The fact that the independent resorts to the same practice does not excuse the chain for doing so, or _vice_ _versa_. Predatory price-cutting is always reprehensible. But the fact that the chains have borrowed a weapon developed by the independents, and used it to better advantage, is no excuse for the elimination of the chain and the retention of the independent. Leaders can never be abolished by the elimination of the chain. To get rid of the leaders, they must be attacked directly.

Is the consumer deceived by such a policy? The practice

9. Klein, Julius, former assistant secretary, Department of Commerce, "The Outlook for the Chain Store", Chain Store Age, Vol. V, (Nov., 1929), p. 55.
10. Hearings Before the Special Committee to Investigate the American Retail Federation, 74th Congress, 1st session, June, July, Aug. 1935, p. 259. Government Printing Office, Washington, D. C.
11. Economics of Retailing, 3d edition, Vol. I, p. 259. 1930, Ronald Press Company, New York.

is so widespread and so universally recognized that most consumers
know that leaders are sold only to get customers into the store. As
a result, the customer goes from store to store and buys the leaders and nothing else. E. D. McGarry,[12] of the University of Buffalo, found that the customers of chain stores tended to shop around
among a larger number of stores than did the patrons of independent stores, and that the chain customers bought a smaller proportion of their total groceries from a single store. This is due largely to shopping for specials. With the prices in chains all plainly
marked the consumer has every chance to take care of herself.

The chains do not sell all, or nearly all, of their identified merchandise at less than total cost. A large proportion of
their business is done in nationally advertised products.[13] Since
the chains do make profits, they can not cut all their identified
merchandise below cost. With a large proportion of national brands
sold at a normal profit, the consumer has an excellent opportunity
to compare the prices of different retail outlets. Of course, some
will be deceived by a policy of a few leaders, but not enough to

12. Mortality in Retail Trade, p. 108. University of Buffalo Studies in Business, No. 4. 1930, University of Buffalo, Buffalo, New
York.
13. Steffler, C. W., estimates that in 1927 the chains did eighty
per cent of their sales in nationally advertised products. "Do
Chain Methods Menace Free Competition?", Commerce and Finance, Vol.
XVII, (July 4, 1928), p. 144.
A report by the Bureau of Advertising of the American Newspaper
Publisher's Association estimated that nationally advertised products account for three-quarters of the total retail business done
by chains. (Quoted by Nichols, J. P., Chain Store Manual, 1936 edition, p. 105. 1936, Institute of Distribution, New York, Figures
unchecked.)
Zimmerman, M. M., reports that sixty-five to seventy per cent of
the standard items in an "A & P" store are national brands (The Challenge of Chain Store Distribution, p. 108. 1931, Harper and Brothers, New York.)

account for the success of the chain.

It may not be unfair for the chain store to push its own brands. It is no more unfair competition to push one's own brand than to use advertisements which say that the customer will get stung if she does not use nationally advertised products. The consumer is not necessarily hurt if she takes the chains' private brands. The chains take pains to put under their own name articles of merit for the grade specified, articles which are often of greater value, quality, and price considered, than nationally advertised products.[14] The chains admit that they obtain a higher gross margin on their private brands than they do on their nationally advertised products, but deny that the consumer is hurt thereby. They claim that the difference in price can be explained, not by the difference in quality, but by the excessive burden of advertising charges which the nationally-known product bears. The above mentioned studies tend to bear out this contention, although they are not conclusive.

There are many claims of the substitution of private brands for national brands, but, in general, substitution is against chain policy. It is not good business. Such tactics would soon alienate the customer and drive her from the store. Once the asked-for article is put on the counter, the merits of the chain-store brand are extolled and the customer left to her own choice. The chain, moreover, is interested in cutting labor costs. It takes time for a clerk to sell a different brand than that for which the customer asks. It also takes sales ability, a quality which is not demanded

---

14. See Federal Trade Commission, "Quality of Canned Fruits and Vegetables", op. cit., and Vaile, R. S., and Child, A. M., op. cit. (surveyed on page 56 ff.)

in chain-store clerks. To obtain this sales ability higher wages
would be necessary. When a customer asks for a product by brand
name, she gets it; when she asks for a product without specifying
the brand, the clerk suggests the chain brand. Such a policy is
not unfair competition.

There is some question as to what constitutes a store's
total cost on any one item. If it means the average cost of doing
business, then any item sold below the average margin is a leader.
Not all items have the same cost to sell.[15] The cost to sell varies
with different items and depends on the rapidity of turnover, the
amount of suggestion required, etc. What constitutes a leader depends, not on average selling cost, but on the actual selling cost
of the particular item. Small margins often yield large profits,
and large margins often do not yield sufficient income to cover the
actual cost. The chains claim to base their markup, to a substantial extent, on the actual cost to handle the item. They also claim
that the independents, when they charge an average markup, ask too
high a margin on some items, and are really the price-cutters on
others, although they do not know it. Many of the "long" items may
actually involve a loss. Independents who try to meet chain prices and still give services are, in reality, using the majority
of their products as leaders, in the sense that the gross margin
does not cover the total cost of each article. There is no accounting system yet devised, however, which would enable a retailer

15. See U. S. Department of Commerce, Bureau of Foreign and Domestic
Commerce, Distribution Cost Studies, No. 2, Bettner, G. E., "Analyzing Retail Selling Time". 1928, Government Printing Office, Washington, D. C.   In a survey of several items in department
stores it was found that the selling expense of each item varied,
ranging from $0.041 per dollar of sales to $0.349 in 1925 and $0.034
to $0.162 in 1927.

to tell his true costs to sell an individual item. The ultimate aim
of retail expense accounting is to obtain these unit costs. Until
such costs are obtained, it is impossible to tell on just what items
the chains and independents are cutting prices. The only criterion
which can be used is the effect of various selling prices on total
profits. Apparently the chains, which have better accounting systems than do the independents, feel that low margins on some items
increase their profits.

The chain does have the financial possibility to practice
local price-cutting. The loss in one city would hardly be felt in
the total profits of a large chain. Chains do have wide variation
in prices between cities, but this might possibly be explained by
other factors, such as the necessity to meet competition, differences in the cost of living, differences in transportation costs,
etc.[16] It is true that independents do not quote different prices
in different stores, but only because they do not have different
stores. A study of independent prices in Washington, D. C., New
York, St. Paul, etc. would show that independents do not charge the
same prices in every city. If it is consistent for individual grocers to charge different prices in different cities, it is also consistent for chains to charge different prices. There may even be
different prices in different sections of the city, for the prices
of independents vary also. Neither local conditions nor competition
can be standardized. The mere fact of variation in prices does not

16. Cover, J. H., _Retail Price Behavior, Studies in Business Administration, School of Business, University of Chicago_, Vol. V, No. 2,
p. 26. 1935, University of Chicago Press, Chicago, reports average
prices in chain drug stores as 100 in Washington, 104 in New York,
108 in St. Paul, 109 in Minneapolis, and 111 in Atlanta.

support a claim of local price-cutting.

Charges persist that one of the reasons for such variation is to drive out of business smaller competitors. The Federal Trade Commission found enough indication of this to recommend that the prohibition of unfair competition in Section Five of the Federal Trade Commission Act be broadened to include unfair or deceptive acts and practices in or affecting interstate commerce.[17] The Commission found that the chains had no consistent pricing policy and that the necessity to meet competition was one of the most important reasons for price variations.[18] Some chains claimed to meet only the competition of chains in the same line of business. No chain professed to initiate price cuts and most of them merely stated that they met competitive situations as they arose. The Commission concluded:

"The competitive advantage of chains over single-store competitors, arising from the fact that chains do business in many localities, is most aggressively pursued on those occasions when chains cut their prices locally below the prices of their competitors in that locality, while maintaining prices in their other stores. Discussion of this question by officials of leading chain organizations indicates that it is quite a usual practice among them to cut prices locally not only to meet, but to go below, the prices of their competitors. A few chains say that this is against their rules, but exceptions to the rule appear even among these few. Others refer to such undercutting of competitors' prices as a matter of course, while a few of them illustrate the effective use that may be made of this powerful competitive device. In addition to these competitive price cuts, it is apparent that the pricing of specials and the reduction of prices to stimulate the volume of business of a particular store also lead the chains to sell at different prices in different communities. Whether or not price reductions made for the latter purposes result in prices lower than those of competitors is a matter with which the chain-store executives interviewed do not seem to be particularly concerned. And in this connection it is interesting to note that, although perhaps aware of their existence, chain-store officials in discussing their price policies make little or no mention of State or Federal laws against price discrimination as influencing or limiting such policies."[19]

17. "Final Report of the Chain-Store Inquiry", op. cit., p. 97.
18. Ibid., p. 33.   19. Ibid., p. 34.

Thus, it is evident that chains have used local price-cutting. However, the effectiveness of this policy is limited by the competition between chains themselves. Such a policy would be effective only if there were inter-chain agreements, of which there is no evidence.

One significant fact remains in favor of the chains. The Clayton Act forbids local price-cutting and the Federal Trade Commission exists primarily to reach unfair business practices which the anti-trust laws do not reach. If chain competition has been flagrantly unfair, the Federal Trade Commission should have found something in it long ago to have warranted interference. Thus far they have not seen fit to do so. Neither have there been any prosecutions under the Clayton Act. Either the law-enforcing agencies have been lax or the chains have not been engaging in such practices as openly as is supposed. At least there are laws on the statute books which, if enforced, would put an end to this one particularly potent form of unfair competition.

If chain competition were as vicious as is supposed, it would seem that more independents would be failing today than failed before there were many chains. Retailing has always been a business with a high death rate. When independents were putting each other out of business, the passing of a small retailer was noiseless; now his passing is marked by the cry that the chain has committed another crime. Retailers have always failed and succeeded and they fail and succeed today in just about the same proportions as ever.

A number of studies have been made of the failure rate of independents and all bear out two facts-- that the mortality of retail stores is high and that the mortality has stayed the same, or even decreased, as chains have developed. As far back as 1840 General

H. A. S. Dearborn, collector for the port of Boston, made a statement
that out of one hundred merchants and traders not more than three
were likely to acquire independence.[20] In 1845, in Worcester, Massachusetts, it was estimated that for retail business in general at
least one-fourth failed within five years, one-half in ten years,
and two-thirds within fifteen years.[21] A book published in 1873[22]
asserted that ninety-seven out of one hundred retail stores were
bound to fail sooner or later. In 1900 John Wanamaker testified
before a Federal body that only about four per cent who started in
the mercantile business succeeded.[23] The magazine, System, in 1916
undertook a study of business failures in eight fields from 1886 to
1916 in three representative towns.[24] Table XXIV shows the number of
firms which dropped out of business within each five-year period.
Not all of the firms which left business failed, but the great majority of the passings were because of lack of success. This shows
that practically one-half of the businesses (almost three-fifths of
the grocery stores) passed out of existence every five years. This
table probably understates the mortality, for by the choice of five-
year periods, many firms which started after the count was taken
and which failed before the next count would not have appeared in the
tabulations. In Waterloo, Iowa the same study showed the average

---

20. Quoted in Nystrom, P. H., Economics of Retailing, 1st edition,
pp.301, 302. 1915, Ronald Press Company, New York.
21. Ibid., p. 302.
22. An Old Merchant, Mercantile Failures, 1873. Mercantile Publishing Company, St. Louis.
23. Nystrom, P. H., op. cit., p. 302.
24. Dennis, S. A., "What Can We Do About the Business Death Rate?",
System, Vol. XXIX, (January 1916), pp. 3-14.
    "Will You Have a Business in 1924?", System, Vol. XXI, (January,
1917), pp. 107-109.
    "When Will My Business Die?", System, Vol. XXXII, (October, 1917),
pp. 523-526.

Table XXIV

BUSINESS MORTALITY: PERCENTAGE OF STORES IN EIGHT FIELDS
OF RETAILING WHICH LEFT BUSINESS WITHIN SELECTED
FIVE-YEAR PERIODS IN A "REPRESENTATIVE CITY"

Field	1886–1891	1981–1896	1896–1901	1901–1906	1911–1916
Grocery	44	61	56	61	63
Hardware	40	45	50	36	66
Drug	37	51	45	30	39
Jewelry	33	46	36	41	65
Dry Goods	50	59	65	57	39
Clothing	45	80	40	52	56
Boots and Shoes	53	53	48	57	58
Furniture	70	50	37	62	61

Source:
Dennis, S. A., "When Will My Business Die?", System, Vol.
XXXII, (October, 1917), p. 525.

failure rate for five-year-periods to be forty-five per cent in groceries, forty-three per cent in drugs, sixty-eight per cent in dry
goods, fifty per cent in jewelry, forty-nine per cent in shoes, forty-eight per cent in hardware, forty-eight per cent in meats, thir-
ty-nine per cent in cigars, thirty-eight per cent in furniture, and
thirty-five per cent in clothiers.[25] In 1910 it was stated that over
twenty per cent of the listing in Bradstreet's retail credit list
were taken off each year and that changes were made in a large number more, some of them due to weakness.[26] A study of Oshkosh, Wisconsin[27] from 1890 to 1912 in seven fields found a similar rapid death
rate of retail stores. The results of this study are presented in
Table XXV. This shows a steady decline in the number of original
stores which remained in any one year and also a steady inflow of

25. System, Vol. XXIX, op. cit., p. 6.
26. Quoted in Nystrom, P. H., op. cit., p. 303.
27. Ibid., p. 307.

new stores to keep the total number approximately the same.

A study by Nebraska University of the failure of grocery stores in Lincoln and its suburbs in 1926[28] found a large turnover in this field. The annual withdrawl rate, not all of which involved bankruptcy or loss, was usually over twenty per cent and ranged to about thirty-five per cent. About two-thirds of those who went out of business were failures in the sense that they had not made expenses. Table XXVI gives the failure rate per year from 1900 to 1923. There seems to be a slight upward trend in the failure rate but this is due to the post-war depression.

A study of business mortality in Buffalo, 1918 to 1928, by E. D. McGarry of the University of Buffalo is the best known of such studies.[29] It includes grocery, drug, shoe, and hardware stores. The method was to take the number of stores listed in the directory each year and to compare the lists of a number of years. Not all of those leaving business were failures but the large majority were. Table XXVII shows the percentage which withdrew each year. There is only a slight evidence of an increase in the failure rate of grocery stores, the field in which chain compeition is the greatest. There was a considerable increase in drugs, a slight increase in shoes, and a slight decrease in hardware, a non-chain field. It may be that as the retail business grows older one might expect a decline in the failure rate, except for the influence of chain competition. The fact that failures are not decreasing may really mean,

28. Nebraska Studies in Business, No. 14, "Some Aspects of Grocery Store Failures". 1926, University of Nebraska, Lincoln.
29. McGarry, E. D., Mortality in Retail Trade, University of Buffalo Studies in Business, No. 4, 1930, University of Buffalo, Bureau of Business and Social Research, Buffalo, New York.

Table XXV

BUSINESS MORTALITY: DECLINE IN ORIGINAL NUMBER
OF RETAIL STORES BY SELECTED PERIODS IN OSHKOSH, WISCONSIN,
1890 TO 1912

Year	Number of Original Stores Remaining in Business									
	1890	1893	1895	1898	1900	1903	1905	1908	1910	1912
Existing Stores										
1890	145	117	91	73	50	37	29	27	18	18
New Firms, 1893		43	24	18	15	12	11	9	8	8
1895			61	33	20	19	17	16	13	9
1898				52	34	26	20	15	15	13
1900					45	31	19	13	10	9
1903						35	24	19	16	13
1905							32	19	13	10
1908								35	24	20
1910									41	34
1912										38
Total	145	160	176	176	164	160	152	153	158	172

Source:
Nystrom, P. H., Economics of Retailing, 1st edition, p. 307. 1915,
Ronald Press Company, New York.

not that chains have no effect on the failure rate of independents,
but that they actually are driving out independents who otherwise
would have survived.

Dr. P. D. Converse studied the mortality of retail stores
in eleven fields in 255 Illinois towns, 1925-1930.[30] This study was
based on the rating books of R. G. Dun and Company and probably understates the withdrawal rate for two reasons. First, the smaller
stores, among whom most failures occur, are sometimes not given a
rating; and secondly, the counts were made as of July of each year,
so that firms which remained in business only a short time would not
have been counted. Table XXVIII shows the number of original stores

30. "Business Mortality of Illinois Retail Stores, 1925-1930", Bureau of Business Research, University of Illinois, Bull. No. 41. 1932,
University of Illinois, Urbana, Illinois.

Table XXVI

BUSINESS MORTALITY: PERCENTAGE OF GROCERY STORES
IN LINCOLN AND SUBURBS WHICH WENT OUT OF BUSI-
NESS EACH YEAR, 1900 to 1923

Year	Per Cent Leaving	Year	Per Cent Leaving
1900	26	1912	23
1901	19	1913	25
1902	28	1914	26
1903	28	1915	22
1904	15	1916	19
1905	20	1917	21
1906	27	1918	36
1907	28	1919	a
1908	20	1920	34
1909	31	1921	22
1910	30	1922	31
1911	26	1923	33

a No data available.

Source:
Nebraska Studies in Business, No. 14, "Some Aspects of Gro-
cery Store Failures", p. 7. 1926, Committee on Business
Research, College of Business Administration, University of
Nebraska, Lincoln, Nebraska.

Table XXVII

BUSINESS MORTALITY: PERCENTAGE OF STORES IN BUFFALO, NEW YORK
IN FOUR SELECTED FIELDS WHICH LEFT BUSINESS EACH YEAR, 1918-1928

Year	Groceries	Drug	Shoe	Hardware
1918	29.6	6.7	19.0	18.5
1919	37.0	14.9	15.3	17.2
1920	32.8	7.2	22.8	14.2
1921	32.8	14.1	14.1	21.2
1922	39.1	12.1	26.3	16.2
1923	38.8	11.8	30.4	18.7
1924	36.3	14.3	28.0	11.4
1925	34.9	11.7	17.7	18.7
1926	42.2	11.6	20.2	13.7
1927	32.8	19.2	22.5	12.9

Source:
McGarry, E. D., Mortality in Retail Trade, p. 60. University of Buffalo, Studies in Business, No. 4. 1930, University of Buffalo, Bureau of Business and Social Research,
Buffalo, New York.

Table XXVIII

BUSINESS MORTALITY: PERCENTAGE OF RETAIL STORES WHICH EXISTED
IN JULY 1925 IN ELEVEN FIELDS IN 255 ILLINOIS TOWNS GONE
FROM BUSINESS IN JULY OF EACH YEAR FOLLOWING, 1926 to 1930

| Trade | Per Cent Gone Each Year | | | | |
	1926	1927	1928	1929	1930
Furniture	8.7	18.5	24.5	30.2	36.2
Grocery	17.5	28.5	38.0	43.8	49.5
Meat	14.1	25.0	33.2	41.1	46.3
Dry Goods	7.9	15.5	24.0	31.6	35.5
Hardware	5.2	12.0	17.0	23.8	27.8
Garages	17.2	30.5	39.9	44.8	51.0
Drugs	7.0	11.3	16.4	20.3	24.3
Department Stores	9.7	19.4	22.6	29.0	38.7
General Stores	14.4	32.8	29.6	35.4	40.5
Clothing	8.8	17.6	25.7	30.4	36.2
Restaurants	28.5	44.5	53.7	60.6	64.7
Total	15.9	26.7	35.2	41.0	46.3

Source:
Converse, P. D., "Business Mortality of Illinois Retail Stores,
1925-1930", p. 14. Bureau of Business Research, University of
Illinois, Bulletin No. 41. 1932, University of Illinois, Urbana, Illinois.

---

of each type gone from business in July of each year. In a comparison of these results with those of the study by System[31] it is apparent that retailers have been passing from business in about the
same numbers for the last fifty years. Dr. Converse concluded that
"the inference from these facts is that the growth of chain stores
has not increased the number of dealers quitting business".[32]

Two other studies bear out this conclusion. H. D. Greer[33]
found the percentage of meat stores which left business each year to
be declining, especially since 1928. Table XXIX summarizes this
study. R. S. Vaile[34] found that in Minneapolis, St. Paul, and Duluth

31. See Table XXIV.   32. Converse, P. D., op. cit., p. 31.
33. "Business Mortality Among Retail Meat Stores in Chicago Between
1920 and 1933", Journal of Business, University of Chicago, Vol. IX,
(1936), pp. 189-209.   34. Grocery Retailing, University of Minnesota, Studies in Economics and Business, No. 1, 1932, University
of Minnesota Press, Minneapolis.

in 1926 twenty-four to twenty-eight per cent of all grocery stores disappeared or changed ownership. He also found that from 1926 to 1930 there was a definite and material reduction in grocery store mortality.

Several studies have attempted to compare the mortality rate of a recent period with one before the chains were very important. P. C. Olsen found the range of grocery store failures per year in Louisville, Kentucky from 1921 to 1929 to be from twenty-one to twenty-seven per cent with an average of twenty-four per cent, whereas for the period 1891 to 1899 there was exactly the same range and an average of twenty-three per cent.[35] For drug stores the range was six to fourteen per cent in the '20's whereas in the '90's it was from ten to nineteen per cent.[36] The same author found that in Texarkana, Texas, home of Representative Patman, co-author of the Robinson-Patman anti-discount bill, thirty-seven per cent of the independent food and grocery stores which originated in the period, 1925 to 1935, were out of business in one year, and that between 1901 and 1911 forty-six per cent failed each year.[37] R. L. Furst[38] found that during 1917 to 1930 individually-owned grocery stores went out of business at almost exactly the same rate as during 1891 to 1904 when there were no chain grocery stores in the city. The percentages of failures were 21.6 per cent and 21.8 per cent.

From these studies it is apparent that something besides chain competition is responsible for the withdrawal of independents

---

35. "Louisville Blues", Chain Store Progress, Vol. II, (August, 1930), p. 2.   36. "Independent Mortality Unaffected By Chains", Chain Store Progress, Vol. III, (February, 1931), p. 3 .
37. Reported in Nichols, J. P., Chain Store Manual, 1936 edition, p. 17, 1936, Institute of Distribution, Inc., New York.
38. Grocery Stores in Fort Wayne, Indiana, M. A. Thesis, University of Chicago, 1931.

Table XXIX

BUSINESS MORTALITY: PERCENTAGE OF MEAT STORES IN CHICAGO
WHICH LEFT BUSINESS EACH YEAR, 1920 TO 1933

Year	Per Cent Which Left
1921	37.4
1922	31.0
1923	25.6
1924	23.1
1925	21.5
1926	23.7
1927	24.8
1928	21.9
1929	21.5
1930	22.6
1931	18.4
1932	17.9
1933	15.9
Average	23.3

Source:
Greer, H. C., "Business Mortality Among Retail Meat Stores
in Chicago Between 1920 and 1933". Journal of Business,
University of Chicago, Vol. IX, (1936), p. 194.

from business. It is impossible to isolate the effects of chain competition on independent mortality but the growth of chains does not
seem to have had as serious effect as has been charged. Particularly significant is the fact that most failures of independents occur within the first two years of business. If unfair competition
were responsible for a large part of the store "deaths", it would
seem that old established stores would fail about as often from such
a cause. Such does not seem to be the case. E. D. McGarry[39] found
that on an average 60.3 per cent of the grocery stores passed out
of existence in their first year and 11.9 per cent in their second
year. From then on there was a declining percentage; 5.4 per cent

39. Op. cit., p. 11.

in the third year; 2.8 per cent, the fourth; 1.5 per cent, the fifth; 0.8 per cent, the sixth; 0.6 per cent, the seventh; 0.2 per cent, the eighth; and 0.2 per cent, the ninth. Once a store survived its first few years and proved its right to exist, the withdrawal rate was almost negligible. Such small percentages as did exist might well have been successful withdrawals. It would seem that if chains were using local price-cutting flagrantly, they would use it most often to drive out the very successful independent. It is reasonable to expect that the independents who live the longest are the successful ones, although they may be small neighborhood stores in whose trade the chain is not interested. If a store proves its efficiency and weathers the first few years, it has an excellent chance to continue. P. D. Converse[40] found that of new concerns of all types which entered business in two typical towns, 31.4 per cent quit in the first year, 47.4 per cent in two years, and 58.7 per cent in three years. Table XXX shows the percentage of meat stores in Chicago which closed in each year of existence. R. S. Vaile[41] found that only sixty per cent of the grocery stores survived one year and only thirty per cent four years. Dr. Olsen found that in Louisville[42] an average of forty-five per cent of the grocery stores passed out of existence in their first year during 1921 to 1927 and that an average of forty-three per cent did the same during 1891 to 1899. R. L. Furst obtained similar results in his study as Table XXXI shows.

A study of the causes of retail failures will show the

40. Op. cit., p. 33.
41. Op. cit., p. 13.
42. Op. cit., p. 2.

Table XXX

BUSINESS MORTALITY: PERCENTAGE OF MEAT STORES IN CHICAGO
WHICH LEFT BUSINESS IN EACH YEAR OF EXISTENCE, 1920 TO 1933

Year	Per Cent Which Left
1	24.9
2	20.2
3	14.5
4	7.5
5	5.7
6	3.8
7	2.9
8	2.3
9	1.8
10	1.1
11	.9
12	.8

Source:
  Greer, H. C., "Business Mortality Among Retail Meat Stores
  in Chicago Between 1920 and 1933", Journal of Business, University of Chicago, Vol. IX, (1936), p. 199.

part the chains play in causing independents to fail. The great majority of the failures of independents are due to inexperience,
inefficiency, and lack of capital. Many people think anyone can run
a store, especially a grocery store. As a result, many people open
stores who do not have a chance for success. Tables XXXII to XXXVI
summarize various studies of the causes of retail failures. It is
obvious that the part of management is a leading one. Insufficient
capital is really an indication of inefficient management, a result
of trying to do too much business on a given amount of capital.
Competition does not seem to play a large part in the cause of failures. In most cases where competition is charged as a cause, it is
found that other causes were the underlying reasons for the failure.
Competition only brings out inefficiency more rapidly. Table XXXVI
shows how much unwarranted blame is placed on competition. Whereas

Table XXXI

BUSINESS MORTALITY: PERCENTAGE OF GROCERY STORES IN FORT WAYNE, INDIANA WHICH WENT OUT OF BUSINESS IN EACH YEAR OF EXISTENCE FOR THE PERIODS, 1916-1930 AND 1890-1904

Year	1916-1930	1890-1904
1	40.3	38.7
2	12.1	13.2
3	7.4	5.4
4	5.5	4.8
5	3.0	2.6
6	1.4	1.6
7	0.7	1.4
8	0.5	1.8
9	0.3	1.8
10	---	.2
11	0.1	.4
12	0.1	.2
13	---	---
14	---	---
15	---	---
In business after 15 years	0.4	0.8

Source:
Furst, R. L., "Relationships Between the Numbers of Chain and Individually Owned Grocery Stores in Fort Wayne". Journal of Business, University of Chicago, Vol. V, (1932), p. 342.

55.5 per cent of the owners said competition contributed to their failure, the creditors thought competition a factor in only 14.6 per cent of the cases. In a study at Louisville, Kentucky[43] it was found that out of thirty failures in only two was chain-store competition an important factor. In a similar study in New Jersey[44] it

---

43. United States Department of Commerce, Bureau of Foreign and Domestic Commerce, Trade Information Bulletin No. 627. Plummer, W. C., "Credit Extension and Business Failures", p. 2, 1929. Government Printing Office, Washington, D. C.
44. United States Department of Commerce, Bureau of Foreign and Domestic Commerce, Domestic Commerce Series. No. 54, "Causes of Business Failures and Bankruptcies of Individuals in New Jersey in 1929-1930", p. 2. 1931, Government Printing Office, Washington, D. C.

Table XXXII

BUSINESS MORTALITY: PERCENTAGE OF FIRMS
WHICH FAILED BECAUSE OF SPECIFIC CAUSES

Cause	Per Cent Which Failed	
Beginner's Handicaps		
Lack of Capital	29.7	
Incompetence	30.2	
Inexperience	4.6	
Unwise Credits	2.0	66.5
Personal Faults of Character		
Fraud	10.3	
Neglect of Business	2.0	
Personal Extravagance	.7	13.0
Factors Threatening Success		
Competition	1.9	
Failure of Others	1.3	
Speculation in Other Business	.8	
Disasters, etc.	16.5	20.5

Source:
Nystrom, P. H., Economics of Retailing, 1st edition,
pp. 313-314. 1915 Ronald Press Company, New York.
(Adapted from a classification by Bradstreet.)

was found that competition did not occupy an important place and that where competition was alleged to be the cause, one or more other things were found to be more important.

In the study of business mortality by Professor Converse[45] the failure rate was given for cities of various sizes. If chain competition were the chief cause of failure, it would seem that the failure rate would be greatest where chains were the most numerous, that is, in the larger cities. Table XXXVII summarizes the findings. In the grocery field the greatest failure rate was in the small towns; in the drug field it increased with the size of the town, except for towns under 400, where the failure rate was greater than in the lar-

45. Op. cit., pp. 13, 14.

Table XXXIII

BUSINESS MORTALITY: PERCENTAGE OF FIRMS
WHICH FAILED BECAUSE OF SPECIFIC CAUSES

Cause	Per Cent Which Failed	
Beginner's Handicaps		
Lack of Capital	29.5	
Incompetence and Inexperience	24.0	
Unwise Credits	4.4	
General Expense Too High	3.0	
Poor Location	2.2	
Expansion	2.0	65.1
Personal Faults of Character		
Fraud	4.0	
Neglect of Business	4.0	
Personal Extravagance	4.8	
Intemperance	2.0	14.8
Factors Threatening Success		
Disaster	10.3	
Failure of Others	3.4	
Speculation	2.1	
Competition	1.4	
Miscellaneous	2.9	20.1

Source:
 Nystrom, P. H., Economics of Retailing, 1st edition, p. 314.
 1915, Ronald Press Company, New York. (Adapted from classification by O. W. Mayer, Credit Manager, Steel, Wideles, and
 Company, in System, February, 1914.)

---

ger cities. The same characteristic failures seem to occur even where chain competition is not strong. E. D. McGarry,[46] after charting chains by wards to see where chain competition was strongest, concluded that there was little indication that the competition of chains increased the mortality rate of independents. Dr. Julius Klein of the Department of Commerce, says, "The plain truth appears to be that the influence of competition in occasioning retail disasters is enormously exaggerated."[47]

46. Op. cit., p. 47.   47. Quoted in Le Boutillier, P., "The Position of the Independent Store", p. 101. Boston Conference on Retail Distribution, 1929.

Table XXXIV

BUSINESS MORTALITY: REASONS FOR THE FAILURE
OF 167 INDEPENDENT STORES IN THIRTY TOWNS, 1927-1931

Cause	Number Which Failed
Bankruptcy	29 stores
Unsuccessful Retirement	57
Chain-Store Competition	8[a]
Independent Competition	1
Voluntary Retirement	13
Successful Retirement	21
Sold Out	1
Fire	3
Death	10
Remodeling	1
Changed to New Line	1
Merger of Two Independents	1
Sold to, Succeeded by, or Merged with Chain	21

[a] Contributed to four others.

Source:
Federal Trade Commission, Chain Store Inquiry, Vol. 1. "Chain
Stores in the Small Town", 73d Congress, 2d Session, Sen. Doc.
No. 93, p. 14. 1934, Government Printing Office, Washington,
D. C.

Much of the failure of independents is due to the fact
that too many enter the field. In fields where a large amount of
capital is required, such as hardware, or where technical experience
or an examination is required, as in drug stores, the failure rate
is very low. The inefficient and ill-prepared do not start. In
fields where little capital or technical experience is required many
enter only to fail and have still others take their places. The
rate of openings approximates that of closings. In the McGarry
study[48] it was found that most of the failures were in the small
general convenience neighborhood stores, or the "fill-in" grocery

---

48. Op. cit., p. 65 ff.

Table XXXV

BUSINESS MORTALITY: PERCENTAGE OF STORES
WHICH FAILED BECAUSE OF SPECIFIC CAUSES

Cause	Per Cent Which Failed
Lack of Capital	37.2
Incompetence	31.4
Inexperience	4.9
Unwise Credits	2.1
Fraud	1.7
Neglect of Business	.9
Personal Extravagance	.5
Speculation	.3
Competition	3.9
Exigencies	15.6
Failure of Others	1.5

Source:
Nichols, J. P., Chain Store Manual, p. 63. 1932, National
Chain Store Association, New York. (The figures are those
of the Domestic Distribution Division of the United States
Chamber of Commerce. Unchecked.)

---

stores. Of those checked forty-two per cent of the owners had had
no training even closely connected with retailing. A great difficulty with independents is that they are too small. In 1926 twenty-
eight per cent of the grocery stores had annual sales of less than
$5,000.[49] In 1929 forty-three per cent of the stores were doing
less than $10,000 business a year,[50] while in 1933 sixty-four per
cent did less than $10,000 business.[51] When one realizes that a gro-
cery store makes net profits of only about two per cent of sales, it
can be seen readily that stores with a volume of under $10,000 are
in a very vulnerable position. Many enter with no experience. In

---

49. United States Chamber of Commerce, Domestic Distribution Department, Retail and Wholesale Trade of Eleven Cities, p. 119. 1928,
Chamber of Commerce of United States, Washington, D. C.
50. Bureau of Census, Fifteenth Census of the United States, 1930,
Distribution, Vol. I, Part I, p. 14. 1933, Government Printing Office, Washington, D. C.
51. Bureau of Census, Census of American Business, Retail Distribution, 1933, Vol. I to V, p. 34. 1935, Government Printing Office,
Washington, D. C.

Table XXXVI

BUSINESS MORTALITY: PERCENTAGE OF TIMES SPECIFIC FACTORS
CONTRIBUTED TO BUSINESS FAILURES,
CLASSIFIED BY OWNERS' AND CREDITORS' OPINIONS

Cause	Owner's Opinion	Creditor's Opinion
Business Depression	76.1	33.2
Insufficient Capital	55.5	36.2
Competition	55.5	14.6
Excessive Overhead	40.8	13.1
Domestic and Personal	39.9	30.7
Poor Location	28.0	5.5
Changes in Trading Area	24.3	3.5
Inefficient Management	21.6	54.8
Bad Debt Losses	21.1	16.6
Decline in Value of Assets	14.2	---
Excessive Interest Charges	14.2	0.5
Too Much Credit Buying	11.9	4.5
Losses From Signing Notes	11.0	1.0
Expanding Too Rapidly	9.6	2.5
Lack of Adequate Books	7.8	2.0
Real Estate Losses	7.3	2.0
Speculation Losses	4.1	3.5
Auto Accident Judgment	2.3	0.5
Insufficient Insurance	1.8	---
Unusual Expenses	1.4	0.5
Dishonesty and Fraud	---	27.1

Source:
    United States Department of Commerce, Bureau of Foreign and Domestic Commerce, Domestic Commerce Series, No. 69. Sadd, V., and Williams, R. T., "Causes of Commercial Bankruptcies", p. 15. 1932, Government Printing Office, Washington, D. C.

---

the Nebraska study[52] it was found that over sixty per cent of the failed merchants had had no previous retail experience before opening their stores. Almost all investigators report the same condition. In the Department of Commerce studies of Louisville and New Jersey it was found that over one-half of the failures kept no books and that over one-third never took an inventory. In addition, credit losses were eight or nine times those of active firms. Independent

52. Op. cit., p. 11.

Table XXXVII

BUSINESS MORTALITY: PERCENTAGE OF ORIGINAL STORES
GONE FROM BUSINESS AS OF JULY OF EACH YEAR,
CLASSIFIED BY SIZE OF TOWN

Size of Town	Grocery Stores				
	1926	1927	1928	1929	1930
Under 400	29.4	42.4	48.2	50.6	57.6
400 - 1,000	17.6	28.4	42.0	50.6	58.0
2,000 - 5,000	16.7	30.7	36.4	43.9	49.7
7,000 - 15,000	19.1	28.8	38.9	46.9	52.1
Over 35,000	15.6	26.3	36.8	39.6	45.2
All Towns	17.5	28.5	38.0	43.8	49.5
	Drug Stores				
Under 400	14.3	23.8	28.6	42.9	42.9
400 - 1,000	8.0	8.0	16.0	22.7	25.3
2,000 - 5,000	7.8	9.4	12.5	15.6	21.9
7,000 - 15,000	4.5	10.8	15.3	18.5	22.3
Over 35,000	7.3	13.3	19.3	22.0	25.3
All Towns	7.0	11.3	16.4	20.3	24.3

Source:
Converse, P. D., "Business Mortality of Illinois Retail Stores,
1925-1930", pp. 13-14, Bureau of Business Research, University
of Illinois, Bulletin No. 41. 1932, University of Illinois,
Urbana, Illinois.

---

grocery stores are often poorly financed. R. S. Vaile[53] found that
twenty-one to forty-eight per cent in the three cities studied were
unrated by credit bureaus; fifty-five to seventy per cent had a net
worth of $1,000 or less each. A number of other studies give simi-
lar indications of weakness on the part of the independents. It is
no wonder that they fail in large numbers.

Thus, it is not the chains but his own inefficiency that
puts the independent out of business. Chain competition merely makes
faulty management show up sooner. Most of the stores which fail are
doomed to fail; the chain only speeds up the process. The remedy is

---
53. Op. cit., p. 13.

not to curb chain competition, but is mainly to educate the independent.

As long as competition is clean and open, it is welcome. It is by competition that the consumer profits. The chain is bringing a keener type of competition and many merchants are finding themselves unable to meet it. To the extent to which chain competition is fair it should be encouraged even though it hurts existing businesses; to the extent that it is unfair it should be curbed. In many cases the agitation to curb the chains is not designed to curb unfair competition but to stop all competition. The objection is only against unfair competition.

To tax the chains will not stop unfair competition. If the taxes are not severe enough to eliminate the chain, the chains will have all the more incentive to be unfair; if the taxes eliminate the chains, both good and bad competitors will suffer. Probably some chains are unfair; probably some are entirely fair. It is not just that both be treated alike. The remedy is direct legislation against whatever bad practices exist. What such legislation should be does not concern this study.

The charge most often made against the chains is that their ability to sell at low prices is based, not on superior efficiency of operation, but on ability to buy more cheaply. Such an advantage is said to be due not to economies permitted, but to coercion of the manufacturer. The process is supposed to be as follows: The chain dangles a huge order before the manufacturer's eyes at a fair price. Of course, the manufacturer accepts. Each year the chain increases its order until it finally takes the major share of the output. This is just what the chain is looking for. At this point it goes to the manufacturer and informs him that it has an opportunity to buy similar merchandise elsewhere and will do so unless the manufacturer will meet the terms of the chain. The producer then must choose between two evils: sell to the chain at a loss or see most of his business slip away, to be regained only by reviving his sales organization (which was allowed to languish when there were only a few buyers) and by soliciting the business of independents again. A variation of the same theme is to look for weaknesses on the part of the manufacturer and take advantage of them. H. B. Teegarden, attorney for interests which pushed the anti-discount law, made the following statement before a House committee:

> "Spies are placed or subsidized in banks, in the manufacturer's own offices, or in other quarters of confidential information, to learn when his notes are falling due, so that a large offer of business or a threat of its withdrawal with consequent gain or loss of case resources may be laid on the manufacturer's doorstep at the critical moment."[54]

The manufacturer supposedly sees that added volume will reduce his operating costs, takes the chain's order at a low price, and charges all the overhead to the other buyers. Hence, the manufacturer is said to make his profits from the independents and to get his volume from the chains.

Two groups of people are directly hurt by this practice -- the competitors of the chain and the employees, etc. of the manufacturer. Out of such discounts and allowances is said to come the chains' ability to undersell the independents. Such a practice also contributes to the leader policy. Chains are enabled to sell pro-

---

54. _Committee on Judiciary_, on H.R. 8442, H.R. 4995, H.R. 5062. House of Representatives, 74th Congress, 1st session, Part I, p. 35, July 10, 11, 17, 18, 19, 1935. 1935, Government Printing Office, Washington, D. C.

ducts far below the usual selling price without a loss. When the manufacturer finds his gross income reduced he has only one opportunity to save himself, that of paying less for the products and services which he buys. This way out usually takes the form of a reduction in the salaries of employees.

Indirectly the public is said to suffer from such discounts. As one type of outlet is given a concession and so enabled to sell more cheaply, goods linger on the shelves of their competitors. Finally, the rival channel is closed and the favored distributor finds itself in the position of a monopoly with the ability to raise prices.

It is also charged that the chains make their profits, not from merchandising, but from certain allowances. The allowances which the chains are said to receive are for cash payments, volume purchases, advertising, brokerage services, and promotional activities. Cash discounts are open to both types of distribution. Wholesalers get volume purchases but supposedly not to the extent that chains do. The other allowances are usually peculiar to the chain.

Do chains actually receive special discounts? Undoubtedly. E. F. Witte, in a study of the purchasing policies of chain drug stores,[55] found that some manufacturers admitted that they gave drug chains special discounts. Most manufacturers denied such a practice but the author felt that they were not sincere. In another part of the same study,[56] there is reproduced a lengthy questionnaire sent

55. Purchasing Policies and Practices of Chain Drug Stores, p. 40, University of Chicago, Studies in Business Administration, Vol. III, No. 2. 1933, University of Chicago Press, Chicago.
56. Ibid., p. 63 ff.

by one chain to all of its sources of supply, which shows to what great lengths chains will go in asking for such discounts. This particular questionnaire asked the manufacturers for their maximum allowances for a large number of services, such as volume, advertising, display, etc. If the chain in question, or competing chains, had not been in the habit of receiving discounts, there would have been no reason for such a document. Mr. B. Silliman, who represented the Chain Food and Grocery Stores, an association of chains, admitted[57] that one company in one year paid $360,000 to the "A & P" as an advertising allowance. The Patman investigations[58] disclosed that many chains were getting large allowances. The Federal Trade Commission made two studies of this problem.[59] Table XXXVIII shows the buying advantage of the chains on the items which the Commission used in its price survey. Greater differences are shown if the figures are unweighted. The chains seem to have a buying advantage of about two per cent in groceries and three per cent in drugs, although not all of this advantage is due to special discounts. Table XXXIX shows the amount of discounts which were given by a large number of selected manufacturers to various types of buyers. This shows a somewhat smaller advantage of chains in respect to discounts, the advantage being about one per cent of total purchases in groceries, two to two-and-a-half per cent in drugs, and almost three per cent

---

57. Hearings Before the Committee on Judiciary on H.R. 8442, H.R. 4995, H.R. 5062, op. cit., p. 187. 58. Hearings Before the Special Committee on the Investigation of the American Retail Federation, 74th Congress, 2d Session, 1935. 1935, Government Printing Office, Washington, D. C. 59. Chain Store Inquiry, Vol. IV, "Prices, Margins, etc. of Chain and Independent Distributors", (eight different surveys). 1933 and 1934, Government Printing Office, Washington, D. C. "Special Discounts and Allowances to Chain and Independent Distributors" (grocery, tobacco, and drug trades). 1934, Government Printing Office, Washington, D. C.

Table XXXVIII

CHAIN-STORE BUYING: BUYING ADVANTAGE OF CHAINS OVER WHOLESALERS
DUE TO SPECIAL DISCOUNTS AND ALLOWANCES ON SELECTED
GROCERY AND DRUG ITEMS IN FOUR CITIES

			Chain Advantage[a] (Percentage)	
Item	City	No. of Items	Before Special Discounts	After Special Discounts
Groceries	Washington, D.C.	274	1.375	1.720
"	Cincinnati	120	0.547[b]	0.023
"	Memphis	193	2.250	2.860
"	Detroit	183	2.015	2.310
Drugs	Washington, D.C.	226	0.370	3.269
"	Cincinnati	268	0.499[b]	1.809
"	Memphis	212	0.084[b]	1.379
"	Detroit	256	0.753	3.877

[a] Using geometric average of actual prices weighted by independent and chain quantities.
[b] Disadvantage.

Source:
    Federal Trade Commission, Chain-Store Inquiry, Vol. IV, "Prices Margins, etc. of Chain and Independent Distributors", (eight surveys). 73d Congress, 1st and 2d Sessions, 1933 and 1934, Government Printing Office, Washington, D. C.

---

in tobacco.

The controversy is not as to whether the chains receive such discounts; it is as to whether such discounts are earned. Theoretically, discounts for volume, advertising, and promotional activities can be justified.

Discounts for bulk buying are legitimate for some economies result. It is an accepted theory that lower prices are justified on larger purchases by the reduced costs of producing, selling, and handling large quantities.[60] Some of the advantages of quantity discounts are: it brings some tendency to exclusive purchasing; it

---

60, Stevens, W. H., "Some Laws of Quantity Discounts", Journal of Business, University of Chicago, Vol. II, (1929), p. 406.

often leads to increased purchases; large orders bring manufacturing, selling, and distributive economies. Production economies are: better utilization of plant capacity; savings in raw material purchases and in interest and carrying charges on raw material and finished goods; standardized production methods; and operation during dull seasons. Numerous selling and distributive economies are realized. There is a saving in salesmen's time; bookkeeping and billing expense are less; there are savings in the shipping department; insurance is cheaper where there are large lots. These economies depend, however, upon the manner of ordering, how the goods are to be shipped, etc.

It is well known that the small buyer is costly to sell, and it is not at all unlikely that he actually is being favored. It costs money to get new customers. The Dartnell Corporation says:

> "It is estimated that it costs anywhere from $100 to $5000 to secure a new dealer . . . . A stove manufacturer reporting states that it costs him an average of $300 to secure a new account and that his dealer turnover in the last two years has been over 100 per cent."[61]

R. E. Wood, the president of Sears, Roebuck, and Company, reported[62] that, in their own stove factory, from which they supplied one-half million dollars' worth to themselves and one-half million dollars' worth to independents, they charged themselves eight per cent on cost and the independents twenty per cent more. At the end of a year they showed a $40,000 profit on their own business and lost $20,000 on

61. Sales Method Investigation, No. 106, "Plans for Overcoming the Inertia of Dealers and Agents", p. 5. 1923, Dartnell Corporation, Chicago.
62. Hearings Before Committee on Judiciary on H.R. 8442, H.R. 4995, H.R. 5062, op. cit., p. 89.

the dealers' business. The reason for this was that it cost thirteen per cent for salesmen, an extra twelve to fifteen per cent on manufacturing costs because the orders came in in driblets and caused shifting of machines, plus some allowance for credit losses. The Department of Commerce in a study of wholesale distribution costs[63] reported the cost of the Western Electric Company to handle individual orders of different size. Table XL gives the results obtained. It is obvious that orders of over twenty-five dollars should be given more consideration -- or orders under twenty-five dollars, less. Table XLI gives the results of a cost analysis of various-sized orders of a meat dealer. There is no doubt which are the most profitable orders.

Payments for introductory campaigns are also justifiable. No matter how much a manufacturer may advertise a new product, he will not be able to get a wide distribution unless he obtains retailer acceptance. If the retailer pushes his product, his advertising becomes many times more productive.

Cash discounts, of course, are usual to the trade. Often, when a manufacturer is hard pressed for cash, he may be willing to offer even larger discounts in order to turn his stock into cash. Ability to find a cash buyer may mean the difference between failure and staying in business.

Discounts for larger orders given in slack times are not unfair. Under regularized production schedules the manufacturer can cut his production costs and keep his force intact.

---

63. Department of Commerce, Bureau of Foreign and Domestic Commerce, Distribution Cost Studies, No. 1; Millard, J. W., "Analyzing Wholesale Distribution Costs", p. 11. 1928, Government Printing Office, Washington, D. C.

Table XXXIX

CHAIN-STORE BUYING: SPECIAL DISCOUNT PRACTICES OF SELECTED MANUFACTURERS
IN RESPECT TO VARIOUS TYPES OF DISTRIBUTORS IN THE GROCERY, DRUG, AND TOBACCO TRADES

Distributor	Per Cent of Accounts Carrying Allowances (1930)	Percentage Discounts Bear To Total Sales		Percentage Discounts Bear to Sales of Discounting Manufacturers	
		1929	1930	1929	1930
Grocery Chains	30.70	1.89	2.02	3.44	3.58
Grocery Wholesalers	10.50	.87	.91	2.68	2.33
Grocery Cooperatives	18.70	1.00	1.04	2.55	2.54
Drug Chains	17.95	4.48	5.19	8.84	10.05
Drug Wholesalers	10.49	1.16	1.11	5.35	4.45
Independent Department Stores	12.04	2.49	2.73	7.66	7.35
Tobacco Chains	32.50	3.69	3.57	--	--
Tobacco Wholesalers	16.0	1.07	.71	--	--

Source:
Federal Trade Commission, Chain Store Inquiry, Vol. IV, "Special Discounts and Allowances to Chain and Independent Distributors". (Adapted from three different studies.) 73d Congress, 2nd Session, Senate Documents Numbers 86, 89, and 94. 1934, Government Printing Office, Washington, D. C.

Table XL

RETAIL SELLING EXPENSE: COST TO SELL INDIVIDUAL ORDERS
BY SIZE OF ORDER, WESTERN ELECTRIC COMPANY

	Value of Sales				
	Over $25	Under $25	$10 - $25	$5 - $10	Under $5
Average Gross Profit	24.70	2.35	4.48	2.07	0.71
Average Expense	14.58	3.98	5.00	3.74	3.25
Net Profit	10.12	-1.63	-0.52	-1.67	-2.54

Source:
Department of Commerce, Bureau of Foreign and Domestic Commerce, Distribution Cost Studies, No. 1. Millard, J. W., "Analyzing Distribution Costs", p. 11. 1928, Government Printing Office, Washington, D. C.

Table XLI

RETAIL SELLING EXPENSE: DEALER'S COST TO SELL
MONTHLY MEAT ORDERS OF DIFFERENT SIZES

Size of Monthly Purchase	Margin, %	Expense, %	Profit, %
Less than $25	$10.91	43.36	-32.45
$25 - $50	10.70	21.14	-10.44
$50 - $100	9.85	14.02	- 4.17
$100 - $200	10.40	10.21	.19
$200 - $500	9.87	7.85	2.02
$500 - $1,000	8.15	6.04	2.11
Over $1,000	9.20	6.13	3.07
All Combined	9.64	8.76	.88

Source:
Greer, H. C., "Distribution Cost Analysis", Bulletin, National Association of Cost Accountants, Vol. XI, (June 1, 1930), No. 19, p. 1313.

One of the forms of allowances to which most objection is made is that for brokerage. There is no doubt that the broker, when he supplies market information and arranges to bring buyer and seller together, performs an economic function. Whether a broker who represents one of the parties is entitled to compensation for the same services is a matter of controversy.

There is a place for advertising allowances, for example,

for newspaper advertising, window and counter displays, having clerks call attention to the good, etc. All of these services are of value to a company, especially a company which is introducing a new product.

There is a definite place for all such payments; the crime is unearned payment. Allowances should be based on the savings involved and there must be definite contracts and assured performance of services for which allowances are made. Such allowances should be open to all who can perform the same job or afford the same economies. No one has a right to demand more than the economic saving which his order or service affords, but the efficient operator has a right to demand a reduction equal to such savings and free from the wastes in other channels. Cheaper buying is not unfair competition if it is due to economies permitted.

If there is a place for discounts, do the chains earn their allowances? No cost accounting system has yet been devised which would show conclusively how much cheaper it is to sell a big order than many small ones or what is the value of specific services. All that can be done in this study is to see if the manufacturer gets something in return for the discounts he allows. Within wide limits he must be the sole judge of his own expenditures. Flagrant abuses would be decidedly unfair -- relatively minor concessions, unless definitely for no service rendered, are matters the wisdom of which concerns the manufacturer. The reasonableness of concessions which are given the chains will always remain an undecided point.

There is little point to argue that the individual retailer ought to have a price equal to the chain, for the expense to handle many small orders directly would amount to far more than the

proceeds of such sales. The real comparison is between the price
to the chain and the price to the wholesaler. Also, it must be remembered that a contract for a sale has other factors than the sale
of merchandise itself. It may include the sale of other services
and takes account also of the reliability of the different buyers.
All these must be included in any consideration of the fairness of
prices charged.

The value of the chain, from the standpoint of the manufacturer, lies in its disciplined organization. The wholesaler
could ask for a concession, and make a bargain but his ideas are
not carried out except as the independents want to carry them out.
In the chain the executive can compel obedience and has access to
the retailers' records. Thus, the chain is in a better position to
render services.

The chains are entitled to quantity discounts at least as
large as those given the wholesaler and perhaps larger. The larger chains buy in larger quantities than do the wholesalers and at
less selling expense. Of course, some chains buy less than wholesalers and should not receive the same consideration as a large
wholesaler. A list of some of the sales made by "A & P" indicates
how large a volume of orders such a company could give. In 1929
"A & P" sold about thirty thousand carloads of potatoes, five million barrels of flour, ninety million dozen eggs, seventy thousand
tons of coffee, one-hundred-and-fifty million pounds of butter,
twelve thousand carloads of oranges, twenty-four million cans of
salmon, and about five hundred million loaves of bread.[64] Of course,

---

64. Smith, W. H., "A Billion From 'Cash and Carry'", Barrons, Vol.
XI, (January 19, 1931), p. 22.

no other chain approaches this but a good many chains exceed the largest wholesaler in volume.

The chain can do more for the manufacturer than can the wholesaler. The wholesaler can not push the retailer to get volume; the chain has a closer contact with demand so that the manufacturer produces less dead stock. The chain will take on an item and force the retailer to push it; the jobber usually will not carry an item until the retailers force him to carry it. It costs less to sell to a chain. A new chain unit becomes a new customer automatically whereas the wholesaler has to sell each new store that opens. In view of the rapid rate of mortality and new openings of independents this is a great disadvantage of the wholesaler-independent system. Invoices are sent to the central office of the chain and purchases made on blanket contracts just as in the case of wholesalers. With larger orders there is some saving in this cost.

In a good many cases the goods are sent direct to the units of the chains. This involves a greater expense than to send them direct to the wholesaler so that in this case the chain could be required to pay more than the wholesaler. Sixty to sixty-eight per cent of the goods bought by chains are delivered direct to the units; in groceries, only twelve to twenty-five per cent are delivered direct; and in drugs fifty to fifty-eight per cent.[65] It is in groceries that the most violent charge of unfair concessions is made and in this field less than one-fifth of the merchandise seems to be delivered direct to the stores. This consists largely of the perishables.

65. Alexander, R. S., "The Wholesale Differential", Journal of Business, University of Chicago, Vol. IX, (1936), p. 316.

With the exception of an allowance for shipping expenses to the units, the chain is entitled to an equal quantity discount with wholesalers and probably more because of the chains' undoubted selling advantages. There is no question but that the large chain should receive a differential over the independent who tries to buy direct for the chain does much more for the manufacturer, gives greater volume orders, and affords savings in selling and distributive expense.

The greatest advantage of the chain, from the point of view of the manufacturer, comes, not in the quantity of its purchases, but in the above-mentioned selling service, and in advertising and promotional services. The chains, in some fields, are consistent advertisers and it is worthwhile for the manufacturer to tie up this advertising with his national advertising. Advertising at the point of contact between the consumer and the distributive system is essential for the greatest possible distribution. This the chain can supply and the wholesaler can not, for the latter can not control the retail units. Chains use a great deal of advertising space. "A & P" in 1929 used nearly fourteen million lines of newspaper space and in 1930 over seventeen million lines and Sears, Roebuck, and Company for the same years used approximately ten million and seventeen million lines.[66] To have one's product mentioned in these advertisements is a service of tremendous value. The chains also sell window and counter space, a service not offered by wholesalers. Counter displays are of great value. A leader in a volun-

---

66. Zimmerman, M. M., The Challenge of Chain-Store Distribution, op. cit., pp. 138, 139.

tary chain[67] asserts that if a housewife sees a product on the counter, she will buy it sixteen times faster than if she is reminded of it orally.

The independent feels that he is entitled to a similar allowance for it is possible for him to render the same services. The value of this service is not the same in all stores but varies with the size, reputation, and prestige of the establishment. Counter space in some stores would be valueless. An allowance of $100,000 to the "A & P" for advertising space would mean an allowance of only fifty cents per store per month. Even if the same amount of advertising would be done in an independent store, no manufacturer could afford to make a large number of fifty-cent contracts. Only through an organization which can make one contract for a large number of outlets and compel obedience would advertising allowances be feasible. The manufacturer, moreover, is the judge of his own advertising expenditures. As has been suggested,[68] to compel the manufacturer to buy counter space in an independent store just because he buys it in the chain would be the same as to compel a man who buys space in the New York Times to buy a proportional amount of space in the Tribune.

Abuses, however, have crept into such allowances. In many cases allowances have been granted and no effort has been made on the part of the giver to check to see if the service were performed.

67. Lazo, Hector, Cooperative Food Distributors of America, Hearings Before a Subcommittee of Committee on Judiciary. On H.R. 4995, 8442, and 10,486, p. 326. House of Representatives, 74th Congress, 2d session, Feb. 3, 4, 5, 7, 1936. 1936, Government Printing Office, Washington, D. C.
68. Phillips, C. F., "The Robinson-Patman Anti-Price Discrimination Law and the Chain Store". Harvard Business Review, Vol. XV, (Aug., 1936), p. 75.

As one man has said:

> "That advertising allowances had become forms of price concession seems to be fairly clear when it is realized that to a large extent these allowances were never audited; and I find it hard to believe that the average business man is willing to pay $5,000, shall we say, for something, supposedly for advertising, without ever checking in any way to see whether he got it or not."[69]

Advertising allowances are justified but only if a definite contract is made and a definite service rendered. This has not always been done.

Chains are valuable in introductory campaigns. If the big retailer will cooperate, and he will if given an allowance, a a distributor of a new product can get national distribution right away without first having to go through the slow costly process of national advertising. This is almost the only way for a small manufacturer to establish his product. The independent does not have enough stores and the wholesalers do not have sufficient control over their retail outlets to receive such an allowance. An example given by Mr. D. C. Keller, former president of the Dow Drug Company and Associated Chain Drug Stores, follows:

> "A certain manufacturer recently conducted two intensive campaigns as experiments in two cities of about equal size. In the first were 165 dealers reached through the jobber. Four thousand dollars was spent on the campaign with a net sale of fourteen hundred packages. In the other city the same deal was offered through a chain system of about twelve stores. Less than $1,000 was spent on the campaign and the net sale was over five thousand packages. This manufacturer is now making his introductions exclusively through chains where possible."[70]

Chains offer a good opportunity for quick tryout campaigns. Also,

69. Thorp, W. L., "Effects of Robinson-Patman Act on Business Practice", American Management Association, Consumer and Industrial Marketing Series, C.M. 22, Appraisals of Robinson-Patman Act. 1937, American Management Association, New York.
70. Quoted in Witte, E. F., op. cit., p. 23. (There is no way of checking the facts so that this example is not conclusive evidence.)

the big retailer can cooperate with the manufacturer in experiments and in the design of new articles and styles.

Chains often receive brokerage fees. They secure their own market information and eliminate the need for a broker. If the chains did not get the brokerage, the producer himself would. If the manufacturer ordinarily sells through a broker, there is no reason why he should pocket the fee just because the retailer performs the service for himself. If the producer is not in the habit of using the broker, a brokerage fee is not justified.

The average discount to chains is not excessive as the Federal Trade Commission findings show.[71] An advantage of two per cent in the grocery business does not begin to account for the differences in price of the two outlets. But specific discounts and discounts to different companies may have been too large and no doubt abuses have existed. Some chains probably are grasping and greedy. The solution is not to abolish all allowances but to check the unjustifiable ones.

The recent Robinson-Patman Act was designed to prevent unearned discounts. Whether it will be effective is not yet known. Whatever it does, it will force some attempt to find exactly the savings made possible by each of these services. Some even feel that such studies would show that some chains could well deserve larger discounts. Effective legislation to prevent unwarranted discrimination is necessary.

One thing which throws light on this subject is whether the allowances of the chains are obtained through coercion. If there is no coercion, it can be assumed that the manufacturer thinks

71. See Tables XXXVIII and XXXIX.

he is getting his money's worth. M. M. Zimmerman points out[72] that

although the chain will always try to drive hard bargains and get

extra concessions, it takes two to make a bargain. The only coer-

cive force that is used is volume orders which the chains hold before

the manufacturer. If he accepts, he has only nimself to blame. The

same writer concludes with the following:

> "The evidence, however, is conclusive that manufacturers
> who maintain a definite policy in doing business with chains
> and stick to it, find their business profitable and have no
> complaint against the chains' demands."[73]

If coercion obtained the allowances, it would seem that the largest

chains would get the largest discounts. In the Federal Trade Com-

mission's study of discounts[74] received from reporting manufacturers,

out of fifty-eight chains, the largest grocery chains ranked in per-

centage of discounts received as follows: nineteenth, forty-first,

thirty-fifth, twenty-fifth, thirty-second, seventeenth, and thir-

teenth. The Commission concluded as follows:

> "From the preceding discussion . . . , there appears to
> be on the whole only a relatively slight association between
> the total amount of sales reported to the various chains and
> the rates of allowances on such sales. Such tendency as is
> indicated by the figures is one of negative correlation; that
> is, large sales are associated with low average rates of allow-
> ances and vice versa."[75]

If coercion is the sole reason for such discounts, the big chains

do not use their power to the best advantage.

The Commission in its final report concluded that chain

buying practices were legal:

---

72. The Challenge of Chain Store Distribution, op. cit., p. 311.
73. Ibid., p. 311.
74. Chain Store Inquiry: "Special Discounts and Allowances to Chain
and Independent Distribution, Grocery Trade", p. 25. 73d Congress,
2d session, Sen. Doc. No. 89. 1934, Government Printing Office,
Washington, D. C.
75. Ibid., p. 27.

"The 'threats' and 'coercion' used consisted of statements or intimations that unless the manufacturer would grant the chain special concessions in price, the chain would either buy the goods elsewhere, proceed to manufacture its own, or conduct its stores so as to discourage therein the sale of the recalcitrant manufacturer's goods. If it be admitted that the chain has a legal right to adopt any or all of these policies, it seems to follow that it has a right to announce its intention of doing so unless certain conditions are met. Unless the law be so made or applied as to prevent vertical integration, a chain store may engage in manufacturing. As to buying elsewhere, if concessions are not given, it has not been even proposed to deprive the chains of that right. And for a chain in its own stores to encourage or discourage the sale of such goods as it may choose in its own discretion seems beyond legal attack under any existing law. If an attempt should be made to outlaw the use of such 'threats' and 'coercion' without also removing the existing legal right to do the things threatened, it would be abortive and ineffective. For it is the manufacturer's recognition that the chain, with its tremendous purchasing and distributing power, may do these things and not the 'threat' of the chain to do them that is the real inducement for granting the special concession."[76]

Chains have power and have used it but the manufacturer has himself partly to blame. The manufacturer, who gives allowances to one distributor, forces all others to strive for the same thing in order to protect themselves. After a chain gets the good ten per cent or so under the manufacturer's "best" price, he still can not be sure a competitor is not getting it even more cheaply. A law which would force proper costing and prices based on actual costs would eliminate a good deal of the "coercion".

That a chain would deliberately ruin a manufacturer seems inconceivable. No chain would want to ruin its source of supply constantly and so be forced to look for new sources and new merchandise to sell. A buyer who forced down prices until he ruined the manufacturer would soon be unable to find a place in which to buy and he would soon lose favor with the public. The chain depends for its

---

76. "Final Report of Chain-Store Inquiry", op. cit., p. 49.

existence upon having consumer-accepted merchandise. The only resort would be to manufacture the goods themselves. In most cases
the chains have not found it profitable to do so. Although the
chains are too shrewd to hammer down prices so as to ruin the manufacturer one can be sure that they will figure what it will cost a
manufacturer and bid accordingly. The competition of voluntary
chain organizations, supermarkets, etc. makes it more necessary than
ever that satisfactory sources of supply be maintained.

Are such allowances open to the independents? Yes, but
usually not to the same extent. The independent system gets some
allowances in the form of discounts to wholesalers, though these
are not as great as those accorded the chain (see Table XXXIX). The
independent retailer can not get allowances directly for he usually
is not big enough to make it worthwhile for the manufacturer. The
independents' hope lies mostly in the voluntary chains. M. M.
Zimmerman, an organizer of voluntaries in the grocery field, says
that voluntaries often get the same concessions and are, in many
cases, more insistent in their demands.[77] The Naborhood Grocer, a
trade paper for the independent grocers, says that ninety per cent
of the manufacturers who grant allowances to "A & P" accord the same
or greater concessions to wholesalers and voluntary groups.[78] One
marketing text[79] says that voluntary chains in the food field seem
to be able to secure just about the same discounts. Hector Lazo,
who represented an association of over twenty thousand individually-
owned retail merchants, testified before a Congressional committee[80]

77. The Challenge of Chain Store Distribution, op. cit., p. 304.
78. Quoted in Chain Store Age, Vol. XI, (Sept. 1935), p. 12 and no
reference given.   79. Maynard, H. H.; Weidler, W.C.; Beckman, T.N.:
Principles of Marketing, Revised Edition, p. 153. 1932, Ronald Press
Company, New York.   80. Hearings Before a Subcommittee of the Committee on Judiciary on H.R. 4995, 8442, and 10,486, op. cit., pp.310-
321.

that his association got all the various types of discounts that the
chains were getting and that in some cases they got as big a discount as anyone else. Usually their allowances were less than that
accorded the chain. The reasons most manufacturers give for this is
that the voluntaries are loosely put together and can not guarantee
a given volume or specific performance. Whether this differential
is economically justifiable or is based on discrimination can not be
proven. Some differential ought to exist for the chain can do more
for the producer. But the fact that some discounts are given all
types of big distributors would make it seem that discrimination were
not the sole motive for allowances.

The chains' biggest advantage in buying is judicious buying and this is open to the independent. In the words of E. D. Bor-
den, manager of the Domestic Distribution Department of the United
States Chamber of Commerce,

"Whatever advantage the chains have in purchasing power is
not due so much to the size of the purchasing power as it is to
the judicious investment of dollars in merchandise that will
turn over rapidly, and at the same time will afford a fairly
wide selection to the consumers."81

Table XXXVIII shows that the greatest part of the chains' buying
advantage in the grocery field does not come from special discounts
but from better purchasing. The major share of the drug chains'
advantage in purchasing, however, comes from special discounts. The
large chains started without purchasing power and did not develop it
overnight. They prospered because they had good management and expanded and ultimately got buying power. Buying power comes to those
who have first earned it by doing those things that are essential for

81. Proceedings of National Association of Commercial Organization
Secretaries, 1933, p. 102.

success. When the independent uses his merchandise money to the best advantage and runs his store efficiently then, and only then can he say, "The only way for me to make more money is to have buying power."[82]

Buying power and special discounts do not account entirely for the success of the chain. A merchant can be the best buyer in the world, but if he does not also have selling ability, he can not succeed. Chain buying contributes to its success but it also has merchandising economy. Large bank accounts will not take the place of economical management, for if they would, huge successful chains would be created almost overnight to share in the enormous profits chains are supposed to be making. The special allowances given the chains form only a small fraction of the difference in selling price between the chain and the independent. Tables XXXVIII and XXXIX show the chains in the grocery field to have an advantage in special concessions of about one per cent whereas the price difference amounts to eight or twelve.[83] In drugs the chains obtained about three per cent advantage in special discounts as compared to a lower selling price of fifteen to twenty per cent.[84]

Some evils do exist but this does not justify the elimination of the chain. Some way must be found to make chain buying entirely fair and still give it an opportunity to prove that it can merchandise efficiently. Special taxation is not a good method to correct buying advantages. As long as the chains are allowed to remain in business, heavy taxation would be even a greater incentive

82. See Bedell, Clyde, The Seven Keys to Retail Profits, pp. 332-336. 1931, McGraw-Hill Book Company, Inc., New York.
83. See Chapter II.
84. See Chapter II.

to obtain special discounts. If the taxes would put the chains out
of business, the public would lose what advantages chains do afford.
Direct action is a much sounder method of attack.

Chains are said to obtain an unfair advantage by the use
of "coercive" methods to obtain their banking service, their advertising, insurance, rents, and labor at low prices. It is charged
that the chains do not maintain a sufficient balance, especially in
the small town banks, to enable the banks to make a profit on the
accounts. The chains are said to deposit their money and to draw a
draft at once transferring it to a central depository. Chains are
said, moreover, to make unreasonable demands for free services of
the banks, such as making change, cashing checks, etc. Neither do
the chains use the banks' loaning facilities. As a result the banks
can not handle the accounts profitably. The remedy in the eyes of
the banks is to require the chains to carry minimum balances, say
eight hundred or a thousand dollars, and to pay a per item charge for
other services.

Chain practices vary in these respects. Some have entirely
satisfactory accounts and some, particularly the under-financed,
have very unsatisfactory accounts. In an analysis of seventy accounts
C. F. Zimmerman,[85] of the executive committee of the American Bankers'
Association, found twenty-five very satisfactory, twelve fairly unsatisfactory, eighteen unsatisfactory, and fifteen very unsatisfactory. C. B. Hazlewood,[86] when president of the American Bankers Association, in returns to a questionnaire to bankers, found that seventy

85. "The County Bank and the Chain Store Account", American Bankers
Association Journal, Vol. XXII, (Nov. 1929), p. 528.
86. "Chain Stores and the Local Bank", Commercial and Financial
Chronicle, Vol.CXXIX, Part I, (Sept. 28, 1928), p. 2000.

per cent reported their chain-store accounts as satisfactory and thirty per cent as unsatisfactory. Just as the profitableness of chain accounts varies so does the profitableness of the accounts of independents. The accounts of many independents are so small as to be unprofitable. It is doubtful, also, that the money of the independent, who is in a good many cases continually hard pressed to meet his creditors' demands, stays in the banks any longer. This, of course, does not excuse the chain for trying to take advantage of the bank, but it does make it seem that the unprofitableness of the chains' accounts should not be a reason to tax them to a greater extent than the independents.

There is no doubt that the chains should make a fair payment for their banking service, as should the independent. This charge should be based on the cost to render the various services. The bankers' associations seem to think a uniform minimum balance and a per item charge should be agreed upon; the chains insist that the actual cost in each bank should determine the minimum balance and fees. Conferences have failed because the bankers have appeared without being able to present an analysis of their costs. The chains can not be required to pay an amount which would make their accounts profitable for all banks. Too often there are so many banks in a community that none can make a profit on what otherwise would be profitable accounts; too often, as our large number of bank failures show, the banks are inefficiently run. The chains should have to pay no more than it would cost in an efficient bank. A banker has a right to insist that an account be profitable only if he renders the required services efficiently.

In regard to the loaning function, the small individual

country banks have not the facilities to take care of the chains'
borrowing needs. Only the larger city banks can handle this. Many
chains do not need loans. There is nothing anti-social not to have
a need for loans.

It is significant that in reply to a request for literature on this subject the Illinois Bankers Association listed no articles written after 1930. This would seem to indicate that the
problem has been satisfactorily solved, for otherwise some literature would have appeared.

The solution of the problem lies with the bankers themselves and not through legislation or taxation of any kind. No bank
need accept an account which it deems unprofitable. The bank can refuse or accept an account as it sees fit. Banks actively compete
for chain accounts and in doing so carry the accounts at less than
it costs them. Those who do not know their costs and carry unprofitable accounts have only themselves to blame.

Little seems to be known about the relative prices paid
for advertising, but the independents do not advertise much, whereas
the chains use a constant run of advertising. Inasmuch as the same
advertisement will apply to all the stores within a city, the chains
get their advertising per store cheaper than do the independents.

Chains, particularly the larger ones, get cheaper insurance rates than do the independents but there is an economic justification for it. The large chains do not insure their property in
each locality individually but insure on a national plan. Their
many locations bring a spread of risk. They maintain specialists,
not only to look for the best terms, but also to study causes of
losses and so lessen the risks. The chains are also better moral

risks for none of the employees would collect the insurance and none of the stockholders would profit sufficiently to hazard the destruction of property. Some are big enough to be self-insurers.

The chains have been notorious for their high rents. The Federal Trade Commission found[87] that in the food lines chains paid seventy-five per cent more rent than the average independent, twice as much in the variety field, and fifty per cent more in the dry goods and apparel field. Inter-chain competition has put rents for choice locations so high as actually to put the chains at a disadvantage in this respect. During the '30's considerable pressure was applied to reduce the terms of long run leases taken out in the '20's but this fact is not sufficient to justify special taxes on the chains.

Wages form a large part of the total operating expense of a retail store. If the chains pay lower wages and work their employees longer hours than the independents, they would gain a competitive advantage. If chain economies are at the expense of labor, they are not justified.

It must be remembered that many things enter into the determination of wages, including such intangible factors as stability of employment, the chance for promotion, the necessity to move around, etc. In a comparison of the wages paid by chains and independents these things must be allowed for. Also, there are two classes of workers, the managers and their assistants and the clerks.

In respect to the chance for promotion and the necessity to move around there is little to choose, from the point of view of the ordinary clerk, between the chain and the independent. The

87. "Final Report of the Chain-Store Investigation", op. cit., p.71.

counter clerk in both is likely to remain a counter clerk in the
store forever unless he saves enough money to become independent.
With the present scale of salaries in the retail field, this is not
likely to occur very often. In respect to stability of employment
the employee finds the chain better. The chains concentrate on
staple goods and necessities so that there is very little decrease
in their business from year to year and from season to season. Also,
the chains do not pass out of business as frequently as do the independents. From this view the ordinary clerk could well afford to
take slightly less from the chain for similar types of work.

As for the manager and his assistants, there is greater
opportunity in the chain. There is no future for a young man who
goes to work for the average independent in order to learn the business. He gets inadequate training and there is no opportunity for
advancement. The young man who enters the chain to "learn" to be a
manager gets a valuable training and has an excellent opportunity
to be advanced to manager, supervisor, or even executive. For a man
with ability, the way is open to a good job. He can get to run a
store and to a degree be in business by himself, without the necessity to put up any capital and without the risk of losing any funds
he might be able to accumulate. The penalty for failure is loss of
a job; the penalty for failure of an independent may be the loss of
everything. Chains are more stable than independents so that a man
with ability can be sure of a steady pay check. The big drawback
of a chain manager's job is that he has to move around. On the
whole, however, there is nothing in a chain job which would require
them to pay higher wages to hold men. There is considerable to
recommend a job with the chain even at a somewhat lower rate than

could be obtained at independents.

Just what wages do each pay? It is difficult to compare
this for several reasons. Many independents staff their stores with
their families, whose pay consists largely of board and lodging.
Moreover, the employees in chains and independents may not be comparable. The independent who hires only one man hires one who can
do everything from sweeping out and delivering up to keeping books
and rendering selling service. The chain, on the other hand, di-
vides up the jobs according to the abilities required and rewards
only that ability. Thus, they can use a large number of low-paid
employees who could not do the varied tasks asked of an independent
clerk. Also, one must be careful with an average wage for wages
differ in different-sized cities and in different lines of retail
trade.

There is no conclusive study of comparative wages in
chains and independents but there are a few available that throw
some light on the question. The study usually cited to show that
chains pay low wages is one by the Department of Labor in the variety-store field.[88] This study shows that wages in the variety-store
field for the period, 1920 to 1928, were on an average around ten
dollars a week. It is known that the wages in this type of store
are low but no evidence was shown that independent stores paid better wages in the same field. P. H. Nystrom, wrote in 1915:

"On the average, it seems, although the writer relies
only on his own observation for this, that the salaries for
the same classes of labor average somewhat higher in chain
stores than in individual stores."[89]

88. Pidgeon, M. E., "Women in 5-and 10-Cent Stores and Limited-Price
Chains", United States Department of Labor, Bulletin of Women's Bureau, No. 76. 1930, Government Printing Office, Washington, D. C.
89. Economics of Retailing, 1st edition, op. cit., p. 231.

E. G. Ernst and E. M. Hartl[90] found in a study of grocery stores in
ten cities that the average wage of chain clerks was seventeen dollars a week, nearly forty per cent less than that paid by independents in the same towns. These figures do not include chain managers who made thirty-five to forty-five dollars a week.

More reliable for purposes of comparison are the studies
by the Federal Trade Commission[91] and the Census counts of 1929 and
1933 (there are no comparable figures for the 1935 census). In the
Commission's study it was found that in eight lines of retailing in
which chains are strong the weighted average wage of chains was
$21.61 (excluding the managers) and of independents $28.48, a large
advantage for the independent. Two factors, however, tend to miti-
gate this difference. By the exclusion of the managers the Commission excluded the only person in the chain above a package wrapper.
He performs most of the functions that a clerk in an independent
store does, particularly in the grocery field. Also, the sample
taken of independents was not representative. Out of 70,000 ques-
tionnaires only 1,564 could be used, and these were all from large
independents located in the larger cities. How much this fact would
change the result is impossible to say. As the figures stand, they
are not comparable.

The Census figures are more reliable but have the fault
that they average all kinds of stores. In the 1929 Census only
state and city averages for different types of operation are given.
The average wage paid by independents, local chains, sectional chains,

---

90. "Chain Management and Labor", Nation, Col. CXXXI, (Nov.26,1930),
pp. 575-576.
91. "Chain-Store Wages", 73d Congress, 2d session, Sen. Doc. No. 82,
1933, Government Printing Office, Washington, D. C.

and national chains is given in Table XLII. It will be noted that
the national chains, with few exceptions, pay by far the lowest average wage and that the local chains pay the highest. A state average is of little significance, however, for it is an average of
stores in every type of retailing. If one organization had a larger proportion of its stores in fields where the average pay is low,
it would appear at a disadvantage in such an average. It was decided to test for this. Illinois appears to be a typical state as
far as average wages are concerned. The average wage of each organization bears about the same ratio to each other as do the averages for the United States. The correction was made as follows:
the average wages for the seventeen fields of retailing classified
by the Census were computed; the ratio which the sales of each organization in the separate fields of retailing bore to the total
sales in the state were computed and assigned as weights to the
average wage in that field; the results were totaled and divided by
the sum of the weights to get what one would expect the average wage
to be if each type of organization paid exactly the average wage in
each field of retailing. The results were: independents, $1,424;
local chains, $1,456; sectional chains, $1,373; and national chains,
$1,251. The actual average wages were $1,422, $1,632, $1,458, and
$1,234, a very close agreement except in the case of local chains.
Allowance must be made for the fact that some types are more concentrated in the large cities, where wages are usually higher. Since
local chains are mostly in the larger cities, their high average
wage can be readily explained. With some allowance for the higher
wages in large cities, it would appear that the independents paid
almost exactly what the computed average indicated, the sectional

chains somewhat more, and the national chains a little less. The
differences were so small that they could have been due to errors
in the rounding of figures. This would indicate that the chains
paid just about the same wages as independents. The manager's salaries, however, are included in this computation so that the clerks
in the chains probably received less.

In the 1933 Census it was found that the average pay of
independents had dropped 27.5 per cent, and of the chains, 19.8 per
cent. In only three states (Connecticut, Rhode Island, and Utah)
did the chains (local, sectional, and national were grouped together)
have a lower average wage than the independents.[92] In this Census
the average wage in each field of retailing was computed. Table
XLIII gives these results. In the light of these figures the chain
seems to have paid somewhat higher wages than the independents. In
Illinois the average wages paid were independents $932 and chains
$1,118. With the same corrections as for the 1929 figures, if each
had paid average wages, the weighted average of the independents
would have been $981 and of the chains $911. The independents' actual average was fifty dollars under this and the chains over two
hundred dollars above, which shows a decided advantage in favor of
the chains.

Chain wages are low in relation to decent standards, but
not in comparison to independents. Both have to pay the market rate
of wages; otherwise they could not get anyone to work for them. It
can not even be contended that the chain pays all it can afford to
pay. It pays just what it has to pay, as does the independent. The

92. Bureau of the Census, Census of American Business, 1933, op. cit,
"Chains and Independents".

Table XLIII

RETAIL WAGES: AVERAGE WAGES OF CHAINS AND INDEPENDENTS
IN EIGHTEEN RETAILING FIELDS, 1933

Field	Independents	Chains
All Fields	947	1079
Department Stores	1000	995
Variety	665	766
Men's and Boys' Clothing and Furnishings	1261	1394
Family Clothing	1127	1197
Women's Ready-To-Wear Specialty Stores	998	988
Shoe Stores	1172	1255
Furniture	1200	1357
Household Appliances	1136	900
Radio and Music	1095	1278
Grocery Stores	813	1191
Combination Stores	899	1195
Restaurants	649	758
Cigars	858	920
Motor Vehicle Dealers	1024	1338
Filling Stations	838	1130
Drugs	972	1024
Hardware	1059	1216
Jewelry	1379	1340

Source:
Bureau of the Census, Census of American Business, 1933, Retail
Distribution, "Chains and Independents", pp. 3-4. 1935, Govern-
ment Printing Office, Washington, D. C.

---

market rate of wages for people of the ability needed to work in

the standardized chain stores is very low. Chains can hire young,

inexperienced, unskilled clerks, a class of worker that does not

command a high wage because of its abundance. The only way to raise

their wages is to decrease the supply of workers of that class. Spe-

cial taxation of the chains will not do it. Nor will putting the

chains out of business and letting the independents do the hiring

raise wages. Some other type of control is needed.

As four hours worked, Ernst and Hartl[93], who were highly

opposed to chains as a whole, admitted that in the ten cities which

93. Op. cit., p. 575.

they studied the hours worked by the clerks were practically the
same with a slight advantage in favor of the chains, that is, the
chain clerks worked fewer hours. It is usually pointed out, however, that the chain manager works long hours. There is no doubt
that he does. It may be that he has to but extra work certainly is
one way by which a man advances in his profession. The independent
who goes back to the store in the evening to take stock, to do his
buying, and to put things in shape for the next day's business probably does a better job of retailing because of it. An ambitious
independent who gets ahead probably works harder and longer than
any chain manager. The excessive mortality rate of independents
may be due to just this factor of not working long hours over their
business. Excessive night work should not be permitted but working
overtime in a chain is a question of how much a man is willing to
pay for his future.

Working conditions are fairly good in the chains but the
chains are exacting in the efficiency of their employees. Everyone
must know his business and must do a full day's intelligent work.
Inefficiency, idleness, and consuming time with non-essentials are
not tolerated. For anyone who works intelligently and well the average chain is not a bad place to work. But for the others there
is constant urging by the manager and, if the situation does not
improve, dismissal.

No doubt the charges of long hours, low wages, and "driving" of employees is often true. Such conditions need to be reme-
died. Some chains are entirely fair; others are not. The special
taxation of all chains will not cure such abuses as do exist.

CHAPTER FOUR

OTHER SOCIAL AND ECONOMIC EFFECTS OF CHAIN STORES

Certain economic and social results are charged to the
chains. They are said to take money out of the community, not to
hire local help, to restrict individual opportunity, to create technological unemployment, to tend to create a monopoly and to restrict
wealth, and to fail to be good citizens.

The argument that a certain organization or policy "takes
money out of the community" is one that arises time and time again.
Mercantilism was based on an idea that money ought to be kept in
the country; our protective policy has had much of the same philosophy; our trade-at-home campaigns are of the same nature. The ad-
monition to patronize the local independent instead of the foreign-
owned chain is just another phase of the same argument. There is
no better statement of this attitude than an article published by
William Allen White in his own newspaper, the _Emporia Gazette_.

"Look at your dollar, Mr. Buyer, before you spend it. And
when you let it go, be sure that it returns something for your
town, because as your town grows, your business increases, and
as your town declines, your prosperity fades. A penny saved in
the price of a commodity is an expensive penny if in saving that
penny your town loses a dollar.

"By that we mean just this. A merchant is valuable in
just the proportion that his money stays on the townsite. If
he keeps it in the town, he builds up the community's capital.
Even if he gives it to the church, or to his club, or to civic
improvements, it adds to the security, beauty, and substantial
worth of the town. If he builds his home or just adds to his
stock, his taxes put in the public pot decreases the taxes of
his neighbor just that much. And the customer's penny saved
out of his dollar on the price of a commodity is a loss if the
dollar leaves the town and goes to the accumulated dollars
that are poured into Wall Street.

"If your merchant is an alien to the community, merely

> sinking his blood-sucking beak into the veins of the town,
> drawing off its idle dollars, his prices must be weighed against
> his menace to the community's prosperity. The fly-by-night
> peddler of bargains is really selling calamity to the town
> wrapped in his shoddy goods."[1]

The opponents of the chains create the impression that chains buy
their merchandise outside the town, erect no buildings locally, and
send their profits to some faraway place, presumably Wall Street.
This is said to reduce the circulation of money in the town and to
result in a weakening of the trade life. Also, such reduction of
the city's money is thought to undermine the amount of funds available for educational, governmental, and other purposes. In contrast, the independent is supposed to spend his money at home, and
thus afford employment for others, increase the trade life of the
community, and contribute toward the upkeep of education and government.

Leaving, for the moment, the discussion of whether the
chains do take money out of the community, the old fallacy that it
is undesirable for a nation or state or community to send money outside its borders must be considered. In other words, if the chains
do send out more money than the independents, would this be an undesirable situation?

Mercantilism was based on the idea that money is the most
desirable form of wealth and should be kept at home through regulation of the trade of the country. The argument that the consumer
should patronize the independent and not the foreign-owned chain is
of the same nature. People have always confused money and wealth.
The universal use of money as a medium of exchange has given it an

---

1. Quoted in Modern Merchant and Grocery World, Nov. 30, 1935, p.8.

importance far beyond that which it deserves. The important things are the goods, not money. Money is only an instrument used to facilitate the exchange of goods. It is a commodity and can always be obtained by exchanging goods for it. In a classical example, Adam Smith pointed out that pots and pans were articles of some durability and that there was a demand for them, and that they could be exchanged for other goods. In such a sense it was pointed out that they were no different from money, except that the metals used in money had some advantages over pots and pans as a medium of exchange. Yet how utterly foolish it would have been for a nation to have heaped up stores of pots and pans. A more vivid picture of the contrast of money and goods is that given by C. W. Wood in his study of the effects of chain stores on Marion, Ohio.[2] He pointed out that if the pioneers had made the mistake of arriving with money instead of shovels and plows, they would have been in a sorry plight and that it probably was many years before the pioneers had much use for money except to send it out of town for such goods as they could not make themselves. They also found that the only way to get more money was to manufacture some products for which some trader would give money. The economic process is an exchange of goods for goods, with the use of money only to facilitate the exchange. To give money to strangers for goods which they can produce better than anyone in the community, and to obtain money in turn by selling to strangers products which the community can make better than anyone else is the essence of our economic order. To pay out money really gives the outsider money with which to buy in turn from someone else. To buy goods outside, then, though it does send out money, in turn brings

2. The Passing of Normalcy, p. 54. 1929, G. C. Forbes Publishing Company, New York.

in wealth, which is the important thing.

To buy at home is to lose the advantages of specialization and exchange. The way to wealth is through division of labor. Restrictions on trading would force all communities to produce their own needs and so divert the factors of production to less profitable employments. If the theory is sound as applied to chains, why would it not be equally sound to buy one's automobiles, furniture, radios, etc. from a local producer? The producers of such commodities take money from a community. The answer is obviously that it is cheaper to buy out of town. Prosperity is built on an inter-change of goods and services between communities, each supplying the things it can make best. Under such an economy no town or state will lose out unless it has nothing to offer the outside world. Thus, Illinois sends out her corn and receives money in return, which her inhabitants spend in retail stores for products produced in other states and other nations. If it is bad to buy abroad, it is bad to sell abroad. If everyone outside the state of Illinois refused to buy her products she would be in a sorry plight indeed. No one can sell forever and not buy. The money goes out one way and returns another; the trouble is that no one ever sees it returning.

What happens to the dollar spent in a chain and independent store? Neither can hoard their gross receipts but must spend them for more merchandise, transportation, taxes, store fixtures, wages, rent, etc. There is a creditor who is waiting for almost every dollar which is taken in and each store owner must meet his obligations. Each one buys merchandise and probably from the same source. The independent does not buy locally unless it is cheaper for him to do so. Neither does the chain. Both pay transportation charges to a foreign-owned railroad or trucking company and to local cartage companies; both must pay wages to their local employees and meet their local expenses for light, heat, etc. The only difference is that the chain pays salaries to executives who are located in some large city and profits to stockholders who are scattered throughout the country. It is these latter amounts that are said to be draining the money from the communities.

The division of operating expenses for the California Safeway Company is: merchandise, $0.781, salaries and wages, $0.112, miscellaneous expenses, $0.069, rent, $0.022, and profits $0.16.[3] The expenses of the Kroger Baking Company in 1929 were: merchandise 77.25 cents, local payroll, 12.0 cents, rent 2.125 cents, taxes .625 cents, local repairs and depreciation .875 cents, advertising .75 cents, local expenses 4.125 cents, and profits 2.25 cents.[4] The Census Bureau found a central office expense of 1.59 per cent for grocery stores in 1929.[5] Using the Kroger figures the chain would have sent out of town, for every dollar of receipts, 77.25 cents plus 2.25 cents plus 1.59 cents and whatever part of their advertising expense and taxes which were not expended locally. If the same dollars had been spent in an independent store, only the amount spent for merchandise would have been sent out of town. For the same merchandise the independent would have paid somewhat more so that there would have been only a slight saving, if any at all, in

---

3. Lull, R., "The Case for the Chain Store", Industrial News Review, Vol. XLIII, (August, 1935), p. 16.
4. Lyons, R. W., "Chain Association Backs Methods", Sales Management, Vol. XXII, (May 3, 1930), p. 22.
5. Bureau of the Census, Fifteenth Census of the United States, 1930, Distribution, "Retail Chains", p. 21. 1933, Government Printing Office, Washington, D. C.

the amount sent directly out of town. At the same time, the consumers would have gotten less for their money. That is, the lower prices of the chains leave more in the pockets of the consumer than the chains actually send out of town. The independent, moreover, does not have to spend his profits at home and may invest them outside. The chain profits go for expansion and distribution to stockholders. Part of the profits may return to the locality to locate more chain units. The stockholders are scattered throughout the country so that some of the profits may come back to town directly. Those who receive the profits have thereby a purchasing power which they can use to buy goods, perhaps some of the goods which the community in question may have produced.

In the case of some communities the money sent out may never return for the community may not be able to produce anything that outsiders want. Such a town, however, is bound to fail whether a chain or an independent sends out the money. Such a town has lost the reason for its existence and must fail sooner or later. The solution of its problem is for its inhabitants to move to places whose goods are in demand. No matter where money is spent, it is put in circulation and gradually returns to those places which can create a good or perform a service better than anyone else. There is no doubt that in some localities and in some states the chain sells more than it spends. Also, in some states it spends more than it sells. It may even sell more than it buys in a single nation. But, in the world economy it is obvious that the chain must spend (including profits paid out) as much as it receives. Whether a nation or state or locality gets its share depends on how well it can create goods or perform services. Some states profit enormously from direct expenditures from chains; for example, California and Florida with their fruits, Oregon with its salmon factories, Wisconsin and Minnesota with their dairy products. In such states the chains probably spend more than they sell; in other states they buy little or nothing. The situation would be the same if the independent sold all the products.

As a matter of fact, it is the efficient store, whether chain or independent, which keeps business at home. With good roads and automobiles people can go long distances to shop. With traveling so easy people will not tolerate poor stores but will go to towns which have the kind of stores they want. If the chain does a good job of merchandising, it will attract trade from a wide area. Not only the chain, but other businesses as well will share in the trade of such new customers. R. S. Vaile says: "It seems probable that town stores that are affiliated with a chain or a group can better meet the competition of stores in the larger towns than can the independent stores."[6] M. T. Copeland quotes an editorial from _Printer's Ink_ (Feb. 26, 1920):

> "Meanwhile, Woolworth is going right along creating for its competitors almost as much business as it gets for itself. By its tremendously efficient methods it brings about a demand for popular-priced goods which it can fill but partially . . . Woolworth knows this perfectly well. In fact, Woolworth is rather proud of its unquestioned ability to stimulate retail business in neighborhoods or towns where it may locate."[7]

People like to trade in shopping centers and chains often form the nucleus of a shopping center.

The unsuccessful enterprises by wasting capital are the

---

6. "Integrating the Small Town", _The Small City and Town_, Vaile, R. S., (editor), p. 41. 1930, University of Minnesota Press, Minneapolis.
7. _Problems in Marketing_, 3d _revised edition_, p. 75-76. 1930 printing, McGraw-Hill Book Company, Inc., New York.

ones which drain away the wealth of a community. Independents fail
more often than do chains and so waste the localities' wealth.

The charge is made that chains enter a community and do
not hire local people. This is true only of the manager and the
assistant managers. All the under-employees are local people for
there would be no point to import them. The manager and his assistants are sent to a new chain unit from out-of-town, and may even be
shifted from town to town. This comes from a policy of promotion
from within the ranks and it would be unfair to old employees to
depart from this principle. No chain could enter a new town and hire
men without chain experience to run their stores. Once established,
however, they will probably hire young men to start in training to
be managers so that local men have a chance to become a manager
eventually in some town. In the newcomer the town gets a new resident who is probably ambitious, hard-working, and experienced in
business. He pays rent and has a family and spends money just like
anyone else. No town ever grew by forbidding newcomers. Many independents, moreover, begin business in towns of which they are not
a native. The shifting of chain managers, moreover, is probably
no more rapid than the mortality of independents. There seems no
reason to tax the chains on the basis of the residence of the people
whom they hire.

It is said that chain stores restrict individual opportunity and initiative. With the growth of chains, there is said to be
less opportunity for an individual to go into business for himself;
the individual becomes an employee, a "servant of a great corporation,
a cog in a machine, receiving and obeying orders from New York"; all
opportunity for the exercise of initiative and individuality is

taken away by the impersonal and standardized merchandising of the chain.

An independent can be successful. In Chapter Two it was seen that the individual store still has a place in retailing. If the individual proprietor sticks to the phases of retailing in which chains are at a disadvantage, or, if he is an exceptional man, he can succeed. Few chains started big and most of the big companies were once small. If the efficient retailer is not hurt, the only opportunity which is denied the individual is that to engage in inefficient and unscientific retailing. The latter is an end greatly to be desired. That the independent still has a place is seen from the fact that the independents still do the great majority of all the business. As a matter of fact, the independents between the Census years of 1933 and 1935 not only increased in total numbers but also did a larger percentage of the total business.[8] Whether the chain will eventually result in huge monopolies and drive out the independents entirely is a question to be discussed below.

Will the same ability get a man farther in a chain organization or in an independent field? The chain offers a wide-open field for advancement. A man can go from the stock room, to an assistant managership, to manager, to supervisor, to executive. His rise is limited only by his ability and willingness to work. The chains have a policy of filling the higher positions from the ranks so that advancement depends more on personal qualities which fit a man for such higher positions than on one's capital or influence. Most of the present chain officials started in at the bottom and worked their ways up to large-salaried jobs. Every chain is full

8. See Chapter I .

of success stories of men who worked their ways up from the stockroom. Of course, these are only a small percentage of the number
who started in the stockroom, but there is the opportunity open to
these few with ability.

The single store does not offer enough return on brains
and capital to attract men of this calibre. A group of stores does.
For the exceptional man there is greater opportunity, measured in
money and power, in the large chain. For the average man there is
just as good an opportunity. He probably can reach a managership
at an earlier age in a chain than in an independent store. It takes
about four years of apprenticeship in the variety field and one year
in the grocery field to train the average man to be a manager. Few
men can obtain enough capital in such a short length of time to set
up their own businesses on a scale large enough to yield an equivalent income. In the words of W. T. Grant, founder of a successful
dry goods chain,

> "Men who started with us at $12 a week, today are execu-
> tives in great positions with fortunes already amassed while
> they are still young men. I worked in an individual store for
> 30 years to amass $1,000 with which to start this business."[9]

In a comparatively few years a chain manager can be making a good
salary.

Some men would never make successful independent merchants
even if they had adequate capital. Most men do not get far under
their own power but bog down and fail to progress. They need pushing, training, and discipline. In the chain there is no such thing
as standing still. The man either progresses with the chain or his
place is taken by someone who will. Some men who otherwise would

9. "Fill a Need or Fail", Printer's Ink, Vol. CXLIII, (June 14, 1928),
p. 30.

have been failures respond to this pushing and become successful
chain managers. Many independents fail because of inexperience and
inefficiency. The chain could have saved these by offering the advice and supervision of older experienced men. In the chain the man
furnishes the ability and willingness to work; the chain furnishes
the merchandising ability and experience and the capital. The successful independent must possess all these requirements. Most men
are lacking in them. The supervision of the chain may be less
bothersome than the constant prodding of the creditor and banker
The chain offers an opportunity for the man who is a good salesman
and nothing else. Also, there is a chance for men with special
talents to specialize and give full scope to their special abilities.

If a man does not want to enter the employ of either a
chain or independent as a career, but merely for training prepara-
tory to opening his own business, there is no doubt but that the
chain offers superior opportunities. The chain has a far superior
knowledge of the factors that make for success in retailing and has
an incentive to make their "learners" acquainted with them. There
is no incentive for an independent to push his clerk or train him
to be able to run a business for it would mean only another competitor. The success of the chain depends upon "graduating" a constant
stream of new men trained in the most efficient business methods
known to the chain. For a man who plans to open his own business
there could be no better investment than a training course in the
employ of a chain.

Is working for a corporation undesirable? Opportunity
does not lie solely in the ownership of a business. To work
for a corporation is the order of the day, more so in

production than in distribution. In all fields business is managed
and manned by paid employees and great careers have been carved out
in banking, transportation, etc. by men who were employees all their
lives. Few great railroad men ever owned one, yet opportunity has
not been denied young men in the railroad business. Perhaps as significant statement as any is one by H. T. Parsons, one-time president of the F. W. Woolworth Company.

"The idea that it is necessary to own a store in order to
achieve success in the retail field has absolutely nothing to
support it. Compared with the uncertainty which confronts the
average independent storekeeper, the many risks he runs, and
the obvious limitations of his vocation, the opportunity offered by a strong corporate retail enterprise, whether it be
in the chain-store field, the department-store field, the
mail-order field or any other branch of the business would
seem to me to be far superior.

"Of course, if a man lacks ability, or character, or per-
severance, or ambition, or any of the other basic qualities
that are essential to success, he can not expect to go very
far no matter what line of endeavor he follows. Certainly he
could hope for little in the chain-store field, while if he
accumulated sufficient capital to open a store of his own,
it would only be a question of time before his own shortcomings
would put him out of the picture--another failure added to the
long list which exacts such a heavy toll from the public."[10]

Nor does the chain method of operation take away all initiative from its employees. Chains establish maximum and minimum
limits for a man to use his brains but have set up certain instructions and guide-posts as warning signals. A considerable amount of
routine and definite instructions must be followed so as to secure
minimum standards of performance. Beyond this a manager and employee
have all sorts of opportunity to make their store a better store.
The initiative is thus directed in certain lines and is not allowed
to wander at will. If the chain business required only following out

10. "Why Chain Stores Command Public Favor", Chain Store Age, Vol.
IV, (January, 1928), p. 131.

of directions, it would not take four years to make a manager. The
man who is a mere order-follower gets no place in the chain business.
It takes initiative in that, as well as any other business, to make
a man stand out among his fellows.

How much initiative a chain manager is allowed depends on
the type of chain. Where specialty goods are handled or where the
distance between units is great, the manager has all the characteristics of a unit store operator. In some fields, particularly the
grocery field, the average manager need do little but follow instructions. The good manager can, and does, do more than this.

The discipline of the chain as against the free-will of
the independent is often criticized. More discipline is needed in
business. The anarchy which has been characteristic of our business
life has been very costly. Self-discipline by business is one step
in the correction of such a situation. Inspection is rigid in the
chain to insure minimum standards. Inspection is even more severe
on the railroad in order to insure safety, yet no one seems to object strenuously to that. Although not as imperative as on railroads
it is essential to the people that the standards of operating efficiency of our retail stores be raised. The independent has never
seemed willing to do it by his own free will. Supervision seems
necessary. As has been said,

"The only difference between the executive who apparently
has all the freedom of thought in the world, and the average
clerk is that the executive is usually a big enough man to be
a self-disciplinarian . . . . It is only when a man has learned
to check himself up and then can start to check others up that
he begins to become an executive."11

Until enough independents learn to pay close attention to every

11. Blauvelt, H., "What Chance Has a Man in a Chain?" Chain Store
Age, Vol. IV, (November, 1928), p. 44.

detail of their business, operating efficiency will improve only under the supervision of chain officials.

To tax the chains would limit opportunity rather than increase it. The only ones that would be benefited by such an action would be the inefficient, and they have no right to protection. To tax multiple-units really limits the individual's opportunity and initiative. A grocer can only draw so much trade to him in a single location. Once he has attained such a size, he can grow bigger only by opening a second store, a third, and so on. Heavy taxation would limit this possibility of growth.

The chain system is said to cause technological unemployment. Just as in production an increase in efficiency in merchandising is said to displace workers, with the result that greater production and distribution are accomplished with fewer workers. This in turn is said to result in decreased buying power and eventually a widespread depression. Unless the masses are supplied with sufficient purchasing power to absorb the products of our mass production system, goods will accumulate on the shelves and depression will result.

There is no doubt that the chain system of operation takes fewer workers than the old wholesaler-independent system. Some jobs have been eliminated, for example, the wholesalers' salesmen. The ability of a chain organization to correlate the activities of the wholesaler and retailer requires fewer men than when the two are under different heads. The chains use fewer clerks per dollar of sale because they locate their stores so that they are of the optimum size to secure the greatest sales per employee. The chains split jobs so that to a large extent they can hire people of lower

average standards of intelligence. The chains reduce the amount of
services rendered, and thus eliminate jobs. Multiple ownership requires fewer accountants, fewer lawyers, etc. As a result, chain
wages per dollar of sale are less than in the independent system.
A great deal of capital which is tied up in the old distributive
system may be destroyed. Seemingly, this would reduce the purchasing power of the people. It might be, however, that if all the
stores now operated by chains were turned over to the managers, the
managers would work longer hours and so eliminate the need for one
man or part of a man. Such was the experience in Iowa when the chain
oil companies sold their stations.

      The traditional answer to such an argument is that such
new devices result in lower prices. As a result consumers can buy
either more of the same articles or spread their income over more articles, and increase their expenditures in those fields. As production increases in these fields, the men displaced from the other
fields are rehired. The result is as much, or even more, employment
and more goods for all. The change will bring some distress but
eventually all will be rehired someplace else.

      This supposes that the new device actually reduces prices
and that such low prices can be immediately spread through the economic system. Even if lower prices result, it takes time for their
effects to be felt. Workers, moreover, do not shift readily and
some of those displaced may never find a job again. Eventually, as
many men will be at work but this does not help those men who never
are rehired. Men have always fought the introduction of new devices
for they have not been willing, even if able, to make the necessary
adjustments. Even if they see the change coming, they want to main-

tain the status quo and not undertake a change. All this brings temporary hardship and misery to some. Progress contributes enormous benefits but it also brings much suffering.

The chains claim to sell at lower prices than do the independents and also to have forced the independents to sell at less than they would otherwise. In Chapter Two it was seen that the chains do sell at a somewhat lower price. What effect they have had on the prices of independents can not be determined. If this continues, the new movement will, in the long run, increase employment; if prices do not remain down, the economic system will be headed for disaster. Thus far the prices have stayed down, and they will stay down unless a monopoly should develop.[12] As a whole, the chains do not appear to have contributed seriously to the problem of technological unemployment.

The question is how to bring progress with the least loss and suffering. It is not fair that a few pay the entire cost of economic progress while society as a whole benefits. It is equally unfair that society should be asked to forego an improvement for the benefit of a few. We should permit the change and make society take care of those who are unable to adjust themselves. As long as competition is not legally unfair, one competitor must be allowed to put another out of business. How best to take care of those who are unfortunate enough to fall behind is a matter that has not been solved satisfactorily as yet.

For those whose existence seems to be threatened by a new device the way to meet such competition is to withdraw from such

---

12. See page 188 ff.

competition and concentrate on phases of the business that the new device can not enter. When automatic machinery entered the shoe-making business, the old hand-workers did one of two things. Some tried to compete with the machines and made cheaper products; some made only extra-quality and special order shoes. For the former it meant increasingly longer hours and lower pay and, finally, extinction; for the latter, it meant continued existence. The independent likewise has two alternatives. He can compete directly against the chain or he can sell those things that the chain can not handle efficiently. Only the superior independent can survive the former choice.

Special taxation would not solve the matter of technological unemployment. For every chain unit that was closed a few employees would have to make the same kind of painful adjustment. Such an act would also result in higher prices which would cause unemployment in other lines. If all the new inventions and discoveries that have been made since, say 1500, were eliminated, it is true that no one would be unemployed. All would be busy all day long trying to gather together enough to eke out an existence. All would be busy but they would have by no means as much to show for their efforts as do most of the so-called poor classes today. The most fortunate individuals of those days were scarcely to be envied by anyone today. If it is fair to scrap one improvement, it is fair to scrap all of them.

One of the most frequently heard charges against the chains is that they are tending to form monopolies in the necessities of life. They are charged with planning to drive out the independents and then to combine and raise prices. With a monopoly of the necessities the chain would have complete control over the lives of the people.

The essence of monopoly is the control of supply. No one can set the price of an article unless he can control the amount of that article that will be thrown on the market. The food field deals largely with staples, which are so widely produced by individual farmers that no one can hope to control the supply. The sources of supply in the retail field in general are so many and varied and scattered that any effective control for purposes of monopoly is practically impossible. If no chain can obtain this control, there can not be a monopoly.

The real test of monopoly is whether the field remains open to competition. As was seen in Chapter One the chains have never done over twenty-five per cent of the total business. In comparison to the amount of business done by independents the chain total does not look impressive. The independent is having a difficult task in many quarters yet he still can compete if he is willing to work and progress. The last census figures even showed that the independents were increasing both in number and in the proportion of business done. Much of the fear of the chains is based, not on the share of the business that they do at present, but on the assumption that chain growth will continue at the rate of the twenties. In a comparison of the amount of business done by chains in 1929, 1933, and 1935 it is evident that chain growth is slowing down. It is possible that the chains have reached maturity and will continue to do about the same proportion of the total business year after year. The census figures, moreover, failed to reveal a city in which any chain organization, or even chain stores as a group, had a monopoly

of the retail business. If the chains were seeking a monopoly, it
would seem that they would have established one in some region of
the country. In some of the retail fields, particularly in the
variety-store field, the chains have attained a virtual monopoly.
It is significant that in this field, where the chains do practically
all the business, no serious charge of monopoly has been made. The
chains do a large share of the business in certain fields in some
cities as Table III shows, but in no case do the chains actually
have complete control of the business. It is not fair, moreover, to
lump together all chains and consolidate their figures. There are
national, sectional, and local chains. The problem of monopoly
arises only in the case of the national and larger sectional chains.
When the business done by the local chains is deducted, see Table V,
the threat of chain monopoly seems very much diminished.

The "A & P", which is four times as large in volume of
business as any other chain, did somewhat over a billion dollars of
business in 1929, out of a total food business of about ten billions. The volume of this largest chain does not seem to indicate
that there is any danger of a monopoly in the near future. It was
seen in Chapter Two that there are economic limits to chain-store
expansion, that once they have absorbed the business for which they
are best fitted and the independents have grown efficient enough to
take care of the share for which they are best fitted the chain
will stop growing and take its place in the retail work. Chains
will not monopolize the retail field but will settle down and take
their place in the scheme of distribution. As long as it is as easy
to open retail stores as it is, monopoly will be impossible. The
chains could not practice unfair competition in enough places and

for long enough a time to keep out all independents. They would spring up as fast as they were eliminated and eventually the chain would exhaust its resources in its attempt to eliminate each new competitor.

The chains, moreover, actively compete among themselves. No evidence of collusion between these has ever been presented so it can be assumed that they are in active competition. The lines between chains of differenttypes are growing hazier and hazier, for example, drug chains are expanding into other lines such as the restaurant and variety business, variety stores are handling groceries and drugs, grocery stores are carrying tobacco products, and some tobacco stores are carrying general merchandise. If any organization should absorb all the grocery stores, chains in all other lines could stock groceries in a short while and enter into competition. Inter-chain competition itself would prevent monopoly. The competition of progressive independents, department stores, mail-order houses, super-markets, etc., are further protection against the formation of any monopoly in the retail field.

The prices that chains charge are not monopoly prices. Intense inter-chain competition has tended to keep prices down and not up. Table XXIII shows the small profit made by the chains on net sales. Although the profit on invested capital is large, the profit per sale is small. The chains are run on the basis of a small mark-up and rapid turnover. Such a policy is not characteristic of a monopoly. Even though the chains should eliminate their competitors, it is doubtful if they would change their policy. It seems to be generally agreed that the chain principles can only be a success when the business is conducted on a low-markup and rapid-turnover

basis.   Furthermore, a glance at the tables in Chapter One will show
that the chains are most numerous in the lines of retailing in which
competition is most severe and the margins the lowest.

What if the chains, or any one chain, should become large
enough to dominate a particular branch of retailing? Whether this
would be good or bad would depend upon the manner by which such a
size were acouired. There would be two main ways to gain control of
the retail field -- by unfair competition and by efficiency. A firm
which attains its position by efficiency is not to be condemned. It
is a general belief that under free competition big business always
crushes smaller businesses. It is seldom considered that both can
live side by side. All big business is not bad. If a firm grows
big because it gives the people what they want, there is no need to
worry about the preservation of competition. What would be needed
then would be legislation to stop bad practices. The way to check
undesirable monopolies is to stop unfair practices and let the best
man win. Taxation will not stop those methods that lead to undesirable monopolies. That the chains have been more efficient than
the average independent seems beyond doubt. That the chains will
prove so much more efficient than the independent that they will
obtain a monopoly seems very doubtful. If one is not burdened unfairly by taxation and unfair practices are prohibited, each will
take its proper place in retailing. It seems strange that after
our trust-busting days corporations should be prosecuted for selling
too cheaply. In many cases this has been the chief crime of the
chains.

The chains do not violate the present anti-trust laws and
so can not be accused of being monopolies. It is an accepted

practice to assume a man innocent until he has been proven guilty.
The chains do not have a monopoly in the present meaning of the law
and so can not be deemed guilty. The chains have never been prosecuted under the anti-trust laws. It is doubtful if such a suit
could be successfully prosecuted. The Supreme Court allows reasonable monopolies based on efficiency. There is nothing in our anti-
trust laws that prevents a firm from becoming large; such laws merely
limit the use to which the power which comes from such size is put.[13]
As long as the chain is fair and honest and puts out a good product
at a reasonable price, it can not be prosecuted. The anti-trust
laws were not designed to permit the inefficient to exist.

Before such a charge could be sustained, one would have
to wait until any one chain had something less than four or five
hundred competitors of the same type and until all these stores combined did over two-fifths of the business within their field, as is
the case in the grocery field. The Federal Trade Commission was
charged to find in its inquiry whether the chains were exhibiting

13. As the Federal Trade Commission said in its final report (op.
cit., p. 19) " . . . . However one may view the economic question
of monopoly, it is futile to treat the legal question of monopoly
as one that is determinable from size or the proportion of business
controlled. Under the principles announced by the Supreme Court a
concern may do all the business in its field of operation and have
no competition without infringing section two of the Sherman Law,
which makes it a penal offense to monopolize, ... (etc.)
"The broad prohibition of the Sherman Law against monopoly has
been narrowed by interpretation of the courts to mean that only actual, as distinguished from potential, monopoly is unlawful, and
that the mere possession of monopolistic power in the absence of
overt acts indicating an illegal use thereof, is not a violation of
this statute. . . . Under the principles of these decisions, if
there should develop one gigantic all-inclusive chain-store system
for each line of distribution, its status as a lawful monopoly could
be attacked only to the extent it had violated the law as a means of
attaining monopoly, and exercised its monopolistic power contrary to
law. . . . . "

any tendency toward monopoly. Their survey was exhaustive enough that if any such tendency had existed they would have found it. On the conclusion of their work they found no such tendency and asked only for more power to prevent any possible threatened monopolies and unfair practices.[14] If the present laws are such that undesirable monopolies can be formed without a violation of them, the remedy is not taxation but additional legislation to plug up the loopholes. If chain monopolies did develop, the public would immediately pass legislation to correct them, especially since they would be a monopoly of necessities. Such laws would effectively block any tendency to monopoly that ever developed and there would be no need of taxes to help out. The charge of monopoly is founded not on the present situation but on a possible future monopoly. The opponents of the chains point to the past growth of the chains and say that if such a growth continues, it will absorb all the trade. This is merely a prediction or opinion and is not a matter of fact so is not actionable under any laws. The charge of monopoly is a ghost and is not to be feared until it actually appears.

Since the chains take the corporate form, they do promote concentration of control in the retail field. Their stocks are widely held but public ownership does not mean public control. As a matter of fact, it may mean that it is easier for a few to control large amounts of money. There is nothing wrong with such concentration of power. The evil lies in the misuse of such power. There is need for some control over this phase of the chain business to prevent the occurrence of any evils, but taxation will not furnish such a control.

14. "Final Report, etc.", op. cit., pp. 94 ff.

Taxation would not increase competition. Before the chains developed, there was not as keen competition to reduce prices. Such competition as did exist took the form of the addition of more and more unnecessary services. If the chains were taxed out of existence, one form of competition would be eliminated. Under a system of independents there would be only local competition with few superior intellects in charge of any of the units. It would leave a distinctly inferior competition. Furthermore, with the chain out of the way the wholesalers would have an even better opportunity to obtain a monopoly. The possibilities of monopoly do not lie wholly with the chain.

In summary, there is no reason to accuse the chains of monopoly and raising prices when they have not done so, merely because they might some day do it. There is just cause for complaint only when and if they employ wrongful practices and seek to develop an illegal monopoly. At the present writing legislation to outlaw the chain is uncalled-for. The dangers of monopoly by the chain are negligible compared to the wastes of distribution which existed before the chain appeared. A more serious question today than a possible monopoly is the high cost of distribution. Any organization which successfully attacks distributive wastes deserves a chance to prove its worth.

The Federal Trade Commission reached the following conclusion:

"In the grocery group, where chain-store systems have reached their largest development, it has been shown . . . . that the large national and sectional chains participate proportionately with smaller sectional and local chains in retail grocery sales falling to these types. The competition which they furnish to each other, supplemented by that of independent stores, would seem to negative monopoly by any individual

chain. The same is true as to the larger chains in the drug
group, where the two large national chains in active competition
with each other at various points together control but 6.8
per cent of total retail drug sales.

"A study of the extent to which chain-store companies have
invaded the general field of retail distribution of commodities
does not indicate a monopolization of that field, taken as a
whole. For the year 1929 total chain-store sales represented
19.3 per cent of the aggregate retail sales of the United
States as against 80.7 per cent for all other methods of distribution. Local chains accounted, however, for 6.7 per cent
and sectional chain companies only 12.6 per cent of the United
States aggregate sales."[15]

Chains are accused of being lax in their community re-

lationships. In addition to his other duties, the retailer has the

function of helping to develop the community from which his business

comes. This help takes the form of contributions to civic and

charitable organizations. In doing this the retailer supposedly

builds up the town and so helps his own business. The merchant is

also supposed to lead a normal personal life and to take part in

community affairs. It is charged that the chains do not contribute

to organizations. The chains are said, moreover, to make such de-

mands on their employees that the men can not lead normal home and

community lives. Chains move their managers often and the uncer-

tainty of tenure makes them hesitate to own homes, prevents them

from making friends, and keeps them from getting attached to any one

town. With so little interest in any one town the individual has

little incentive to take part in any of its activites. On the other

hand, the independent is pictured as a liberal contributor to and

participant in all community affairs and a leader of community life.

This has been the point at which the chains have been the

weakest but they have found it good business to support the locali-

---

15. "Final Report of the Chain-Store Inquiry", op. cit., pp. 19-20.

ties and have undergone a change of heart. During the period of their expansion they gave no time and attention to this phase of retailing but many are contributing now to some extent in an effort to convince the public that they have as great an interest in the community as the independent. The chain executives realize that their stores need more than price appeal and that they need "community personality", that is, that stores are often judged by their representation on business club rosters, their contributions to charity, and their local spirit. On the whole, it is probably more difficult to find a chain-store executive who does not realize the value of community relationships than it would be to find an independent who did not.

Community contributions are only a secondary function of retail stores, albeit an important one. The first and most important service of any business to its community is efficient performance, elimination of waste, and the provision of the greatest value possible for the consumers' dollar. The real builders of a town are those who build up their own businesses. A modernized and efficient store does more for a town than membership on a committee. Good stores do in a direct way what associations propose to do -- bring more trade into the town. Although running a profitable store is the retailer's first duty, he can not overlook his other function. As someone has suggested, it is like the husband who works hard to be a good provider and wonders why his wife becomes cross because he forgets to send her flowers on their anniversary. Although it is unfair to emphasize the secondary function of community relationships, no store will be forgiven if it overlooks such activity. The chains are awakening to this and are contributing more than they once did.

Chains vary in the degree to which they support such activities. Some are very generous and some even niggardly. A survey by the New England Association of Commercial Executives in fifty-six New England cities showed the Kresge Company belonged to civic associations in ninety-six per cent of the cities in which it had stores; W. T. Grant in eighty-four per cent; Liggett, eighty-four per cent; Penney, eighty-three per cent; Walkover, seventy-five per cent; Mohican Company, sixty per cent; Waldorf, fifty per cent; Woolworth, forty-three per cent; "A & P", twenty-one per cent; United Cigar, thirty-one per cent.[16] Several chains belonged to none at all. In a survey conducted by the National Association of Commercial Organization Secretaries in which seventy-nine per cent of its total active membership, representing every state in the union, supplied material, almost eighty per cent said that aside from financial support the chains and managers were cooperating with their fellow merchants.[17] The same study showed how various chain organizations stood with respect to commercial organization support. Table XLIV summarizes these findings. It will be seen that there is no correlation between cooperation and size, geographical location, or type of chain. Many chains are leaders in public work and are outstanding for their cooperation. The Federal Trade Commission found that ninety-four out of 164 reporting chains were represented in local civic organizations.[18]

Some chains allot a certain percentage of their sales for

16. Reported in "What's Your Policy?", Chain Store Age, Vol. IV, (March, 1928), p. 97.
17. "Report of the Chain-Store Committee", Proceedings of the National Association of Commercial Organization Secretaries, 1932, p. 50.   18. Chain-Store Inquiry, Vol. I, "Chain Stores in the Small Town", 73d Congress, 2d Session, Sen. Doc. No. 93, p. xiii. 1934, Government Printing Office, Washington, D. C.

Table XLIV

COMMUNITY RELATIONSHIPS: RECORD OF SUPPORT GIVEN BY VARIOUS CHAIN
ORGANIZATIONS TO CHAMBER OF COMMERCE ORGANIZATIONS, 1932

Chain	Number Supported	Number Not Supported
Jas. Butler Grocery Stores	1	14
Childs	11	0
Cities Service Refining Co.	14	7
Crane Co.	19	2
W. L. Douglas Shoe Co.	8	30
Eastman Kodak	11	0
Endicott-Johnson Corp.	8	18
Enna-Jettick Shoe Stores	4	18
Fanny Farmer Candy Shops, Inc.	14	12
Firestone Tire and Rubber Co.	25	15
First National Stores Inc.	23	8
Goodyear Tire and Rubber Co.	11	9
W. T. Grant Co.	111	10
Great Atlantic and Pacific Tea Co.	283	31
Jewell Tea Co., Inc.	20	13
S. S. Kresge	179	2
S. H. Kress Co.	83	3
G. R. Kinney Co.	100	25
Kroger Grocery & Baking Co.	87	15
Lerner Stores Corp.	48	16
Louis K. Liggett Co.	98	5
Mangel's Inc.	42	11
Martha Washington Candy Co.	15	19
Thom McAn Shoe Co. & Melville Shoe Corp.	51	31
McCrory Stores Corp.	41	14
McLellan Stores Inc.	59	12
Montgomery, Ward & Co.	193	11
J. J. Newberry Co.	60	10
J. C. Penney Co., Inc.	250	8
Piggly Wiggly (various companies)	55	20
Safeway Stores Co.	65	1
D. A. Schulte Co.	38	17
Sears, Roebuck Co.	162	6
Singer Sewing Machine Co.	2	45
Standard Oil of N. Y.	46	14
Swift & Co.	29	18
United Cigar Stores Co.	28	73
Walgreen Co.	38	17
Walk Over Shoe Co.	23	14
Western Auto Supply Co.	60	6
F. W. Woolworth Co.	306	59

Source: "Report of the Chain Store Committee", Proceedings of the National Association of Commercial Organization Secretaries, 1932, p. 55 ff.

community cooperation to be administered by the local district manager according to his own judgment. Others give only the executives
the right to make contributions. Others permit the local manager
to contribute to certain associations but to refer all unusual requests to the home office. The Melville Shoe Company, for example,
sets aside one-tenth of one per cent of gross sales for this purpose.[19]

The chains' attitude toward the support of such civic organizations is indicated in the answers to a questionnaire sent out
by Sears, Roebuck and Company.[20] According to this, chains look
with favor on Chambers of Commerce and join those bodies that are
effective in their work. Chains permit managers to serve when fric-
tion and antagonism does not follow, although some reserve active
participation for older men. The chains, however, frown on managers
who devote too much time to such activities. Many do not support
Chambers which tend to town selfishness, "ride" the chains, or ask
too high contributions from the chains. The chains are shrewd buyers and if they do not buy a particular chamber membership, it may
be that the goods are not properly presented or are not up to quality.

The chains probably support the chambers and similar activities about as well as anyone. The fact that some chains do not
contribute is offset by the fact that many independents also fail to
belong. Before anything is said against the chains, the independent
should be sure that he who has lived in the town all his life is

19. Dovell, R., "Chain Stores Can Be Good Citizens", Nation's Business,(June, 1931), p. 82, Vol. XIX.
20. Mowry, D. E., "How Large-Scale Organizations View the Chamber of
Commerce", Proceedings of National Association of Commercial Organization Secretaries, 1932, pp. 166-174.

doing his bit. In a study in San Francisco of grocery stores it was found that 69.0 per cent of the chains and only 29.8 per cent of the independent stores were members of the Chamber of Commerce.[21] The chain-store committee of the National Association of Commercial Organization Secretaries reported that, "On the whole, it appears that chains are probably supporting commercial organizations at least as well as are other progressive interests."[22] Chains may not be doing as well as they might but they are doing as well as the independent.

The chains probably contribute less to other types of requests but in many cases their refusals are justified. Many of the requests made of merchants are more or less polite blackmail and the merchant gives against his will. The chain organization is such that it can refuse such requests. The independent merchant is afraid to offend a friend or customer and so is forced to give under pressure. One chain-store manager was asked to contribute to over two hundred causes.[23] A chain-store editor says there are in Philadelphia forty-six different organizations which are trying to do Chamber of Commerce work.[24] If such is the case, the chain can hardly be blamed for selecting the organizations to which to contribute.

Chains also have a varied record in respect to their contributions to charities and community chests. Some are entirely fair while others contribute nothing. In Chattanooga, Tennessee in 1930, fourteen, or twenty-two per cent, of the sixty-eight chain organizations made no contributions to the Community Chest.[25] As a

21. Faville, D. E., "Comparison of Chain and Independent Grocery Stores in the San Francisco Area", Journal of Marketing, Vol. I., (October, 1936), p. 87.   22. Op. cit., p. 52.
23. Ernst, E.G. and Hartl, E. M., "Chain Stores and the Community", Nation, Vol. CXXXI, (Nov. 14, 1930), p. 545.
24. Lebhar, G. M., "As We See It", Chain Store Age, Vol. V, (May, 1929), p. 37.   25. Phelps, C. W., "Some Limitations and Disadvantages of the Chain Store System", Progressive Grocer, Vol. X, (April, 1931), p. 83.

whole, the chains contributed less than one-thirtieth of one per cent of their sales. It was found that some chains set aside from one-fourth of one per cent to three-fourths of one per cent of their total sales for this purpose but such chains were exceptional. The majority of the chains were very niggardly. The Federal Trade Commission found that out of 153 chains which reported, 126 made contributions to local charities.[26] The total sum contributed amounted to about seventy-seven dollars per year for the stores which contributed or sixty-five dollars for those which reported. In a study of corporation contributions to community chests[27] it was found that for 1929 out of almost fifty-nine million dollars which was raised by 129 community chests about twenty-two per cent came from corporations, 2.9 per cent of which came from chain stores. It was found that 64.1 per cent of the total contributions received from chain stores and 73.7 per cent of the total amount came from thirty-four national chain-store concerns.[28] Although chain contributions were small, they were found to be growing steadily.

Some chains have excellent records. J. P. Nichols lists a few of these in a pamphlet put out by chain stores.[29] In 1931 United Cigar Stores Company and the Shulte Cigar Company pledged five per cent of their sales for one day to unemployment relief; Sears, Roebuck gave its seventh gift of $100,000 to the Joint Emergency Relief Fund and Julius Rosenwald, Chairman of the Board, gave $250,000 for the relief of the unemployed in Cook County, Illinois;

26. "Chain-Stores in the Small Town", op. cit., p. xiii.
27. Williams, P. and Croxton, F. E., Corporation Contributions to Organized Community Welfare Services, 1930, p. 11. 1930, National Bureau of Economic Research, Inc., New York.   28. Ibid., p. 12, 167, 168.   29. Chain Store Manual, pp. 66, 67. 1932, Institute of Distribution Inc., New York.

W. T. Grant Company contributed $45,000 to charity; Safeway gave
$660 per store in Portland, Oregon; The MacMarr Stores donated $1,500
per unit; the Western States Grocery Company subscribed $440 per
store; and the Grand Union Company pledged $100,000 to the relief
fund. These are the exceptional stores, however. Relief is a public function and should not be supported by individual contributions.
The funds should be raised by taxes and not by levies on merchants
and individuals. For those who hold such a view there can be no
criticism of one who does not contribute.

As for the home and community life of chain-store managers
they are human beings with interests comparable to any other similar
group. Each manager joins in home, religious, civic, and fraternal
life according to his own personal bent. Chain managers probably
participate in about the same proportion as do independents. The
chain manager must live somewhere, pays taxes on what he owns, sends
his children to school, and votes the same as any other man. He
may move around and be less attached to a single town but the subject of local patriotism can be overdone. The independent, moreover, does not have all the virtues he is supposed to have.

In a study of Safeway Stores employees (7,555), of whom
sixteen per cent were women and eighty-four per cent men, sixty-six
per cent were married, there were 10,550 dependents, the average age
was 29, thirty per cent owned their own homes, eighty-one per cent
owned radios, sixty-seven per cent owned automobiles, and seventy
per cent personally paid taxes with an average tax of $54.87 (average
per capita tax for the country, $18.37). Thirty-eight per cent had
lived in the state over fifteen years; twenty per cent, eleven to
fifteen years; twenty-two per cent, six to ten years; sixteen per

cent, two to five years; and four per cent, less than one year.[30]
In another survey of the 2,663 Safeway Stores[31] the average age of
over 21,000 employees was found to be 28.2 years; sixty-seven per
cent were married; thirty-six per cent lived in the state in which
they were born while the average length of residence of the remaining in their present homes was sixteen years; twenty-eight per cent
owned their own homes; fifty-one per cent owned their own radios;
sixty-four per cent owned automobiles; 15,430 were qualified voters;
sixty-four per cent paid taxes of $43.36 apiece; thirty per cent
were members of fraternal organizations; ninety-seven per cent regu-
larly read the local newspapers; ninety-one per cent were affiliated
with some religious group; and seventy-three per cent contributed to
charity an average sum of twenty dollars, over half of which went to
community chests.

In a survey of 2,242 store managers and supervisors of
the First National Stores[32] twenty-two per cent had been with the
organization over ten years; practically one hundred per cent were
citizens or had applied to be; eighty-four per cent were registered
voters; twenty-four per cent owned their own homes; seventy-four
per cent paid local, state, and federal taxes other than poll and
auto; 1,828 belonged to local organizations such as Boards of Trade,
Chambers of Commerce, Legion posts or other local, civic, and fraternal organizations and 248 were officeholders; and eighty per

30. Lull, R., "The Case for the Chain Store", Industrial News Re-
view, Vol. XLIII, (Aug., 1935), p. 17.
31. Reported in Lyons, R. W., "Social Aspects of Chains are Sound",
Chain Store Progress, Vol. III, (April, 1931), p. 1. "A Chain Puts
Its Links Under the Microscope", Business Week, (June 10, 1931),p.14.
Proceedings of the National Association of Commercial Organization
Secretaries, 1931, report by Lyons, R. W., p. 48.
32. "A Chain Turns the X-Ray On Its Store Managers," Business Week,
(Oct. 14, 1931), p. 10.

cent had bank accounts.

In a study of grocery stores in San Francisco[33] chain-store employees averaged thirteen-and-a half years' residence in California and independent, twenty; the most typical length of residence in a community was four years for chain employees and ten-and-a-half years for independents; both had an average of 1.9 dependents. The differences are somewhat lessened when it is considered that the chain employees were of a much younger average age. Forty-seven per cent of the chain employees were under twenty-five, and only 29.8 per cent of the independents; only 16.7 per cent of the chain employees were over thirty-six and 37.1 per cent of the independents. Table XLV continues the comparison. The relatively minor differences can be explained in large part by age differences for it is reasonable to believe that older men would be more capable of owning homes, autos, etc., and would belong to more clubs. The conclusion from these studies is that there is little or no difference in the activities of chain-store employees and independents.

In summary, the chain store meets a want but to be most successful it must make itself a part of the community. Although the chains do about as well as the independents, they do not support the towns as they should. Some progress has been made but more is needed. That the independent is slightly more interested in the community than the chains does not mean that the community would be better off without the chains. The independents do not contribute so much more that the field ought to be left to them. Taxation would only lead the chain to believe that the community was against chains

---

33. Faville, D. E., op. cit.

Table XLV

COMMUNITY RELATIONSHIPS: PERCENTAGE OF GROCERY CHAIN MANAGERS
AND INDEPENDENT GROCERYMEN IN SAN FRANCISCO WHO ENGAGED
IN CERTAIN ASPECTS OF COMMUNITY LIFE

Activity	Chains	Independents
Owning Houses	11.8	29.8
Owning Homes or living with Parents Who Do	32.8	43.6
Owning Autos	66.7	74.8
Owning Radios	83.2	82.3
Paying Taxes Previous Year	66.7	78.2
Contributing to Charity Previous Year	85.0	86.8
Registered As Voters	67.7	74.2
Member of Social Club or Lodge	42.2	54.5
Belonging to a Church	69.3	66.7

Source:
Faville, D. E., "Comparison of Chain and Independent Grocery
Stores in the San Francisco Area", Journal of Marketing, Vol.
I, (October, 1936), p. 89.

---

so that the chain would have even less reason to contribute.

Thus, the charges that the chain stores take money out of the
community, do not hire local help, stifle individual opportunity
and initiative, bring technological unemployment, tend toward monopoly and concentration of wealth, and do not do their share in community projects can not be used to justify the special taxation of
chain stores. Only in respect to the latter can the chain be said
to lag behind the independent. The essentially isolationist policy
of trying to keep all the money possible in a community and of
hiring only local help harms rather than helps a town. There is
just as much chance, and even more, for a man to succeed now as
there was before the development of the chains. Technological unemployment results from chain policies but the public will be better
off in the end. What to do with the displaced workers must be
solved, however. There is no evidence of an illegal monopoly. The

chains are weak in their community relationships but are improving.
The independents are little, if any, better in this respect. This,
moreover, is a secondary function of retailing and does not deserve
the importance it has been given.

CHAPTER FIVE

SUMMARY AND CONCLUSIONS OF THE USE OF SPECIAL TAXES
TO REGULATE CHAIN STORES

The real test of the desirability of the use of special taxes to regulate chain stores is whether such taxes are a benefit to the consumer. From the consumer viewpoint the test to be applied is whether the chain fulfills an economic need, that is, whether it performs a service which the public wants. In addition, the chain must so operate that its competitors are given a fair chance to vie with the chain to serve this need. The rights of the competitor are important but it must be certain that it is a right that is being violated and not that a less efficient system is unable to keep up with the chain. The consumer is injured whenever an efficient competitor is put out of business unfairly; the consumer gets a benefit when an inefficient competitor is put out of business fairly. The real differences in this question are really not between the chain and the independent but between the community and any interest that hurts it. No one form of distributive organization is as important as the people to whose wants it administers. The sole question then is whether the public wants the chain and the deciding point is whether the chain benefits or can benefit a large group of consumers without unfairly hurting other interests.

It is significant that the consumers do not urge special taxes on chains but that such taxes have been supported by wholesalers and independents. Many efficient wholesalers and independents, however, do not favor such taxes. There is some tendency for those who go out of business, and most of these are inefficient operators, to work for the passage of such legislation. Others who find their profits lowered also desire the same thing. Those who want legislation would rather have the help of law to put their competitors out of business than to try to improve their own methods. Such laws are a subsidy to certain groups and only such groups will benefit. If those who urge such laws had been as perfect as their propaganda would lead one to believe and as free from blame for their failure as they claim, there never would have been a chance for the chains to grow. The special taxation of chains would give many inefficient merchants a chance to survive and live off the consumer.

The opposition to chains comes largely because of successful competition and only partly because of unfair practices. For the old system of distribution to compete it must use ability, energy, and thought. This is the only way to attain efficiency, but efficient merchandising does not come easy and it is much easier to ask for legislation. In all periods and in all groups there has been similar opposition to advanced methods. The craftsmen protested against power machinery in England, the stagecoach drivers fought the railroad, and so did all who found their security threatened by a new innovation. It is only natural that people strive to protect their own interests but it is just as natural that the consumers try to protect their interests and to see that a successful innovation is allowed to take its proper place. Just as the power machinery and railroad benefited the consumer and should not have been held back for the benefit of the displaced workers so the chain, if it does benefit the consumer, should be allowed to take its place. No group has a right to say that its method of operation is the only way to do a thing and to combine to force through legislation to prevent another group from taking over its job. The consumer should be allowed to be the judge of whom it wants to perform the necessary services.

The chain does fulfill an economic need efficiently. The integration and specialization of the chains offer buying, operating, and selling advantages which make them the most economical means yet offered the consumers to buy their necessities. By saving the consumer money the purchasing power of the people is increased, the standard of living improved, and the maintenance of mass production aided. This lowered price of merchandise is the fundamental justification of the chain. In addition, the chain has introduced new efficient methods in distribution, especially in the mechanical aspects; has increased the attractiveness and cleanliness of stores and merchandise; and has made available a non-service type of store for customers who desire the savings involved. The chain has brought a keener type of competition to the retail field. The consumer benefits from such rivalry for the wastes in distribution will only disappear when there is active competition between different types of retailers. The crying need of the day is for less waste in distribution and the chain has done more to eliminate waste than any other agency. Our distributive system is far from perfect and any legislation which proposes that the most efficient type of distributor be taxed, with no idea of the effect of such a tax on the cost of distribution, is not in the public interest. Until our distributive system is perfect, such legislation is not in order.

The situation is this: the chains have developed for economic reasons; the chains have certain advantages over independents and the independents certain advantages over chains; there is

a place for both if they do their job well; in case both try to do
the same job the real issue is not between chain and independent but
between the competent and the incompetent. Consumer acceptance
proves the right of the chain to exist. It meets the demands of a
certain class of customers and to eliminate the chain would deprive
many of something they have welcomed.

Thus, the chain offers possibilities of being a benefit to
the consumers and is not all bad. If the good of the chain can be
preserved and the evil eliminated, the consumer will gain by the existence of the chain. Evils have arisen in some cases but such evils
have been only incidental to the chain success. The evils said to
belong to the chain system of operation are short-weighting and short-
changing; inferior goods; local price-cutting, loss-leader selling,
and other unfair practices; coercive buying; poor employee relationships, including low wages; taking money out of town; destroying
individual opportunity; helping to create technological unemployment;
tending to form monopolies; and failing to take an active interest
in the local communities. The question is whether the good of the
chain does, or can, outweigh the evils said to exist.

It is true that some of the above evils have existed to a
degree but it can not be proven that any of the evils mentioned are
inherent in the chain system. Isolated cases of every evil of which
the chain is accused can be pointed out but several cases do not
make a condition true for all chains. The same evils could thus be
found in any system of retailing. Almost any type of activity could
be condemned by the same reasoning -- restaurants would have to be
condemned because a few serve faulty meals, automobiles would have to
be condemned because a few break down. In an investigation such as

this care must be taken not to generalize from the particular. A
label can not be applied to a whole group because of the actions of
individuals who may belong to the group. The chief interest in this
study is to see whether the alleged evils are inherent in the chain
system.

There are all sorts of chains, national, sectional, and
local; large and small; good and bad. All five thousand or more
chains do not operate in the same manner or deal with all factors
identically. They are not like peas in a pod but differ as widely
as do independents. The same treatment should not be accorded to
all. To class all chains together is to miss the first essential in
dealing with them correctly. The chains are capable of the misuse
of power but all do not avail themselves of the possibility. Only
the bad deserve punishment. Though evils may, and do, arise, there
is nothing inherently sinister or vicious in the theory of chain organization. The special taxes that are proposed are just as disas-
trous to useful chains as to bad ones. Moreover, most of the evils
suggested would not be true of chains of the least number of stores
at which the maximum tax rate takes effect. If the existing schedules are designed only to stop abuses, most of them are illogically
arranged.

The chains are not one hundred per cent perfect but neither
is the wholesaler-independent system. The average wholesaler and
independent are not so much superior to the chains in respect to each
of the conditions advanced as reasons for the special taxation of
chains that he deserves to be allowed to stay in business despite his
inefficiency. The average independent is not such a virile force
that he deserves artificial encouragement.

In respect to each of the alleged abuses, how does the chain stand? It has been shown that for the grade specified the chains carry fully as good quality merchandise as the independent. They cater to the lower grades of merchandise but give good values in those grades. Since there is a demand for this type of merchandise, the chains fulfill an economic need. Various studies found that chains were no more guilty of short-weighting and short-changing than were independents. The actions of both left much to be desired but there was not enough difference to justify the extinction of one and the survival of the other. The chains were found to be using the loss-leader and local price-cutting more than the independents but not as extensively or as effectively as was alleged. This is one abuse of the chain system of operation that needs correction.

Chains were found to buy cheaper than independents but no evidence was found to support a view that the concessions granted the chains were not equal to the economies permitted. It can not be said, however, that the special concessions which have been obtained have always been justified. This situation also demands correction. "Coercion" of sellers was not proven. In view of the absence of cost data it is not known whether chain bank accounts are unprofitable to the banker, or whether they are more unprofitable than those of the average independent. It was found that chains pay as high salaries as independents for the same grade of work, considering stability of employment, the chance for promotion, etc. No difference in working conditions was proved. Chains do not appear to have an unfair advantage in buying advertising, insurance, etc.

Chains do not seem to take more money out of town directly than do independents, and, even if they should, such a condition does not seem to be undesirable. Chains hire local people, except store managers, but all localities have an equal opportunity to supply men who have a chance to become managers. Chains do not lessen individual opportunity for the efficient are still able to compete. In addition, the chains open a new kind of opportunity for people who are too big for one store or who are unable to get along without someone to direct them. Directly, the chains cause some temporary unemployment but, in the long run, their decreased prices can be expected to increase employment. No single chain has a monopoly of its line of business. The business of all national and sectional chains combined is not enough to enable them, even by agreement, to control retail prices. No evidence of inter-chain agreements has been found. The chains have been weak in their community relationships but are improving. The aid which they give, however, is largely a mechanical bid for favor and is not a genuinely heart-felt gift to aid the town. The chain is but one more phase of the increasing delocalization of business and business outlook.

Over against the abuses that have sprung up are the undoubted assets of the chain of low prices and efficient distribution. The question is whether the good outweighs the bad, or rather, whether the abuses that exist can be eliminated without the elimination of the good of the chain. Some discussion of this will be made later.

The method that has been followed in some instances to remove the abuses of the chain system is to impose upon the chains special taxes which are designed to drive all chains out of business or else raise their costs to an extent that they will be handicapped

in competition. Several questions are involved. Do the chains need
to be regulated? Is taxation for social purposes justified? Is
special taxation the way to remove the alleged abuses of the chains?
Is the government ever justified in interfering between competitors,
except to see that each competes fairly? Is special taxation the
best way for the independents to attack the chain problem?

The evils that are found in the chains do need to be regulated. Whether the chain or the independentdoes things contrary to
the public interest they should be prosecuted. The chains have done
things that are not in the public interest; so have the independents.
It is the evils that ought to be regulated and not a type of operatin
of which some members have practiced the evils. Wrongdoing must be
stopped no matter who does it. Special chain-store taxation does
not attack the right thing; it attacks an organization and not evil
practices.

It is doubtful if it is ever justifiable to use taxation
to encourage goods or to restrain evils. M. H. Hunter defines a tax
as follows:

> "A tax is a compulsory contribution, exacted by public
> authority according to some general rule, the expenditure of
> which is presumably for the common good without regard to bene-
> fits to special individuals."[1]

The definitions of a tax given by all other writers are in substantial agreement. All emphasize the revenue feature of taxation and
none define a tax so as to include the regulatory feature. The two
ends of revenue and regulation are not consistent. To accomplish
either purpose effectively, a tax must be used solely for revenue
or solely for regulation. The tariff is the most prominent example

1. Outlines of Public Finance, p. 125. 1926, Harper and Bros., New
York.

of a tax that has been used for purposes of both revenue and regulation. To the extent to which the tariff protects it raises no revenue. Revenue is only raised if the rates are such that goods can
come into the country. If it is agreed that a particular thing needs
to be regulated, it must be proven that taxation is the best way to
attack the problem under consideration.

H. L. Lutz[2] says that the use of taxation for non-fiscal
purposes violates the modern conception of the true nature and purposes of taxation and that when taxation is used deliberately for
regulatory objectives, a vast amount of guesswork as to the final
effects is inevitable. He says that when regulation or discrimination is the primary purpose of taxation, it is impossible to apply
the canons of fair and equitable taxation and that the extensive use
of taxation for regulatory purposes means either the erection of a
costly and relatively unproductive administrative machine or the
overloading of the regular tax-administering bodies so that they will
not be able to perform their legitimate functions properly.

At least three questions must be asked before such taxation
can be applied. Is regulation necessary? Will such taxation correct the abuses and have no other evil effects ? Is there a superior alternative method for the correction of the abuses? In addition, care must be taken that such use of the taxing system does not
overload the tax administrative machinery so that it can not function
properly and efficiently; that such taxes are really in the public
interest and not for the benefit of a particular group; and that

2. Public Finance, 3d edition, pp. 371, 372. 1936, D. Appleton-
Century Company, New York.

the government would have the power to do the same thing through direct action. Taxes have been used before for social purposes, for example, the tariff, the tax on state bank notes, sumptuary taxes, etc. In some cases the end has been accomplished but frequently such taxes only effect a compromise with the evil. In such a case it is difficult to justify social taxation.

In the application of these principles to the use of special taxation to curb chain stores it is concluded that such taxation is undesirable. It has been pointed out that there are conditions, or at least the possibility that conditions might arise, that need correction. Special chain-store taxation is not the way to correct such abuses. Such taxation does not require any change in method of operation as long as chains are able to survive at all and their competition would presumably take the same form with or without taxes. In fact, heavy taxation might drive the chains to more desperate methods. Only by the elimination of the chains would taxation stop what abuses do exist in the chains. Such a particularly vicious tax would bring more abuses and evil effects than it would correct for it would eliminate the advantages of the chain. It is not in the interest of the public to pass a tax which would destroy an organization without any regard at all for the efficiency of the taxpayer. There is no excuse to use the tax system to handicap organizations that a minority regard as undesirable to themselves. Only when it is clearly in the interest of the majority is the extinction of any organization justified. It is felt that the consumers as a whole can benefit from the chains when they are run properly. H. L. Lutz says:

"Severely regulatory taxation is part of the general idea

of regimentation, of determining, on the basis of pre-conceived
notions or on the basis of favoritism, the character of business or the line of conduct deemed to be good for the people,
and of keeping everyone in the established channels by heavy
taxes on variations and departures."[3]

The use of the taxing power to eliminate the chains is a
dangerous precedent for the enactment of similar legislation for the
elimination of other business activities by those who find themselves
hard-pressed by competition. The use of political power to settle
economic issues is dangerous. Our laws should be just instead of
favoring one organization against another. Such legislation would
hurt the innocent as well as the guilty.

There is nothing in the legislation that would make the
independent more efficient and so enable him to fill the place of
the chain. If the chains were broken up, the chain ideas and supervision and control would be abandoned. A number of the managers who
would find themselves store owners probably would fail soon because
they would fail to maintain efficient operation without supervision,
would be in constant lack of capital, etc. As a result there would
be little progress in retailing and prices would be higher. If the
taxes are designed merely to prevent chains from growing large, they
also hinder the efficient operation of the chains because the maximum rates often are imposed at twenty stores or lower, a number of
units too small to afford the maximum efficiencies. There is no
reason to check the opening of new stores. There are too many stores
but not enough good stores. To limit new ones would be to subsid-
ize existing ones, good or bad. It is a good thing to lose inefficient stores.

3. Op. cit., p. 373.

It is not proved that the conditions would be any better in respect to each alleged abuse of the chain if all the business were handed over to the independents. Thus, special taxation does not solve the chain problem satisfactorily: it fails to remove the abuses unless all chains are removed; if the chains are removed, the public loses an efficient organization and there is no certainty that the abuses will not continue to exist.

There are superior ways to deal with each problem directly and at the same time the better parts of the chains' methods may be retained. Inasmuch as the chain method is sound, an attempt should be made to retain the advantages and remove the abuses. Improper practices should be picked out and legislation passed against them. Legislation of this sort would eliminate such unfair practices no matter which form of distribution practiced them. The chain system should be studied and watched. It is capable of great good and great bad. If the bad features are eliminated, the chains will serve the public better and will fully deserve the patronage of the consumer.

Specifically, what can be done about the alleged abuses? Legislation exists to prevent the sale of inferior merchandise, short-weighting, and short-changing. Such legislation needs strengthening, particularly in the case of the labelling of goods. A conspicuously-placed statement of the grade of good would protect the consumer. There is a place for high-grade and low-grade merchandise if the consumer knows exactly for what she is paying and getting. The special taxation of the chains would not protect the consumer for the independents are just as guilty of these practices as are the chains.

The great need in dealing with the chain-store problem,

and also with all other organizations in the retail field, is to make more rigid the unfair trade practice statutes. The standards of big business, and of small business, are not as good as they ought to be and it is up to the government to tackle the problem. Business ethics only improve when the law forces them to improve. The usual business man goes as far as he can go legally and even farther if the law is not enforced, and the chain and the independents are not exceptions. The remedy is stringent laws to forbid all unfair practices, in this connection particularly against local price-cutting, loss leaders, misuse of corporate power, etc. The only way to ensure that retailing will be carried on in the public interest is to enforce rigidly fair competition. To this end the anti-trust laws and the Federal Trade Commission Act should be altered so as to make them collectively a comprehensive policy concerning the standards of conduct in business. What is wanted is a regulated competition, one in which competitors can conduct their businesses under conditions of equal opportunity and freedom. Any practice that lessens true competition must be eliminated. Our efforts should be to restore competition, not to prevent it; to set up rules of action to guide it; to eliminate its destructive forces. When this is done, the chain will take its true place in distribution and many independents who are not touched by special chain-store taxation will also be forced to deal more fairly with their competitors and consumers or go out of business. The special taxation of chains will do none of this.

The way to prevent the abuses of buying is to prohibit unearned discounts. This would force all producers to set their prices on the basis of a cost analysis. Earned discounts, no matter how large, should be permitted. The special taxation of chains pre-

vents firms from getting large enough to give the producer the benefit of large orders. The chains that do manage to exist would not
be forced by taxation to stop asking for buying favors.

The remedy of the abuse of banking services lies with the
bankers themselves, or possibly in a reform of the banking system.
The banks should analyze the cost of all accounts, chain and independent and try to handle such accounts as efficiently as possible.
When this is done, a charge equal to the cost of an average efficient
bank should be determined as the maximum to be charged each account.
In addition, further attention ought to be given the banking problem
to see whether a more efficient type of banking system might be developed.

If labor conditions are not good in the chain, neither are
they good in the independent system. What type of labor legislation,
if any, is necessary to relieve this situation is a matter of doubt.
The only way to raise the low wages of a group of workers is to decrease the number of those workers or increase the demand for them.
To eliminate the chains would do neither. Organization to restrict
artificially the number of workers is impossible for the workers are
so unskilled and so scattered, and the hirers of labor so small and
scattered that no union would be effective.

No one has yet found the solution to the problem of technological unemployment. Thus far we have allowed all innovations
without regard to the temporary suffering which they have caused.
Progress should not be stopped but some provision should be made for
those who are displaced. What the form of this shall be is a matter
of controversy.

The special taxation of the chains would prevent future

monopolies but there are better ways to handle the problem. There
is nothing wrong with combination but with the way combinations
sometimes work. What must be done is to stop the possible evils of
large combinations and to this end more effective laws are needed.
What is needed are laws to stop, not bigness, but badness. If bad
practices are stopped, no undesirable monopolies will grow. The
best way to break monopolies is to enforce rigidly fair competition.
If competition were to be based on efficiency alone, companies would
grow only until they reached the optimum size economically. Under
such conditions it is doubtful if any chain could survive to grow
large enough to do a majority of the business in any one field. Most
small business men claim that they are not afraid of bigness if only
the big company would compete fairly. Big firms should have a right
to beat smaller ones in an honest race. It is as unfair to give an
advantage to one as another. By concentrating on mere size and
by breaking up the "trusts" unfair competition is invited again and
the evils of the monopoly continue to exist, but on a smaller scale
and from many sources. If minimum standards of conduct are set,
the monopoly problem will take care of itself.

There can be no legislation to make the chains and their
employees better citizens, just as there is none to make the independents better in the same respect. Special chain-store taxation
will do no better. The only remedy for this is public opinion. The
chains' laxity in this respect is no more serious than that of the
independent, surely not so much so as to justify the extinction of
the chain. The remedy may well be, not to make the chains give more
to such causes, but to prohibit exactions from private individuals
and business establishments for many purposes of a public nature and

to raise the funds by general taxation. Some of the things for which the chains and independents are asked to contribute money are more properly governmental functions.

Continuing to apply the principles laid down for the justification of a tax for social purposes, special chain-store taxes load the tax-administrative bodies with an unproductive tax.[4] The tax commissions could spend their efforts to better advantage if they administered more just and productive taxes. It has been pointed out previously that such taxes are for the benefit of a particular group and not for the benefit of the public as a whole. The special taxes placed on chain stores attempt to do something that it is doubtful whether the government could find constitutional justification for doing directly. To pass legislation under the guise of a revenue measure to accomplish a forbidden end does not seem justifiable. If such powers are necessary to protect the people and the people want their governments to have such powers, machinery exists whereby any constitution can be changed so as to do so. Until authorized by the people to exercise a certain power, the governments should not accomplish the same thing indirectly.

The government is not justified in interfering between competitors except to see that each competes fairly. The part of government is that of a referee and not that of a partisan. The part of government is not to take sides but to lay down rules of competition and then to see that both parties are prevented from using undue restraints or unfair methods to interfere with the other's right to trade.

---

4. See Chapter Six.

One of the criterions of a good tax is that it weigh as evenly as possible on competing businesses. The arbitrary selection of one class violates one principle of just taxation and all principles of just treatment of its subjects by the government. Any such legislation which is beneficial to one group at the expense of another is class legislation and should find no part in government activities. It is proper to tax business and to regulate business but such taxation and regulation should be just and uniform. Chains should pay reasonable taxes and obey all laws but should not be made the object of an extra tax burden for the benefit of their competitors. If legislatures through the pressure of one group can enact statutes to cripple a business such as has been attempted in the case of the chains, then other groups just as organized and militant as the independents will have obtained a precedent to force the destruction of their business rivals by the same methods. Any such tendency should be discouraged. Most of all, legislation against progressiveness is a dangerous thing in a democratic government.

Especially is such legislation to be frowned upon when it is passed under the guise of a revenue measure. If legislation is passed under the police power and upheld under that power, such legislation can be condoned, but when it is passed under the guise of a revenue measure and upheld under the revenue power it is indefensible. The taxing power should be limited strictly to raising revenue and any departure from equality in treatment should be justified under the police power.

Whether the chain or the independent ought to survive if it competes fairly should be left to the public. To let the politician decide assumes for him too much wisdom. In final analysis

the question will be settled by the American people by their patronage. The public sooner or later will test each feature of the distributive system on the basis of whether it serves the wants of the
public. Many will feel that the chain serves them best and spend
their money in the chain store. This ability to perform the distributive functions so as to satisfy a large group of consumers should
determine whether any retailer deserves to survive. The right to do
business should depend, not on one's identification as a chain or an
independent, but upon merchandising ability and fairness. Public
sympathy for the little fellow and antagonism toward "big business"
will make the chain earn its way. The fact that people patronize
the chains in large numbers shows they do not want them legislated
against. The need in settling this problem is not legislation to
put the chain out of business, but legislation to stop unfairness
plus education of public opinion.

The coming of the chains has meant much to the independent retailers and wholesalers. It has created new problems and
forced new methods. It has compelled the independents to reduce
their costs. It has eliminated agencies that could not meet the new
competition. It has brought new experiments, such as the voluntary
chain, into the retail field. The weaker competitors of the chain
became panic-stricken, the stronger units studied the chain methods
and improved.

With the arrival of a new competitor came the question of
how to meet the new competition. Three remedies were tried -- sympathy, legislation, and improved efficiency. The latter is the
best course. The first method proved ineffective for the public did
not feel that it owed the independent a living. When appeals to

sympathy failed, the independents turned to taxation so as to handicap the chains. If the independent really needs taxes to survive,
his right to do so is problematical. The independent has been at-
tacking the wrong thing. The reason for the predicament of the independent does not lie in the chain but in the inefficiency of the
independent-wholesaler system. What the independent system needs
is to improve its own efficiency rather than to try to lower that of
the chains. There is nothing constructive in trying to limit the
other fellow. The less time that the independents give to tearing
down the chains the more time there will be for building up themselves. The independents are in business to serve the public and
not to tax the chains. If the independents do succeed in taxing
the chains out of existence, their troubles will not be over for
some new form of retailing, such as the supermarkets, will arise to
compete with them. The only permanent relief that the independents
can hope to find is to improve their own efficiency so much that no
new retailing organization can find an opportunity to rise to challenge them. Competition can be met only by successful competition.

The present taxes have not been effective in eliminating
the chain except in the filling-station field in a few states and,
to some extent, in the grocery field. The chains have been handicapped but not eliminated. The chains seem to do about as large a
proportion of business in the states where there are special chain-
store taxes as where there are not. Thus far the money and time and
effort spent by the independents to have special tax bills passed
does not seem to have done them much good. At the same time no bad
practices have been eliminated nor has the public received any benefit. But the taxes are getting more and more severe so that in time

they may succeed in forcing the chains out of business. The chains'
only hope is to arouse the consumer who benefits from the chain. As
M. M. Zimmerman has said:

> "In our final conclusion, we question whether the chain-
> store system of merchandising with all its modern methods of
> scientific economy and efficiency is as serious a detriment
> to the best interests of our country as many anti-chain propa-
> gandists claim. . . . However, the sooner we make up our minds
> to accept the chain as a legitimate branch in our system of dis-
> tribution and accept it as just another retail competitor, -
> accepting its innovations and improvements in scientific ar-
> rangement and management, its excellent system of stock con-
> trol, its numerous other contributions to modern merchan-
> dising, utilizing them in the fullest possible manner, - the
> quicker will the disturbed conditions and the unfairness of
> the chains' competition which the independent merchant com-
> plains about, be adjusted."[5]

The independents are beginning to worry that their efforts
to tax the chains may prove a boomerang. As the states need more
revenue the independent may be taxed now that classifications have
been made which set the independent, the voluntary chain, and the
chains apart. Already several states have considered tax bills that
would definitely include voluntary chains. In each succeeding chain-
store tax bill the amount assessed the owner of one store has been
increasing.

No better conclusion can be given than that of the Federal
Trade Commission after years of study of the problem. The Commission's investigation was made in response to a Senate Resolution which
directed them to see whether the chains were doing anything that
needed to be controlled. The Federal Trade Commission did not find
that the chains ought to be abolished and specifically disapproved of
special taxes. They found weaknesses but concluded that public interest demanded that the legitimate advantages inherent in the chain

---

5. The Challenge of Chain-Store Distribution, p. 318. 1931, Harper
and Brothers, New York.

store should be retained. In the words of the Federal Trade Commission itself:

> " . . . . Advantages or disadvantages such as manifest themselves in profits, margins, quality of goods, services rendered, managerial efficiency, and low overhead are purely economic in character. Under a competitive system such advantages and disadvantages are presumably not subject to removal by law and it is to be expected that the type of distribution which gives the greater sum total of advantages to the consuming public will increasingly prevail.

> "In general, it appears that chain-store merchandising has substantial economic advantages which under existing law are clearly legal. If, aside from lower cost of its goods, the system is characterized by a lower cost of distribution in proportion to volume of sales, that is not open to attack on legal grounds. If, by eliminating certain services rendered by independents, the cost of doing business is lowered, the consuming public is the judge whether it is willing to forego those services or pay for them elsewhere in the form of higher prices. When it comes to reducing costs of doing business by reducing wages and salaries, it is becoming widely recognized that the law may impose limitations upon employers in the public interest.

> . . . .

> "In more recent years state attempts to control the development of chain stores took the form of special license fees and taxes. . . . .

> "The reason assigned, in most instances, for the enactment of such laws is the increasing of revenue, but their main purpose is to obstruct the development of chain-store operations in the various states which have enacted them.

> . . . .

> "If the main purpose of graduated taxes on chain stores is to protect the independent merchant and offset the advantages of the chain by heavier taxation, that purpose can be fully accomplished only through increasing the tax by the full amount of the chain's advantages. Otherwise the effect is merely to slow down the rate of chain-store development and postpone the date of chain-store supremacy. Theoretically, it is possible to so graduate the tax as to more than offset the chain's advantages and thus force a reversal of the evolution which brought about its present challenging position. Such a policy, however, would involve destruction of the chain's ability to make lower prices than independents and would provoke wide protest from consumers. Pro tanto, any tax on chain stores which substantially lessens their ability to undersell independents is open to the same practical objection. If ability to undersell based

on greater efficiency or on elimination of credit and delivery
costs is destroyed by taxation, it is the consuming public
which will really pay the tax and not the chain.

" . . . . The laws created by the Federal Government for
the prevention and control of monopoly and combinations in
restraint of trade have been paralleled by constitutional
declarations in many of the States and legislative enactments
in nearly all of them. Most of the States have laws forbidding
price discrimination. A number of States prohibit acquisition
of competitors. Many States have laws against false and misleading advertising and all but one have statutes penalizing
short weights and measures. It is a striking fact that only
a negligible use of the above State laws has been made in dealing with the chain-store problem. . . . .

. . . .

" . . . . To tax out of existence the advantages of chain
stores over competitors is to tax out of existence the advantages which the consuming public have found in patronizing them,
with a consequent addition to the cost of living for that
section of the public. That portion of the public which is
able to pay cash and is willing to forego delivery service in
return for the advantage of lower prices will be deprived of
that privilege, generally speaking, although there are exceptions both ways. It will also tend toward an arbitrary
frustration of whatever saving in cost of production and distribution results from integration of the functions of producer, wholesaler, and retailer. So on the whole the number
of people adversely affected by such a tax would constitute a
very substantial percentage in comparison with the number adversely affected by present conditions. The graduated tax on
chain stores can not accomplish fully the social ends aimed
at by such legislation without producing incidentally these
results."[6]

---

6. Chain Store Inquiry, Vol. V, "Final Report of the Chain-Store
Inquiry," 74th Congress, 1st Session, Sen. Doc. No. 4, pp. 66,
78-97 passim. 1935, Government Printing Office, Washington, D. C.

CHAPTER SIX
SPECIAL CHAIN-STORE TAXES AS REVENUE MEASURES

Although special taxes on chain stores are indefensible
as regulatory or discriminatory measures, it is possible that something may be said for them as revenue measures. Not all of the present taxes have been levied with a design to handicap the chains.
Some few have been passed to supply funds to the state. Others have
been passed to equalize the tax burdens of the chains and independents, on the theory that the chains escape their fair share of
taxes, especially in respect to the property tax. These latter two
motives will be analyzed in this chapter.

Wisconsin has paid particular attention to the use of special chain-store taxes to equalize the tax burden of chains and independents. It is believed that the chains pay less than independents in property taxes and that the state does not receive an
equitable share of the corporation net income tax. L. B. Krueger
of the Wisconsin Tax Commission gives this argument in a published
article.[1] He says that a "gross income tax at a uniform rate would
result in extending the chain-store movement rather than to curb or
control it", and further that "the imposition of such a tax usually
results in a further handicapping of struggling independent merchants". As for property taxes, the large national chains frequently own no real estate in the state. They may own warehouses and
factories "but these may not be located in the state imposing the
tax." Moreover, the large national chains do not pay their just
share of personal property taxes. They operate with a high rate of

1. "How Should Chain Stores Be Taxed?" Bulletin of the National Tax
Association, Vol. XXX, (Dec., 1935), pp. 75-80.

turnover so that the business done is large in proportion to the
value of stock on hand on any one day; the purchasing expense is
often charged to central office expense rather than to the merchandising account so that the goods are listed as of lower value; the
local assessor can reach the books of the independent merchant whereas the books of the chain are in a central office in a distant city
so that comparable information is not available with which to check
the adequacy of the returns. Other reasons that have been advanced
are that chains can manipulate their stocks between states on taxing day; they buy for less and so get assessed less. The corporation
net income tax would be an equitable tax if the proper amount of income could be allocated to the states. It is impossible to determine the amount of income actually earned within the state by a far-
flung national chain. The accounting and auditing would be very
involved and it would be costly to see if the chains had figured
their profits correctly. By manipulation of accounting the chains
could take their profits in any states they pleased. The equality
of burden of the flat-rate sales tax was dismissed by Krueger with
the statement that such a tax was one on the consumer and not on
business. Thus, in respect to most of the taxes used in Wisconsin,
the chain is said to pay less taxes than the independent. Moreover,
as a chain increases in size, it is thought that the practices and
policies which enable chains to pay less taxes also increase. As
a result it is deemed advisable to pass special chain-store taxes
and to make such taxes progressive so as to equalize the tax burden.

In a study of whether a taxpayer pays his fair share of
taxes two things must be determined. Does the taxpayer escape any
taxes which he is legally bound to pay? Does his total tax burden

which results from all the taxes which he pays give him an undue preference over other taxpayers?

In answer to the latter question one must judge a taxpayer's burden, not from the amount he pays under one particular tax, but from the amount he pays under the tax system as a whole. The chains may pay less under the property tax but their total tax burden may amount to more than the independents' when it is considered that they pay state and federal corporation taxes of various kinds, which most independents do not pay; and that they now pay Federal Social Security taxes, which most independents do not pay because they do not hire enough employees to qualify. In addition, the chains pay every tax a store or corporation can be called upon to pay. The property tax is only one tax with which retailers are faced. Most people have little idea of the number of taxes a retail store, especially if run under the corporate form, is forced to pay. The sum total of the burden of all taxes is significant, but not the burden of one particular tax. This total tax burden varies between industries. The gasoline filling stations already pay heavy taxes, probably heavier than any other line of retailing. If the purpose of special chain-store taxes is to equalize inequalities as between chains and independents in the operation of existing taxes, it would seem that different rates ought to apply to retailers who handle different types of goods. The actual amount of taxes paid by each organization can not be determined but the chain units certainly do not pay less than do the independents. The only objection that can be made as to payments under a given tax is that of illegal evasion. The reports of the Federal Trade Commission investigation of chain stores did not mention that the chains were evading the payment of taxes.

There can be no objection to the lower taxes paid by chains because they can run their business on a lower inventory than can independents and because they can buy more cheaply. It is no crime to avoid taxes by efficiency and the non-ownership of property. The tax rate is the same for all. As long as the chains pay taxes on the stocks they carry and there is no claim that taxes are illegally evaded, there can be no complaint that they pay less than independents whose inventory runs higher. There is no reason to condemn the chains because independents carry much slow-moving stock. It is like criticizing a man who does not earn enough to pay an income tax. The low taxes of the chains may be a tribute to their efficiency.

Chains pay a great amount of property taxes indirectly through rent payments. Someone has to pay taxes on property—if the retailer does not own the store and so has to pay taxes directly, the landlord will have taxes to pay. In the long run these taxes will be shifted to tenants, especially since the inter-chain competition for sites is so great as to force rents to a high level. It has been argued that during the depression the chains were able to lower rents to such an extent that the taxes actually were paid by the landlords. However true this may be, it is dangerous to pass taxes to remedy such shiftings with our present incomplete knowledge of the shifting and incidence of taxes. Unless a time limit is placed on such taxes, they have no place in a revenue system for no one can tell for years in advance just what the condition of the shifting of a particular tax may be. Attention should be given to the probable incidence of a proposed tax but it is doubtful if it is a good policy to pass special legislation because a certain group should find themselves temporarily in a position to shift a tax.

Although an extra tax is not justified because an organization finds a more efficient manner by which to do a thing, there is a different problem if an organization illegally escapes its fair share of taxes. The Wisconsin Tax Commission claims that the chains are evading their just share of the property tax. Because of the difficulty to obtain access to the chains' records there has been little chance to check the accuracy of the chains' lists of property so that the chains virtually assess themselves. Investigations have shown many cases of gross underassessment. The Commission claims that it would cost as much or more to enforce the property tax against chains as it does to administer the special chain-store tax laws. Special taxes are thought to be an easy method to remedy the advantage given chains.

Several defects appear in this reasoning. There is probably a good deal of underassessment of chains but there probably is much underassessment of independents also. No state even pretends to assess all property at one hundred per cent of true value. At how much lower percentage of true value chain-store property is taxed has never been stated. With general underassessment most taxpayers turn in their property at as low a figure as they dare and leave it up to the tax authorities to adjust the amount. He who turns in his property at full value really pays an unfair share of taxes. The tax authorities in Wisconsin seemingly have authority to compel reports from corporations and individuals so that it is not impossible for them to check all assessments and administer the property-tax law. This would be a costly process but is far better than to substitute a tax which can not possibly measure the taxes escaped, which is just

as costly, and which is not a fair tax.[2] The Wisconsin chain-store
tax law imposes a tax graduated by the number of stores, regardless
of the size of store. Each unit of a department-store chain of five
units would pay an average chain-store tax of twenty dollars with a
total amount of taxable property probably running into the millions;
each unit of a grocery chain of the same number of stores would pay
the same amount but would not have a total assessed value of $50,000.
If, which is more likely, there were twenty-five units in the grocery
chain, each unit would pay a tax of $104.00, or five times that of a
large department-store unit which has the opportunity to escape much
more in property taxes. Some chains, moreover, may make perfectly
honest assessments and would get hit as hard by the special chain-
store tax. Although the Wisconsin law permits the chain-store tax
to be paid with property tax receipts, inequalities must arise. A
concentrated local grocery chain has no more opportunity to evade
its taxes than does an independent store. Such a chain of twenty-
five units would have to pay $104.00 per store as a special tax which
would amount in many cases to more than the full personal property
tax bill. Other chains, such as variety chains would have to pay no
special chain-store taxes because their personal property tax would
amount to more than the per unit chain-store tax. Most states, have
laws which carry heavy penalties for dishonesty in tax returns. The
real remedy for the condition of underassessment is to remedy the
administration of the property tax. Although there are numerous defects to the property tax, it does not cause as much discrimination
between competitors in the same line of business as would a special
tax on one group. The Wisconsin Commission has recommended that

2. See below for discussion of the last two points.

chain stores be assessed centrally instead of by local assessors. This promises to be a better solution of the problem than the special taxation of chains.

The difficulties of the assessment of the proper amount of income earned within a state is a problem created by the existence of state lines, a condition of which all large corporations take advantage. There is apparently no way to allocate such income except at enormous expense. This is a problem between states and not between competitors inasmuch as independents ordinarly are not corporations and so are not liable to the corporation income tax laws. Unless there can be developed an extensive system of inter-state agreements or Federal administration with allocation of the receipts to the states or unless the courts will permit an arbitrary allocation of incomes between states, state corporation income taxes always will be ineffective as applied to corporations which do business in more than one state. The substitution of a chain-store tax based on the number of stores would be a poor substitute from the point of view of justice, for the number of stores operated within a state bears no relation to the profits made. Chain-store taxes based on gross income are open to the same objections. Moreover, the chain-store taxes weigh just as heavily on concentrated local chains which have no opportunity to escape the payment of state income taxes. Inasmuch as the large national and sectional chains are the ones which can avail themselves of this opportunity, it would seem that if it is deemed necessary to pass a special chain-store tax to make up for the condition, a tax of the Louisiana type, where the measure of the tax is the number of stores owned by the corporation no matter where they are located, is a more logical type of tax. Such a tax, however, should not be excessive. The present Wisconsin chain-store tax carries a maximum rate of $250 per store for all stores over twenty-five. Grocery chains make average annual profits of about $1,000 per store. Net income taxes do not approach such a high percentage of net income as the maximum chain-store taxes bear to net income. The rates of the Wisconsin law seem to be higher than necessary to make chains pay their fair share of taxes. There is mixed with it a desire to secure as much revenue for the state as possible, and little attention seems to have been paid the inequalities caused.

If a state is to pass laws to correct inequalities in the operation of specific tax laws, it might just as well repeal all tax laws and say to each taxpayer, "This is your fair tax load." The sales tax weighs more heavily on chains than on independents because chains operate on a policy of small margins and rapid turnover. Income taxes hurt the chains worse than independents. Based on a $2400 income a corporation pays $204 to the Federal government whereas the independent, if he is the head of a family, pays nothing; on $7500 income the corporation pays $765 and the independent $200.[3] If a commission should set out to equalize the burdens of every law, it would have to pass a special tax on independents to make up for their advantage under the above laws. The solution is to adopt a tax system, which, as a whole, will be as fair as possible. If, after all taxes are considered, it is found that the chains do not pay a fair share of taxes, a new tax on them could be justified. As yet it has not been proved that the total tax burden of the chains is not a fair share.

3. Nichols, J. P., Chain-Store Manual, 1936 edition, p. 93. 1936, Institute of Distribution, New York.

Almost all of the states are in desperate need of additional revenue. The depression period brought additional needs and declining revenues from old sources. As a result, state finances are in poor shape and any means to raise more money has been sought after eagerly. Taxes on the old sources were pushed almost to the saturation point so that new sources had to be found. Special taxes on chain stores proved to be one of these taxes.

Such taxes obtained a large amount of support because they hit an institution unpopular with a large organized minority. Also, chains are largely foreign corporations, have enjoyed the reputation of earning tremendous profits, and have not been active politically until recently. There is always support, moreover, for a bill aimed at "big business". These elements ensured enough support for such a tax bill to get it enacted. As several states adopted this form of taxation, a source of revenue was revealed to other legislatures which were anxiously casting around for new sources. With the flood of anti-chain propaganda which came at the same time that revenue was sorely needed, it is no wonder that chain stores should be singled out for special taxation.

With this pressing need for revenue as an excuse the selfish aspects of chain-store taxes were easily hidden. The final result of such measures was that what was often proposed for the purpose of revenue was loaded with discriminatory features which made the taxes illogical as revenue measures. Anti-chain prejudice often has influenced the passage of the bills so that many measures were passed without any regard for the merits of the bill or of whom they might hurt or serve. The procedure of this chapter will be to see whether the existing taxes are good revenue taxes and, also, whether

such laws might be framed so as to be good revenue measures. The
biggest problem involved in a decision on the place which the taxation of chains should play in a revenue system is to prevent anti-
chain prejudice from influencing or confusing the solution of a
genuine revenue problem.

Various characteristics of a good tax system have been laid
down by writers on public finance questions. No tax is justified for
revenue for useless and extravagant expenditure. To judge the propriety of a tax one can not consider the merits of a particular tax
alone. A good tax system will have a number of taxes, properly co-
ordinated to form a unified whole. No one tax will fill adequately
all the requirements for a sound tax system and at the same time return ample revenues. An excessive number, however, is as bad as too
few for such a condition would work havoc with administration. What
is required is a proper coordination of the various parts, truly a
tax system and not a collection of isolated acts. The construction
of a good tax system requires careful, systematic study of each element in the tax system and of the relation of every part to each
other. Each tax has different effects and weighs more heavily on
different classes. These effects must be studied and determined.
The solution of good finance calls for a skillful balance of effects.
It is very important that a state in securing its revenue should deal
equitably between its subjects, that each should pay his proper share
and no more. What is a proper share is difficult to define for
there is no absolute standard of equity that can be applied. The
standards that are often advanced are benefit received, ability to
pay, and the cost of service. In addition, the principle that taxes
should be levied so as to be of the greatest benefit to the largest

number is often urged. More likely than not all of these principles
are overlooked and taxes are levied according to the principle of
expediency, or of the collection of taxes wherever it is possible.
There is no agreement as to the meaning of these standards and no
way to measure them.

Justice in taxation is a matter of opinion. In the words
of H. L. Lutz:

> "The strongest case for equity in taxation appears to be
> made when the general good is most clearly being served through
> the expenditure policy, when the power of taxation is being
> exercised reasonably and impartially, and when there is ade-
> quate evidence of regard for some of the elements known or
> assumed to be involved in the distribution of the tax burden."[4]

Justice is done when no person or group is shown favoritism. Justice
depends, not on whom the tax is levied, but upon whom it finally falls.
The equity of a tax system can not be determined without regard to
the principles of shifting and incidence. A good fiscal system should
have no undesirable economic, political, and social effects and
should be imposed for public and not private purposes. A tax should
not crush economic initiative or curtail economic progress. The tax
system should not be administered so as to result in political favoritism or to work injury on states or citizens. No tax should
destroy its base, that is, the tax should not be so heavy as to destroy the source of revenue. The cost of the administration of any
tax should not be excessive in comparison to the returns. Taxes
should produce adequate revenue to meet the just wants of the state,
yet maintain the source of revenue and have no other undesirable
effects. As H. L. Lutz has said:

---

4. _Public Finance_, _3d edition_, p. 350. 1936, D. Appleton-Century
Company, New York.

"The first thing, then, to be asked of a tax is that it
be capable of producing substantial revenue for public purposes.
There is no use in considering any other taxes or forms of taxation than those which possess this merit. Among those which
do possess it, the choice should be determined by applying
various other tests, so that the whole group of taxes actually
used will not only be fiscally adequate to the demands that may
be laid upon them but will possess certain other important
qualities."5

At the same time the cost of administration should consume as small

a part as possible of the total receipts. No tax which is very cost-

ly to administer, or which involves heavy indirect costs of ob-

structed industry or of undesirable economic effects can be excused

on the basis of fiscal adequacy except in emergencies such as war

needs.

The administration of any tax should be simple as far as

is possible with no complicated and elaborate machinery, for compli-

cations hinder the cooperation of taxpayers. The amount to be paid

should be certain and not arbitrary and the manner of payment should

be convenient for the taxpayer. A good tax system should make it

possible for revenues to expand and contract with the need of reve-

nue. It is not necessary that every tax be elastic but there should

be elasticity of the tax system as a whole. A tax should be flexible

and so vary with the need of the times; that is, a good tax system

should maintain continuous harmony with the economic and social or-

ganization. There should be as few exemptions as possible and all

exemptions should have a reasonable justification from the standpoint

either of justice or of administrative difficulties. In case of a

conflict between the different principles the least important should

be disregarded.

The purpose of the chapter will be to see how chain-store

5. Op. cit., p. 338.

taxes measure up to these characteristics. Only rough estimates can be made for such taxes are only one part of the tax system and there is further complication of numerous taxing bodies.

Three types of chain-store taxes have been in use. First, the so-called Indiana type, which consists of a tax per unit, graduated according to the number of units within the state which imposes the tax. Second, there is the Kentucky type, which is probably unconstitutional,[6] which is a gross income tax, graduated according to the volume of sales within the state. Third, there is the Louisiana type, which is a per unit tax on the stores located within the state but graduated according to the number of stores no matter where located. In addition, proposals have been made for flat and graduated net income taxes, taxes graduated both by the number of units and gross income, and taxes per unit graduated by the number of stores but with different rates for each type of retailing. All of these must be considered.

If the chains are to be taxed, a type of tax must be selected that will not be passed on to the consumer. The chains deal largely in necessities and their customers are the poorer classes. To the extent that chain-store taxes are shifted the poor are burdened. A tax on necessities or on the poor is not a good tax unless the other members of the tax family bear heavily on other groups. But such is not the case in the tax systems of the majority of our states. Property taxes and sales taxes bear more heavily on the poor than on the rich so that an additional tax on the poor can not be justified. The problem is whether chain-store taxes are shifted.

6. This type of tax has been declared unconstitutional in Kentucky, Iowa, and Florida. Minnesota and South Dakota still retain this type of tax but both these laws are under attack in the courts.

The situation is this. There is competition between chains and independents, supermarkets, etc. The chains undersell the independents by approximately eight to ten per cent in the grocery field, and by fifteen per cent or more in the drug field. The relative prices in the other fields are not known. Some differential is natural between the two types of retailing for the chains usually sell on a cash-carry basis and the independents on a full-service basis. It is felt, however, that the differential is more than it need be for the chain to hold the great majority of its customers. In such a case, if there were no competition between chains, the chains could raise their prices to some extent and so take care of a moderate tax. If the taxes should be more severe than the amount that could be shifted in this manner, one of two things would happen. The chains could attempt to raise prices so that the tax would be fully covered. If they did, some consumers would shift their patronage to the independents and the less efficient chains would have to go out of business. On the other hand the chains could attempt to maintain the differential that now exists and try to absorb the tax. In such a case chain profits would be lower and capital would be discouraged from being invested in the chain-store business and the number of chain units would be diminished. In either case, trade would be diverted to the independents and average prices would be higher.

There is, however, intense inter-chain competition. Wherever competition exists between chains, their prices are nearly enough alike that none gets an advantage. If a greater tax were imposed on one than another, the total amount of such a tax could not be shifted. Only the amount levied on the chain which bears the smallest amount of tax could be shifted. For example, suppose that in a locality in Idaho there are four chain systems, each operating one store. One is a large national chain with forty units in the state. Each unit would pay $500.00 tax. Another chain has fifteen units in the state; it would pay $350.00 per unit. Also, there is a small chain of ten units which would pay $200.00 a unit, and one of five units which would pay fifty-five dollars per unit. Under such conditions no chain system could shift over fifty-five dollars of the tax or it would lose customers. It may even be that none could shift the whole fifty-five dollars if the independents were successful enough to be selling at a price which just measured the difference in the cost of the extra services offered. In another community the chain with a per unit tax of $500.00 might find itself with no chain-store competition and so could shift more of the tax. The extent to which such taxes would be shifted depends entirely on the competition offered at each point of competition. In some localities the chains will be able to shift the taxes entirely; in others they will be able to shift them only in part; in others they will not be able to shift them at all.

More is involved in this problem than the shifting of taxes. There is also involved economic effects of such taxes. There is only a shifting of taxes where there has been some payment to the government. To the extent that chain-store taxes lessen the number of chain units there is no tax paid to the government and no shifting of taxes. In such a case business is taken from a more efficient distributor and given to a less efficient distributor. The consumer has to pay higher prices and the government gets no tax. The effect on the consumer is the same, part of his income which has

been spent ordinarily to buy other commodities must now be spent in
the purchase of necessities.

Consideration must be given the different types of chain-
store taxes. Gross sales taxes usually are shifted more easily than
are lump sum taxes. Many chains operate on a very small markup so
that they must raise the prices of each good or suffer a loss on
their sale. A tax on sales is a tax on costs and probably would be
shifted excepting for possible competition. The chains are interested in making the greatest profit or the least loss. If they raise
the prices of their goods after a special tax has been placed upon
them, they may make the consumer pay an extra amount for his goods
equivalent to the amount of the tax and the tax can said to have
been shifted. At the same time the chains would find that their
volume of business would decline under such a policy. The chains
will raise prices to the point where selling prices in relation to
the volume of sales yield them the greatest profits. The amount by
which the chains could raise prices would depend on how nearly the
independents were meeting the chain prices, and on the differences
in the amounts assessed chains which may be in competition.

Per unit taxes are harder to shift. Taxes can be shifted
only by a reduction in the supply of goods. A per unit or lump sum
tax is a tax on profits and does not affect the supply of goods. If
there were one chain system which had a monopoly, its prices would
be set where the maximum net income would be returned. If a lump
sum tax were imposed on such a chain, it would not be shifted.
Chain stores are in competition and their prices are not monopoly
prices. Chains are selling at low prices in order to meet the competition of other chains. Under such conditions some part of lump

sum taxes are shifted, the amount of which is determined by competitive conditions.

It is likely, however, if the chains raise their prices, that the independents will also for the chains have been forcing the independents to sell on low margins. With chain competition lessened the independents will not be forced to lower their prices and will attempt to sell at higher margins. To the extent to which they do this, chains will be able to shift more of the tax than they otherwise would.

The extent to which chain-store taxes will be shifted or will affect chain operations depends on the type of retailing. Table XXIII shows that the profit per store in chains in different types varies greatly. Existing taxes are negligible where applied to some fields, for example, the average income per store in department-store chains is $81,546; in furniture chains, $25,275; and in variety chains, $16,163. The highest chain-store tax now imposed is $750.00. In the three fields mentioned even this heaviest tax is so light that it would not hurt the chains to absorb it. In the variety field competition is, to a large extent, between large chains who would pay about the same tax. In this case practically all the tax would be shifted. On the other hand, the income per store is so small in some fields that existing tax rates tend to discourage the inflow of capital into such chains. For example, a tax of $750.00 on grocery chain units, which make approximately $1,000.00 per unit, would discourage the opening of new units or even the continuance of a large number of existing stores. Inasmuch as the chain grocery stores own no capital which can not be shifted from an unprofitable location, they would immediately close all unprofitable units. The chain-store

taxes have not been so heavy as yet that the great majority of chains
have had to break up. However, in the gasoline filling station, and
to some extent, in the grocery field, the chains are breaking up in
the states with the highest taxes. There can be no knowledge of the
extent to which the opening of new units in the various fields has
been discouraged. There is no doubt but that the more severe taxes
prevent the addition of new units. Inasmuch as these units would be
likely to be more efficient than the independents who take their
place, the consumers have to pay more for their goods.

It is concluded that the consumers are hurt by chain-store
taxes unless the taxes are so low that chains find it profitable to
absorb them rather than to try to shift them to the consumer. To
the extent that the independents are permitted to take business
which would otherwise be done by chains the consumer must pay higher
prices. If chains are eliminated, consumers will have to deal not
only with a less efficient distributor but also will lose, to a large
extent, the opportunity to deal with a retailer who sells his goods
without an added charge for services which some prefer to perform
themselves. Light taxes would probably be absorbed by the chains
so that they could maintain the full competitive advantage which
they have at present. What is an excessive tax depends upon the type
of chain. The same tax on a grocery store and variety store would
have different effects.

In addition to being a type of tax which tends to be paid
by the poorer classes or to have such economic effects that the goods
which the poorer classes buy are higher in price, chain-store taxes
do not treat competitors equally. If the intent is an equitable tax,
a tax based on the number of outlets or on gross sales is scarcely

justifiable. If the taxes are shifted, they rest on the poorer
classes of consumers; if they are not shifted, they rest unequally
on different chains. Tax laws should, as far as is possible, treat
competitors equally. It has already been shown that chain taxes discriminate against the chains in favor of the independents. In addition, chain-store taxes discriminate between the chains themselves.
Different rates are imposed upon chains in the same line of retailing.
All per unit taxes but one are imposed according to the number of
stores operated within a single state. A large national chain may
have only three or four stores in a state and pay only a nominal tax
whereas a concentrated local chain may find itself burdened with a
heavy tax. The tax on a chain of two hundred stores may be over one
hundred times that on a chain of twenty-five stores (see Table IX).
If a local chain has the two hundred stores and the national chain
but twenty-five, there can be no possible reason for such a distinction. Even between two large national chains there may be discrimination, for one may have relatively few units in a state whereas the
other may have several hundred. In such a case different rates will
be imposed even though, taking their operations as a whole, both
are similarly situated. Such taxes, moreover, weigh more heavily on
certain types of chains than on others even though such chains may
be in competition. As has been noted, chain-store taxes are scarcely
felt by chains of department stores, furniture stores, and variety
stores, whereas they weigh heavily on grocery stores. The burden of
such taxes is different on each type of chain. Yet there is competition between the different types. Variety stores and department
stores sell groceries; drug stores, grocery stores, and department
stores compete with tobacco stores; department stores and variety

stores compete with drug stores; drug stores and variety stores compete with restaurants; and national bakers who sell their products through outlets which they do not own compete with chain bakeries. In all cases the taxes affect the different types in a different manner. Per unit taxes are ridiculous if equality of burden is intended. Such taxes put a department-store chain in the same class with chains of little candy shops and hamburger shops. Stores which do business with a large number of small stores with a small profit per store are burdened unduly. Gross sales taxes are just as discriminatory. Table XXXIII shows that chains in the various fields operate with different average rates of markup. Grocery stores have an average return on sales of 2.24 per cent, whereas variety stores average 9.42 per cent and department stores 4.88 per cent. Since such taxes are graduated taxes, chains in the same line may be taxed differently.

Taxation has little opportunity to be just and equal unless the taxes are imposed according to a uniform standard. The word, "store", is a very indefinite term and chain organizations have very unequally-sized stores. The number of stores operated by a chain bears no relation to profits, the amount of capital, the size of the enterprise as a whole, the total value of the enterprise, the stock turn, or any aspect of business operation. None of the above factors, moreover, increases in the scale adopted by most of the taxes. When the number of stores operated by an organization is chosen as the criterion of a tax, the principles of ability to pay or benefit received are ignored completely.

Neither the lump sum taxes nor gross sales taxes conform to the principle of ability to pay. If the taxes are shifted, they

are paid by persons in the lower income groups. If they remain with
the corporation, there is no measure of ability to pay. Corporations
do not have ability to pay. Ability to pay is a personal, subjec-
tive matter. Only living beings can have ability to pay for this
quality is a psychological matter inasmuch as it is concerned with
the sacrifice which is made in the payment of part of one's income
to the government. A tax which truly measures ability to pay would
take account of this felt sacrifice. Since this is impossible, ability to pay is measured roughly in our tax systems by the objective
measure of the amount of income earned by individuals. The amount
of income earned by corporations gives no hint as to the amount
which individuals may receive. A small corporation may be owned by
two or three men, each of whom may receive a relatively large amount;
a large corporation may be owned by thousands of stockholders, each
of whom may receive very little. In other cases one stockholder may
receive half a corporation's earnings and the other half may be dis-
tributed among a large number of small stockholders. Although the
one man would receive a very large income, any taxes on the corporation would fall on him at exactly the same rate as on the smallest
stockholder. A lump sum tax or graduated lump sum tax on corporations does not assess, in itself, individuals according to their
ability to pay. For these reasons taxes on corporations must be justified under some different theory than ability to pay. This theory
is that of benefit received.[7] The essence of the benefit theory is
that the action of society or of governments which confer a right or

7. See Hunter, M. H., "Shall We Tax Corporations or Business ?"
American Economic Review, Vol. XXVI, (March, 1936), pp. 84-89.

permit operation enables a business or individual to earn a greater income than he otherwise would. It is, in other words, a payment for benefits received. It must be recognized that it is impossible to measure such benefit as may be received. There is a feeling, however, that society has not received enough of the income that is earned by corporations. Inasmuch as it is impossible to measure the benefits which accrue to the chains from the fact that society allows them to operate multiple units only obvious inequities can be condemned. Such taxes should be limited to the special benefits brought by the chain form of organization.

Chain stores do have large incomes and, apparently, very stable ones. Chains receive no greater benefit from the state in fire and police protection and in general services of government. A charge for benefits received by the chains must be based on the privilege of being able to enter the market with a large number of stores. What this extra benefit is, is impossible to determine. It is not measured by the total profits, for, assuming each unit to be under individual ownership and run with equal efficiency, the total profits would also be large. The advantage of a chain over a group of independents of equal efficiency lies in the integration of the marketing functions. If the chains have received their greater income because they have been more efficient or have adopted a method of operation that is more efficient, the advantage they obtain can not be said to be a benefit conferred by society but an advantage due to personal efforts and intelligence. As A. G. Buehler has said:

> "If chain stores should be taxed more heavily because they are more efficient than certain independent retailers, because they have a faster stockturn, because they may have larger

sales and may earn more profits, then the more capable and successful of the independent retailers should also be singled out for special taxation in order to lessen their advantages over the less efficient and capable retailers."[8]

The only special tax on chains that can be justified under the benefit theory is that on the privilege of exercising their greater talents in a multiple number of stores. The larger profits of the chains and the advantages which accrue to them from the privilege of conducting business under the corporate form supposedly are caught under the corporation net income tax, which is a more equitable type of tax than the special chain-store taxes.

Under the assumption that if special taxes are to be levied on chains, they are to be levied only to the extent that they measure the advantages of the ownership of more stores than one, three questions must be asked. Do the benefits received from the operation of a number of units increase to a greater extent than the number of stores operated? Does a lump sum tax imposed equally on all types of chains measure the benefits received by each? Are the present progressive rates excessive?

The benefits of operation as a chain do increase more than proportionately but the progression is not as steep as the rates of existing taxes. As chains grow larger, they obtain some decreasing costs in performing the retail functions, although this advantage is offset by the added cost of the supervision of additional stores and the added expense of the development of new locations. The greatest advantage of the ownership of multiple units comes from the gain in purchasing power, from the greater profit on capital

8. "Chain Store Taxes", Journal of Marketing, Vol. I, (January,1937), p. 187.

from more rapid stockturn, and from economy in the use of capital
and labor.

Most of the present taxes reach their maximum rate at twenty or thirty stores. The extra benefits of multiple ownership would hardly be felt at this number. The number of stores at which chains begin to obtain advantages from multiple ownership depends upon the type of chain. P. H. Nystrom[9] says that chain-store men believe that in the grocery field the full possibilities of chain-store methods can not be secured without at least fifty stores and that the best results require two hundred or more stores. Beyond this there is some point where additional units yield no additional advantages and may yield diminishing returns for there would be no added gains from quantity purchases, turnover, and economy in the use of capital and labor. At the same time the cost of supervision and control would grow and the system would become less flexible. From this it is evident that the progressions that have been established in most chain-store taxes are unfair. At what number of stores different rates would be justified depends on the type of chain.

It is this difference in the type of chain that makes the use of graduated per-store taxes illogical instruments to measure the special benefit received from the chain form of organization. The gain which comes from the addition of another store differs with each type of chain. There is a greater advantage obtained by the addition of a second department store than by the addition of a second variety store, grocery store, etc. To make such a tax just,

9. _Economics of Retailing_, 3d edition, Vol. I, p. 213. 1930, Ronald Press Company, New York.

in the sense of a measurement of benefit received, a different progression and a different rate should apply to every type of chain.

Because the same rate and progression applies to all types
of chains the present taxes exact more from some chains than the
benefit received, and probably less from other chains. Table XXIII
which shows the difference in the earnings per store of different
types of chains shows how false a measure of benefit received the
present type of tax is. The present taxes, moreover, are all out
of proportion. If the feature of graduation is predicated on the
increased benefit received by the addition of more units, the progression should bear a reasonable relation to this. Otherwise
discrimination will result. No attempt has been made to correlate
the progression with the facts of chain operation. The taxes pay-
able under the Michigan law will illustrate this.[10] Kroger with
858 stores pays 21,082 times as much tax as a two-store chain,
3,011.71 times as much as a five-store chain, 501.95 times as much
as an eleven-store chain, 134.21 times as much as a twenty-store
chain, and 20.93 times as much as a fifty-five-store chain. An
eleven-store chain (J. J. Newberry) pays forty-two times as much
as a two-store chain, six times as much as a five-store chain, and
almost twice as much as an eight-store chain. A twenty-store chain
(Sears-Roebuck Company) pays 157 times as much as a two-store chain,
22.42 times as much as a five-store chain, and 3.73 times as much
as an eleven-store chain. Table IX shows the increase in rates as
applied to chains of various number of stores under the tax laws of

10. Taxes on the various companies presented in the brief for the
chain stores in C. F. Smith Co. vs. Fitzgerald, 259 N.W. 352-362,
March 6, 1935. A Michigan case. The brief is not published with
the case but was obtained on request.

each state which imposes special chain-store taxes. It is apparent
that the progression is most severe as stores are added up to a total of twenty or twenty-five stores. From then on the increase in
the average amount paid per store declines except in those states
which do not impose the maximum tax as early as twenty stores.
Scarcely any progression can be justified for most types of chains
until twenty or fifty units are included in the chain. The rates
to be applied must be determined after further study of the actual
benefit received by chains of different lengths in the various fields
of retailing. In addition to a lack of reasonableness in the application of different rates to various lengths of chains within a
state there is no uniformity as to the rates imposed by different
states, as Table IX will show. There is no reason to believe that
a chain of five units in Idaho receives half the benefit of a chain
of similar length in Florida; that chains of ten, twenty-five, and
fifty units receive approximately the same benefit in both states;
and that a chain of 200 units receives five times as much benefit
in Idaho as in Florida. Similar inconsistencies can be seen in the
rates of every one of the states which impose such taxes. In no way
do the rates seem to bear a reasonable relation to the privileges
given. The rates seem to have been determined by consideration, not
of benefits received, but of what could be pushed through the legislature.

The number of stores operated by a chain within a state
is no measure of the benefit a chain organization receives. Under
the California tax, which was defeated in a state-wide referendum,
Montgomery Ward and Company with fifty stores would have paid $21,011
and Sears Roebuck and Company with twenty stores would have paid

$6,011. As far as their total operations are concerned both probably get the same benefit from the addition of another unit but under this law (and the disparity in rates is probably less in this law than in any other) one would pay over one-third per store more than the other. It is possible for a large national chain with a few units in a state to pay less per unit under a particular tax than a small concentrated chain with all its units located in one state. The Louisiana law which bases the rate to be applied on the number of stores no matter where located is more logical in this respect than the taxes in the other states.

For special chain-store taxes to measure benefit received there should be an attempt to approximate the actual benefit received, a different progression and set of rates should be applied to each type of chain, the rate per store should be based on the total length of the chain, and the rates should not be so excessive as to be discriminatory.

A gross sales tax is no measure of benefit received because different types of chains have different markups and turnovers. A graduated gross sales tax is even more vicious. There is no relation at all between the total sales of an organization and the benefit it receives from the privilege of operation as a chain.

L. B. Krueger of the Wisconsin Tax Commission has suggested at various times that chains be classified on two bases, number of units and gross sales per store. Although this type of tax would be a better measure of benefit received than either a per unit or gross sales tax (providing the rates were logically arranged) it would still permit discrimination. Using Table XXIII as a basis and figuring the average sales per store and assuming classifications to

be arranged so that stores which have average sales of forty to
fifty thousand dollars, fifty to sixty thousand dollars, and so on
would be grouped together, the inequitable results of such a tax
are seen. Under such an assumption, in the $40,000 group would be
men's hats and caps, unlimited variety stores, five-dollar-limit
variety stores and grocery stores. An added unit does not give the
same benefit in each for the return on sales was, for the years
1913 to 1930, a minus .24 of one per cent, .30 of one per cent,
2.97 per cent, and 2.24 per cent respectively. In the $50,000 group
would be men's furnishings, women's accessories, millinery, men's
shoes, and grocery and meat chains. Their return on sales was .75
of one per cent, 2.84 per cent, 2.80 per cent, 4.80 per cent, and
2.96 per cent respectively. Similar results appear in the rest of
the supposed classification. The average sales of a store bear
no relation to net income or to benefit received.

The existing taxes do not conform to the theory that
taxes should be levied according to the cost of service. It costs
the government little, if any, more per store to watch over chain
systems than over independents. From the point of view of the
greatest good to the greatest number the existing taxes are not justified. Chapters Two through Five dealt with the justification of
the use of special chain-store taxes to curb the chains and the
conclusion was reached that there was no justification. Hence,
existing chain-store taxes can be justified under no theory of
equity that has been advanced. The only basis for such taxation
is that of expediency, (the choice of taxes which seems justified
by the need of revenue and the pressure of interests). Expediency
is often the determining factor in the selection of a tax and may

have greater influence than principles of justice. It is necessary
that revenues be raised but expediency should not take the place
of approximate justice and should not be the tool for the promotion
of special interests. A good many of the present chain-store taxes
were passed under the pressure of the needs of the depression years.
As an emergency tax productivity would outweigh abstract principles
of justice, but in such a case the taxes should be abandoned with
the end of the emergency. Even so, these were poor taxes for they
weighed more heavily on the poorer classes who were hard-pressed
without such taxes, especially when sales taxes (which were looked
upon as emergency measures) also were passed in many states.

      The fact of productivity can not be advanced in justifi-
cation of special chain-store taxes, however, for they are not productive, especially in view of the cost of the administration of
them.[11] Chain-store taxes have brought in disappointingly meagre
revenues, so insignificant in view of the needs of the state that
it is doubtful if they have been worth while even without regard
for principles of justice. The amounts received were reported for
ten states. Alabama received $105,808.87 from Oct. 1, 1936 to June
1, 1937; Idaho, $113,208.41 for the two-year period, 1935 and 1936;
Indiana, approximately $600,000 a year for the past few years;
Maine, $45,612.50 (1933-1934), $44,772.50 (1934-1935), $44,266.00
(1935-1936); $43,105.50 (1936-1937); Maryland, $102,000 for the
last year; Michigan, $167,000 in 1936; Minnesota, $223,157.59 (1933-
1934), $398,287.11 (1934-1935), $409,556.90 (1935-1936), $463,189.49

---

11. It is impossible to separate out from most state reports the
productivity of such taxes and the cost of administering them. The
material for this analysis was obtained by request from state officials. Returns were obtained from fourteen states, not all of
them usable.

(1936-1937); Mississippi, $8,670.74 (Jan. 1 to July 1, 1937); West

Virginia, approximately $125,000 annually; Wisconsin $169,745 in

1932, $80,467 in 1933, $188,640 in 1934, $71,052 in 1935, and

$143,316 in 1936.   In addition, A. G. Buehler[12] reports Kentucky re-

ceived $163,771 in 1935 and W. O. Farber[13] lists Florida as having

received $54,871.56 for the year ending August 27, 1933; North

Carolina, $65,347.00 for the year ending May 31, 1933; and South

Carolina, $246,458.00 for the three years 1930 to 1932 and $79,952.00

for the first six months of 1933.   Only one tax yielded as much as

$500,000 and the typical yield was in the neighborhood of $100,000.

Most of the revenues are obtained from a few companies.   These taxes

which yield such small revenues are hardly worthwhile because of

their high cost of administration.   Alabama reported a cost of col-

lection of about 27.1 per cent; Idaho, 6.0 per cent; Indiana, 6.0

per cent; Maine, 25.0 per cent in 1934, 16.0 per cent in 1935, and

15.0 per cent in 1936; Maryland reported that there was no cost

involved; Michigan, 4.5 per cent; Minnesota, 1.07 per cent in 1934,

0.8 of one per cent in 1935, about 1.3 per cent in 1936, and 1.2

per cent in 1937; Mississippi, 0.86 of one per cent; West Virginia,

5.6 per cent; and Wisconsin, 2.9 per cent in 1934, 8.7 per cent in

1935, and 5.0 per cent in 1936.   There is no way to check to see

that every state included every cost involved.   Such costs of ad-

ministration are too high.   One of the canons of taxation advanced

by Adam Smith was that every tax should take out of the pockets of

the people as little as possible above what it brings into the gov-

ernment treasury.   Chain-store taxes violate this canon.   H. L.

Lutz, in his report for the Recess Commission on Taxation for the

12. "Chain Store Taxes", op. cit., p. 180.
13. "State Taxation of Chain Stores", Tax Magazine, Vol. XII, (Jan.
1934), p. 13.

State of Maine[14] after a discussion of the chain-store tax in specific terms said, "The small yield and the high expense put this tax
in the nuisance class."

Another characteristic of good taxation which is violated
by special chain-store taxes is that a tax should have no undesirable economic and political effects and should be imposed for public
and not private purposes. The more severe chain-store taxes are
forcing reorganization in some types of chain retailing, particularly
in filling stations and grocery stores. Here there is a threat,
and some actual examples, that the chains will sell their stores to
the managers and become voluntary chains; will eliminate the small,
unprofitable, and neighborhood stores and will concentrate on centrally located superstores; will concentrate on the profitable and
low-tax areas; or will become wholesale houses. None of these alternatives open to the chain to avoid such special taxes offers
the consumers the same advantages as the chains do. To the extent
that chains are broken up or discouraged business is diverted from
the more efficient to the less efficient, consumers are forced to
pay more for their goods and to go without a type of service which
many of them have wanted, and mass production is slowed up. In
addition, such taxes do not affect competitors equally. Besides
hurting the chain as against the independent it discriminates against
the large chain and the concentrated chain and weighs differently
against different types of chains which may sell, in part, the same
goods. None of these economic effects are desirable.

---

14. The System of Taxation in Maine, p. 61.   State Document, printed
December, 1934.

Such a tax also has a bad political effect in that it sets a precedent for "pressure groups" to push through legislation to foster their own interests. Much of the support for chain-store taxes has come from groups who were interested, not in public purposes, but in their own private interests. Chapters Two through Five indicate that such taxes serve no public purpose and that they are designed to advance private interests.

In respect to the other characteristics of a good tax system there is little to condemn chain-store taxes. Per unit taxes have stood the test of constitutionality so that states are on sure legal grounds in the adoption of them. However, graduated gross sales taxes probably are illegal. The chain-store taxes are simple and easy to understand, the amount owed by each taxpayer is certain, and the manner of payment is not unduly inconvenient. Chain-store taxes are not very elastic but it is not necessary that every tax be elastic. It is enough if the system as a whole is elastic. The matter of exemptions brings some problems for most states exempt certain types of chains. However, the problem is not serious. Also, the yield is relatively stable.

Thus, the existing chain-store taxes fail to satisfy the canon of equity, have undesirable economic and political effects, are unproductive and costly to administer, and weigh more heavily on the poor than on the richer classes. The chain-store taxes, however, must be viewed in the light of the whole tax system in these respects. As has been indicated, a tax system must be judged in its entirety. If the defects in one group of taxes balance opposing defects in another group, no injustice may be done. The chains may escape some of their fair share of other taxes but not to the extent to which they are assessed under the present chain-store taxes. Some special taxation might be justified on this score but not to the amount that is now asked, and especially in view of the fact that such taxes can not possibly bear any relation to the taxes escaped. No tax can be excused if it has undesirable economic and political effects unless it has some strong points in its favor. The latter is not the situation in respect to chain-store taxes. No one tax can be excused if it is unproductive and costly to administer unless some desirable result other than revenue is expected to result. It has been indicated that chain-store taxes do not produce a result which is favorable to consumers or to the public at large. A tax which falls on the poor classes can not be justified unless such classes escape their fair share under other tax statutes. The poor often are considered to pay more than their fair share, inasmuch as property taxes, sales taxes, excise taxes, and the protective tariff are regressive in effect. As revenue measures, the present chain-store taxes are undesirable.

Thus, neither from the standpoint of regulation or revenue or of the equalization of existing tax burdens can the present chain-store taxes be justified. The chains, however, do escape some taxes and do receive a benefit from their opportunity to conduct business in multiple units and some extra taxation is justifiable. To what extent such extra taxes may be imposed with justice is not known for no one has taken the trouble to approximate these advantages. Further study is necessary to determine what amount of extra taxation is justifiable. Unreasonable and unfair rates should be stopped. It is necessary that a sound position be taken in respect to the taxation of chains. The need for revenue is increasing and

it is likely that all forms of taxes will be higher in the future.
Justice in taxation will not be attained by an increase in the rates
of existing taxes under the criterion of charging what the traffic
will bear. The tax system, to be just, requires constant over-
hauling and balancing. In addition, the trend seems to be toward
splitting off different groups for special taxation. This trend
is in the general line of progress if the burdens which are imposed
on special groups are exacted with a reasonable regard for the
principles of justice in taxation. The recognition of differences
in taxable groups, and a levy of taxes with a reasonable regard for
the abilities or benefits of such groups is the first requisite for
the attainment of a just tax system. The special taxation of chain
stores is of this nature. Its special abilities and benefits, if
any, should be studied and taxes levied with due regard to these
factors. The rates imposed will never be more than rough measures
of such advantages but approximate justice can be attained.

More definite conclusions can be drawn as to the form of
such taxation. Whatever type of tax is used should apply to the
national situation rather than to that which exists in one state,
that is, the measure of the tax should not be determined by the
number of stores, the gross sales, or the net income earned within
a particular state boundary. The measure of the tax should be based
on the total operations of the chain and allocation made to the
states. In this respect the Louisiana type of tax is the most
logical. The chains should not be taxed by graduated per unit
taxes which apply the same rates to all types of chain unless such
taxes are very light. If the income yielded is necessary for the
operation of the government, such a tax could be justified on the

basis of expediency. But a government seldom needs revenue badly enough to justify grossly discriminatory legislation. Graduated gross sales taxes which apply alike to all types of chains are also undesirable. This leaves two types of taxes, net income taxes and graduated per-unit taxes with different progressions and different rates for various classifications of chains.

Net income taxes conform most nearly to all the characteristics of a good tax. All advantages which an individual or corporation obtains whether by efficiency, the avoidance of one's just share of taxes, by extra benefits received from the state, or from any other source, are reflected in the net income which is received. A tax on this net income would supposedly reach any special advantages that a taxpayer might have. A greater reliance on this type of tax and a less reliance on such types as the property tax and sales tax would work greater equity between individuals and between competing business organizations. In this particular instance it would lessen the disadvantage which the independent has in respect to property taxes and would reach the results of the advantages chains receive from the operation of multiple units. But difficulties exist in this tax. Chains are taxed by state governments and state boundary lines complicate the administration of a net income tax where a taxable party earns part of its income in two or more states. The determination of net income involves complicated accounting problems and a highly controversial question as to just what profit is. If a net income tax were administered by a taxing body within whose boundaries the chain, or other corporation, earned all, or substantially all, of its income, difficulties would arise in the administration. But such difficulties could be solved satis-

factorily and, in time, a procedure developed that would handle
the matter adequately and with comparatively little expense. There
is a different situation where such a tax is administered by a large
number of taxing bodies, say forty-eight states. None of these has
the capacity to go through the complicated process of the determination of the net income of the various chains and, even when
this should be accomplished, of the allocation of a proper share of
the tax proceeds to itself. The amount received by any one state
would not justify the expense of a thorough administration of such
a law. But administration by one agency would. The solution to
the whole matter would be to have the Federal government administer
the tax, deduct the expenses of collection, and allocate the remain-
der to the states in accordance with some standard formula. Since
the Federal government already imposes a corporation income tax, the
extra costs of administration would be very slight. It is very
doubtful, however, if the various states and the Federal government
could ever agree on the terms of such an arrangement. Some such a
solution would be the ideal one for the problem of the special taxation of chain stores.

          In some respects the most logical type of tax is the sug-
gested per-unit tax on various classification of chains. If the
progressions and rates were made with due regard to the facts of
chain-store operation, such a tax would measure with approximate
justice the extra taxes which chains can be expected to pay. At
the same time the measure of the tax, the number of stores, can be
determined easily and at practically no expense by each state. Thus,
there would be no need for interstate agreements or allocation of
receipts. The difficulty of administration would inhere in the

determination of the reasonableness of the charges. The initial
cost of administration would be high but would be reduced and would
be low thereafter.

The greatest difficulty with such a tax would lie in the
problem of constitutionality. Classification for different treatment under tax laws must be based on reasonable differences between
taxable parties. It probably would be very difficult to get the
courts to see that there were sufficient differences among the operation of grocery chains and department-store chains to justify different rates of taxation. But differences do exist, and economically,
if not legally, there are as great differences in the operation of
these two types of chains as there are among the operations of
chains as a whole and independents. Grocery chains and department-
store chains operate on different markups; have obvious differences
in the volume of sales per store, in their location policies, in
buying methods, in internal management, etc. Economically, there
is a greater difference between the operation of a grocery chain
and a department-store chain than there is between a chain of department stores and a single department store. If a tax law which
provided for such a system of classification should carry the ex-
press provision that the rates and progression on each class should
be limited to the approximate advantages which accrue to each class
by the differences that exist among the classes (turnover, markup,
volume of sales, buying and management policies, location policies,
etc.), it would have some chance to pass a liberal court, especially
one which based its decisions on economic factors rather than on
legal precedents. Such a law has never been passed and until the
courts actually have decided on such a law, its constitutionality

can not be judged. Such a law would do indirectly what a net income tax would do directly but, if legal, offers less difficulties.

One of these taxes, or some other equally as just, should
be adopted. No matter what type is adopted, the rates should be
just and reasonable.

APPENDIX A

CHAIN-STORE TAXES IN OPERATION IN THE UNITED STATES

State	Year Passed	Rate of Tax		
Alabama	1935	1 store		$ 1.00
		2-5 stores,	for each added store	15.00
		6-10 " ,	" " " "	22.50
		11-20 " ,	" " " "	37.50
		over 20 stores,	" " " "	112.50
Colorado	1934	1 store		$ 2.00
		2-4 stores,	for each added store	10.00
		5-8 " ,	" " " "	50.00
		9-15 " ,	" " " "	150.00
		16-24 "	" " " "	200.00
		over 24 stores,	" " " "	300.00
Florida	1935	1 store		$ 10.00
		2-3 stores,	for every store	50.00
		4-6 " ,	" " "	100.00
		7-10 " ,	" " "	200.00
		11-15 " ,	" " "	300.00
		over 15 stores,	" " "	400.00
		Plus gross receipts tax of ½%.		
Idaho	1933	1 store		$ 5.00
		2 stores,	for every store	10.00
		3 " ,	" " "	20.00
		4 " ,	" " "	35.00
		5 " ,	" " "	55.00
		6 " ,	" " "	80.00
		7 " ,	" " "	110.00
		8 " ,	" " "	140.00
		9 " ,	" " "	170.00
		10 " ,	" " "	200.00
		11 " ,	" " "	230.00
		12 " ,	" " "	260.00
		13 " ,	" " "	290.00
		14 " ,	" " "	320.00
		15 " ,	" " "	350.00
		16 " ,	" " "	380.00
		17 " ,	" " "	410.00
		18 " ,	" " "	440.00
		19 " ,	" " "	470.00
		over 19 stores,	" " "	500.00
Indiana	1933	1 store		$ 3.00
		2-5 stores,	for each added store	10.00
		6-10 " ,	" " " "	20.00
		11-20 " ,	" " " "	30.00
		over 20 stores,	" " " "	150.00
Iowa	1935	2-10 stores, for each store		$ 5.00
		11-20 " , " " " added		15.00
		21-30 " , " " " "		35.00
		31-40 " , " " " "		65.00
		41-50 " , " " " "		105.00
		over 50 " , " " " "		155.00

continued on next page

State	Year Passed	Rate of Tax	
Iowa (cont'd)	1935	Plus gross receipts tax ranging from $25 for gross receipts under $50,000 to $1,000 for each additional $10,000 receipts over $9,000,-000.	
Kentucky	1936	1 store	$ 2.00
		2-10 stores, for each added store	25.00
		6-10 " , " " " "	50.00
		11-20 " , " " " "	100.00
		21-50 " , " " " "	200.00
		over 50 " , " " " "	300.00
Louisiana	1934	10 stores and under, no matter where	$ 10.00
		11-35 stores, located	15.00
		36-50 "	20.00
		51-75 "	25.00
		76-100 "	30.00
		101-125 "	50.00
		126-150 "	100.00
		151-175 "	150.00
		176-200 "	200.00
		201-225 "	250.00
		226-250 "	300.00
		251-275 "	350.00
		276-300 "	400.00
		301-400 "	450.00
		401-500 "	500.00
		over 500 "	550.00
Maine (repealed 1937)	1933	1 store	$ 1.00
		2-5 stores, for each added store	5.00
		6-10 " , " " " "	10.00
		11-15 " , " " " "	15.00
		16-25 " , " " " "	25.00
		over 25 stores, " " " "	50.00
Maryland	1933	2-5 stores, for each added store	$ 5.00
		6-10 " , " " " "	20.00
		11-20 " , " " " "	100.00
		over 20 " , " " " "	150.00
Michigan	1935	2-3 stores, for each added store	$ 10.00
		4-5 " , " " " "	25.00
		6-10 " , " " " "	50.00
		11-15 " , " " " "	100.00
		16-20 " , " " " "	150.00
		21-25 " , " " " "	200.00
		over 25 stores, " " " "	250.00
Minnesota	1933	2-10 stores, for each added store	$ 5.00
		11-20 " , " " " "	15.00
		21-30 " , " " " "	35.00
		31-40 " , " " " "	65.00
		41-50 " , " " " "	105.00
		over 50 stores, " " " "	155.00
		Plus sales tax ranging from 1/20% of gross sales on under $100,000 to 1% on sales over $1,000,000.	

State	Year Passed	Rate of Tax		

Mississippi — 1936

2 stores, for each		$ 3.00
3-9 " , for each added store		10.00
10-14 " , " " " "		20.00
15-19 " , " " " "		30.00
20-25 " , " " " "		75.00
26-30 " , " " " "		125.00
31-40 " , " " " "		200.00
over 40 stores, " " " "		300.00

Montana — 1933

1-2 stores, for each	$ 2.50
3-4 " , for each added store	15.00
5-6 " , " " " "	20.00
7-10 " , " " " "	25.00
over 10 " , " " " "	30.00

North Carolina — 1935

2-5 stores, for each	$ 50.00
6-9 " , for each added store	70.00
10-13 " , " " " "	80.00
14-17 " , " " " "	90.00
18-21 " , " " " "	100.00
22-31 " , " " " "	125.00
32-51 " , " " " "	150.00
52-101 " , " " " "	175.00
102-201 " , " " " "	200.00
202 and over, " " " "	225.00

Pennsylvania — 1937

1 store	$ 1.00
2-5 stores, for each added store	5.00
6-10 " , " " " "	10.00
11-15 " , " " " "	20.00
16-20 " , " " " "	30.00
21-30 " , " " " "	50.00
31-50 " , " " " "	100.00
51-75 " , " " " "	200.00
76-100 " , " " " "	250.00
101-200 " , " " " "	350.00
201-500 " , " " " "	450.00
over 500 " , " " " "	500.00

South Carolina — 1930

1st store,	$ 5.00	16th store,	$ 80.00
2nd " ,	10.00	17th " ,	85.00
3d " ,	15.00	18th " ,	90.00
4th " ,	20.00	19th " ,	95.00
5th " ,	25.00	20th " ,	100.00
6th " ,	30.00	21st " ,	105.00
7th " ,	35.00	22d " ,	110.00
8th " ,	40.00	23d " ,	115.00
9th " ,	45.00	24th " ,	120.00
10th " ,	50.00	25th " ,	125.00
11th " ,	55.00	26th " ,	130.00
12th " ,	60.00	27th " ,	135.00
13th " ,	65.00	28th " ,	140.00
14th " ,	70.00	29th " ,	145.00
15th " ,	75.00	30th " ,	150.00
		over 30 " s,	150.00

State	Year Passed	Rate of Tax	
South Dakota	1935	1 store	$ 1.00
		2-10 stores, for each added store	5.00
		10 or more , " " " "	10.00
		Plus gross receipts tax ranging from 1/8% on sales not over $50,000 to 1% on sales over $1,000,000.	
Texas	1935	1 store	$ 1.00
		2nd store	6.00
		3-5 stores, for each added store	25.00
		6-10 " , " " " "	50.00
		11-20 " , " " " "	150.00
		21-35 " , " " " "	250.00
		36-50 " , " " " "	500.00
		over 50 " , " " " "	750.00
West Virginia	1933	1 store	$ 2.00
		2-5 stores, for each store added	5.00
		6-10 " , " " " "	10.00
		11-15 " , " " " "	20.00
		16-20 " , " " " "	30.00
		21-30 " , " " " "	35.00
		31-50 " , " " " "	100.00
		51-75 " , " " " "	200.00
		over 75 " , " " " "	250.00
Wisconsin	1935	2-5 stores, for each	$ 25.00
		6-10 " , " " store added	50.00
		11-15 " , " " " "	100.00
		16-20 " , " " " "	150.00
		21-25 " , " " " "	200.00
		over 25 " , " " " "	250.00
Delaware	1927	$10 plus 10¢ for each $100 of aggregate cost value of goods in excess of $5,000, on foreign corporations maintaining branch stores, warehouses, etc., within the state.	
Tennessee	1931	15¢ on each $100 of average capital invested, minimum $5.00. If average stock less than $800, tax is $7.50 and no ad valorem tax is charged.	
Virginia	1935	An operator of distributing house who sells goods to own retail stores.	
		Sales not over $10,000	$50.00
		Next $10,000	50.00
		Each $100 in excess	.13

Sources: Tax Research Foundation, Tax Systems of the World, 6th edition, 1935, pp. 167-169. 1935, Commerce Clearing House, Chicago.

Nichols, J. P., Retailers' Manual of Taxes and Regulations. 1935, Institute of Distribution, Inc., New York.

BIBLIOGRAPHY

Books and Pamphlets

Alexander, R. S., A Study in Retail Grocery Prices, 1929, New York
    Journal of Commerce, New York.
American Management Association, Consumer and Industrial Market-
    ing Series, C.M. 22, Appraisals of Robinson-Patman Act, W. L
    Thorp, "Effects of Robinson-Patman Act on Business Practice",
    1937, American Management Association, New York.
American Retail Federation. Chain Store Taxes, 1937, American
    Retail Federation, Washington, D. C.
An Old Merchant. Mercantile Failures, 1873, Mercantile Publishing
    Company, St. Louis.
Barnett, H. R. Chain Store Methods Exposed, 1936, Barnett Pub-
    lishing Co., Los Angeles.
_____. Man Management in Chain Stores, 1931, Harper and
    Bros., New York.
Baxter, W. J. Chain Store Distribution and Management, 1928,
    Harper and Bros., New York.
Bedell, Clyde, The Seven Keys to Retail Profits, 1931, McGraw-
    Hill Book Co., Inc., New York.
Bjorklund, E. and Palmer, J. L. "A Study of the Prices of Chain
    and Independent Grocers in Chicago," School of Commerce and
    Administration Studies, Vol. I, No. 4, 1930, University of
    Chicago Press, Chicago.
Bloomfield, D. (editor). Chain Stores, 1931, H. W. Wilson Co.,
    New York.
_____. Trends in Retail Distribution, 1930,
    H. W. Wilson Co., New York.
Borsodi, R. The Distribution Age, 1927, D. Appleton & Co., New
    York.
Bristol, W. F. "Operating Costs of Service Grocery Stores in
    Iowa, 1927, Iowa Studies in Business, No. 6, 1930, College
    of Commerce, University of Iowa, Iowa City.
Buehler, A. G. Public Finance, 1936, McGraw-Hill Book Company,
    New York.
Buehler, E. C. Chain Store Debate Manual, 1931, National Chain
    Store Association, New York.
Cassady, R. and Ostlund, H. J. "The Retail Distribution Struc-
    ture of the Small City", University of Minnesota Studies
    in Economics and Business, No. 12, 1935, University of
    Minnesota Press, Minneapolis.
Chamber of Commerce of the United States, Domestic Distribution
    Department. Retail and Wholesale Trade of Eleven Cities,
    1928, Chamber of Commerce of the United States, Washington,
    D. C.
Cheasley, C. H. The Chain Store Movement in Canada, McGill Uni-
    versity Economic Studies, No. 17, 1930, Packet-Times Press,
    Ltd., Orillia, Canada.
Clark, F. E. Principles of Marketing, Revised Edition, 1932,
    MacMillan Co., New York.
Clark, F. . Readings in Marketing, 1924, The MacMillan Co.,
    New York.

Clark, F. E. and Weld, L. D. H. Marketing Agricultural Products
in the United States, 1932, MacMillan Co., New York.
Comish, N. H. Marketing of Manufactured Goods, 1935, The Strat-
ford Company, Boston.
Committee on Recent Economic Changes, Herbert Hoover, Chairman.
Recent Economic Changes, Textbook Edition, Copeland, M. T.
"Marketing", pp. 321-424. 1929, McGraw-Hill Book Co., New
York.
Converse, P. D. "Business Mortality of Illinois Retail Stores",
1925-1930", Bureau of Business Research, University of Illi-
nois, Bulletin No. 41, 1932, University of Illinois, Urbana.
_____. The Elements of Marketing, revised edition, 1935
Prentice-Hall, Inc., New York.
_____. Marketing Notes, 1933, Daniels and Shoaff, Cham-
paign, Illinois.
_____. Selling Policies, 1928, Prentice-Hall Inc., New
York.
_____. The Automobile and the Village Merchant, Bureau
of Business Research, University of Illinois, Bulletin No.
19, 1928, University of Illinois, Urbana, Ill.
Copeland, M. T. Principles of Merchandising,1925, A. W. Shaw Co.,
New York.
_____. Problems in Marketing, 3d revised edition, 1930
printing, McGraw-Hill Book Co., Inc., New York.
Corbaley, G. C. Group Selling By 100,000 Retailers, 1932, Ameri-
can Institute of Food Distribution Inc., New York.
Cover, J. H. "Retail Price Behavior", Studies in Business Ad-
ministration, Vol. V, No. 2, 1935, University of Chicago
Press, Chicago.
Darby, W. D. The Story of the Chain Store, 1928, Dry Goods
Economist, New York.
Dartnell Corporation. Sales Method Investigation, No. 106,"Plans
for Overcoming the Inertia of Dealers and Agents", 1923,
Dartnell Corporation, Chicago.
Davidson, C. Voluntary Chain Stores, 1930, Harper and Bros., New
York.
Davis, T. C. Chain Stores vs. Farm Problem, 1933, Geo. W. King
Printing Co., Baltimore.
Donald, W.J. Handbook of Business Administration, J. L. Palmer,
"The Chain Store", pp. 301-309. 1931, McGraw-Hill Book Co.,
New York.
Egbert, J.C.; Holbrook, E. A.; Aldrich, M. A. (editors). Ameri-
can Business Practice, Vol. I, 1931, Ronald Press, New York.
Filene, E. A. The Model Stock Plan, 1st edition, 1930, McGraw-
Hill Book Co., New York.
Flowers, M. America Chained, 1931, Montaville Flowers Publicists,
Ltd., Pasadena, California.
Furst, R. L. Grocery Chains in Fort Wayne, Indiana, M. A. Thesis,
School of Commerce and Administration, University of Chi-
cago, 1931.
Gault, E. H. Control of the Retail Units of Chain Stores, 1935,
University of Chicago Libraries, Chicago.
Givins, R. H. Jr. Outlawry of Chainstores, 2nd edition, 1936
Better Business Publishing Company, Tampa, Florida.
Guernsey, J. Retailing Tomorrow, 1929, Dry Goods Economist, New
York,

Hall, T. H. (editor). Current, Conflicting Views on the Chain
    Store Controversy, 1930, National Research Bureau, Chicago.
Hardy, F. K. The Special Taxation of Chain Stores, Ph.D. thesis,
    University of Wisconsin, 1934.
Haring, A. Retail Price Cutting and Its Control by Manufacturers,
    1935, Ronald Press, New York.
Haring, C. E. The Manufacturer and His Outlets, 1929, Harper
    and Bros., New York.
Harvard University Bureau of Business Research. Bulletins of the
    Bureau of Business Research, 1920-1936, The Murray Printing
    Co., Cambridge, Mass.
Hayward, W. S. and White, P. Chain Stores, Their Management and
    Operation, 3d edition, 1928, McGraw-Hill Book Co., Inc.,
    New York.
Hoadley, R. L. The Chain Store, With Special Reference to Iowa,
    Iowa Studies in Business, No. IX, 1930, College of Commerce,
    University of Iowa, Iowa City.
Holtzclaw, H. F. The Principles of Marketing, 1935, T. Y. Crowell
    Co., New York.
Hunter, M. H. Outlines of Public Finance, 1926, Harper and Bros.,
    New York.
Institute of Distribution, Inc. 33 Questions and 33 Answers Im-
    portant To Your Pocketbook, 1936, Institute of Distribution
    Inc., New York.
Jensen, J. P. Government Finance, 1937, T. Y. Crowell Company,
    New York.
Lebhar, G. M. Chain Stores-Boon or Bane, 1932, Harper and Bros.,
    New York.
─────────. How to Meet Unfair Charges Against Chain Stores,
    Second Edition, 1936, Chain Store Publishing Co., New York.
Lutz, H. L. Public Finance, 3d edition, 1936, D. Appleton-Cen-
    tury Company, New York.
McGarry, E. D., Mortality in Retail Trade, University of Buffalo
    Studies in Business, No. 4, 1930, University of Buffalo,
    Buffalo.
Mach, G. R. Some Factors in the Development of Chain Stores, M.
    A. Thesis, University of Illinois, 1922.
Maynard, H. H.; Weidler, W. C.; Beckman, T. N. Principles of
    Marketing, Revised Edition, 1932, Ronald Press Co., New
    York.
Millis Advertising Co. The Menace of the Chains, 1924, Millis
    Advertising Co., Indianapolis.
Nebraska, University of, Committee on Business Research, College
    of Business Administration, Nebraska Studies in Business,
    1922 to 1927, University of Nebraska, Lincoln.
Nichols, J. P. Chain Store Manual, 1932 edition, 1932, National
    Chain Store Association, New York.
─────────. Chain Store Manual, 1936 edition, 1936, Institute
    of Distribution, Inc., New York.
─────────. Retailer's Manual of Taxes and Regulations, 1935,
    Institute of Distribution, Inc., New York.
Nystrom, P. H. Chain Stores, Revised Edition, 1930, Chamber of
    Commerce of the United States, Washington, D. C.
─────────. Economics of Retailing, 1st edition, 1915, Ronald
    Press Co., New York.

Nystrom, P. H. Economics of Retailing, 3d edition, Vol. I and II,
    1930, Ronald Press Company, New York.
Ohrbach, N. M. Getting Ahead in Retailing, 1935, McGraw-Hill Book
    Company, New York.
Olsen, P. C. The Merchandising of Drug Products, 1931, D. Apple-
    ton and Co., New York.
Progressive Grocer Publications. Operating Expenses of 110 Se-
    lected Food Stores, 1935, Butterick Publishing Company, New
    York.
Pyle, J. F. Marketing Principles, 1931, McGraw-Hill Book Co.,
    Inc., New York.
Rost, O. F. Distribution Today, 1933, McGraw-Hill Book Co., Inc.,
    New York.
Seligman, E. R. A. and Love, R. A. Price-Cutting and Price Main-
    tenance, 1932, Harper and Bros., New York.
Shideler, E. H. The Chain Store, Ph.D. Thesis, University of Chi-
    cago, 1927.
Somerville, J. Chain Store Debate Manual, 1930, National Chain
    Store Association, New York.
Tax Research Foundation. Tax Systems of the World, Sixth Edition,
    1935, Commerce Clearing House, Inc., Chicago.
United States Chamber of Commerce, Domestic Distribution Depart-
    ment. Retail and Wholesale Trade of Eleven Cities, 1928,
    Chamber of Commerce of United States, Washington, D. C.
Vaile, R. S. "Grocery Retailing", University of Minnesota, Study
    in Economics and Business, No. 1, 1932, University of Minne-
    sota Press, Minneapolis.
_____, (editor). The Small City and Town, R. S. Vaile,
    "Integrating the Small Town", 1930, University of Minnesota
    Press, Minneapolis.
_____ and Child, A. M. "Grocery Qualities and Prices", Uni-
    versity of Minnesota, Studies in Economics and Business, No.
    7, 1933, University of Minnesota Press, Minneapolis.
Williams, P. and Croxton, F. E. Corporation Contributions to Or-
    ganized Community Welfare Services, 1930, National Bureau of
    Economic Research Inc., New York.
Witte, E. F. "Purchasing Policies and Practices of Chain Drug
    Companies", University of Chicago Studies in Business Ad-
    ministration, Vol. III, No. 2, 1933, University of Chicago
    Press, Chicago.
Wood, C. W. The Passing of Normalcy, 1929, B. C. Forbes Publish-
    ing Co., New York.
Zimmerman, M. M. The Challenge of Chain Store Distribution, 1931,
    Harper and Bros., New York.
Our Taxes and Your Pocketbook, 1935, Institute of Distribution,
    Inc., New York.
The Fifty Thousand Per Cent Chain Store Tax, 1936, California Chain
    Stores Association Inc., Unpublished.

Periodicals and Newspapers
    Alexander, R. S. "The Wholesale Differential", Journal of
    Business, University of Chicago, Vol. IX, (1936), pp. 314-
    346.
    Beard, Chas. A. "Planning and Chain Stores", New Republic,
    Vol. LXXIII, (Nov. 30, 1932), pp. 66-67.

Becker, S. and Hess, R. A. "The Chain Store License Tax and the Fourteenth Amendment", North Carolina Law Review, Vol. VII, (1929), pp. 115-129.

Blauvelt, H. "What Chance Has a Man in a Chain?" Chain Store Age, Vol. IV, (Nov. 1928), pp. 44-45 ff.

Brewster, M. R. "Chain and Independent Store Prices in Atlanta", Georgia Business Review, (Jan. 31, 1931), pp. 9-10.

Buehler, A. G. "Anti-Chain-Store Taxation", Journal of Business, University of Chicago, Vol. IV, (1931), pp. 346-369.

——————. "Chain Store Taxes", Journal of Marketing, Vol. I, (Jan. 1937), pp. 177-188.

——————. "Trend of Taxation of Distributive Enterprise", Boston Conference on Retail Distribution, 1933, pp. 39-43.

Christianson, T. "When Main St. Becomes Chain Street", Commercial Law Journal, Vol. XXXV, (Dec. 1930), pp. 729-733.

Converse, P. D. "Prices and Services of Chain and Independent Stores in Champaign-Urbana, Illinois", Bulletin National Association of Teachers of Marketing and Advertising, Oct. 1931.

Copeland, M. T. "Some Present-Day Problems in Distribution", Harvard Business Review, Vol. ix, (April 1931), pp. 299-310.

Cox, R. "Inadequacies of Chain-Store Taxation", National Tax Association Bulletin, Vol. XIX, (Feb. 1934), pp. 132-141.

Criscuolo, L. "Forces Affecting the Future of Chain Distribution", Boston Conference on Retail Distribution, 1931, pp. 20-25.

Dennis, S. A. "What Can We Do About the Business Death Rate?" System, Vol. XXIX, (Jan. 1916), pp. 3-14.

——————. "When Will My Business Die?" System, Vol. XXXIII, (Oct. 1917), pp. 523-526.

——————. "Will You Have a Business in 1924?" System, Vol. XXXI, (Jan. 1917), pp. 107-109.

Deute, A. H. "Do Jobbers Deserve the Same Price as Chains and Mail Order Houses?" Printer's Ink, Vol. CLIV, (Feb. 12, 1931), pp. 3-4 ff.

Donovan, W. J. "How the Anti-Trust Laws Affect Chain Stores", Printer's Ink, Vol. CXLIX, (Oct. 3, 1929), pp. 133-134.

Dovell, R. "Chain Stores Can Be Good Citizens", Nation's Business, Vol. XIX, (June, 1931), pp. 78 ff.

Dowe, D. "A Comparison of Independent and Chain Store Prices", Journal of Business, University of Chicago, Vol. V, (1932), pp. 130-144.

Engle, N. H. "The Marketing Structure in the Grocery Industry", Harvard Business Review, Vol. XII, (1934), pp. 328-338.

Ernst, E. G. and Hartl, E. M. "Chain Management and Labor", Nation, Vol. CXXXI, (Nov. 26, 1930), pp. 574-576.

——————. "Chain Stores and the Community", Nation, Vol. CXXXI, (Nov. 14, 1930), pp. 545-547.

——————. "Chains versus Independents", Nation, Vol. CXXXI, (Nov. 12, 1930), pp. 517-519.

——————. "The Fighting Independents", Nation, Vol. CXXXI, (Dec. 3, 1930), pp. 606-608.

Farber, W. O. "State Taxation of Chain Stores", Tax Magazine, Vol. XII, (Jan. 1934), pp. 10-14 ff.

Faville, D. E. "Comparison of Chain and Independent Grocery Stores in the San Francisco Area", Journal of Marketing, Vol. I, (Oct. 1936), pp. 87-91.

Filene, E. A. and Schmalz, C. N. "Status and Prospects of the Chain Store", American Economic Review, Vol. XXI (supplement), (Mar. 1928), pp. 19-34, 27-28.

Fiske, R. T. "Retail Development", Proceedings of the National Association of Commercial Organization Secretaries, 1933, pp. 98-101.

Flynn, J. T. "Chain Store: Menace or Promise?" New Republic, Vol. LXVI, (April 15-May13, 1931), pp. 223-226; 270-273; 298-301; 324-326: 350-353.

Fulton, H. A. "Anti-Chain Store Legislation", Michigan Law Review, Vol. XXX, (Dec. 1931), pp. 274-279.

Furst, R. L. "Relationships Between the Numbers of Chain and Individually Owned Grocery Stores in Fort Wayne", Journal of Business, University of Chicago, Vol. V, (1932), pp. 335-345.

"R. G." "Chain Store Taxation", Pennsylvania Law Review, Vol. LXXX, (1932), pp. 289-295.

Grant, W. T. "Fill a Need or Fail", Printer's Ink, Vol. CXLIII, (June 14, 1928), pp. 17-20.

Greer, H. C. "Business Mortality Among Retail Meat Stores in Chicago Between 1920 and 1933", Journal of Business, University of Chicago, Vol. IX, (1936), pp. 189-209.

_____. "Distribution Cost Analysis", Bulletin National Association of Cost Accountants, Vol. XI, No. 19, (June 1, 1930).

Grether, E. T. "Market Factors Limiting Chain-Store Growth", Harvard Business Review, Vol. X, (Apr. 1932), pp. 323-331.

Hardy, F. K. "Legal and Economic Aspects of Chain Store Taxation in Wisconsin", Wisconsin Law Review, Vol. IX, (July 1934), pp. 382-387.

_____. "Taxation of Chain Retailers in the United States", Journal of Comparative Legislation, Vol. XVIII, (Nov. 1936),

_____. "Wisconsin's New Chain Store Tax and Its Relation to Personal Property Taxation", National Tax Association Bulletin, Vol. XIX, (Dec. 1933) pp. 66-72.

Hazlewood, C. B. "Chain Stores and the Local Bank", Commercial and Financial Chronicle, Vol.CXXIX, Part I, (Sept. 28, 1928), pp. 2000-2001.

Heer, C. "Taxation as an Instrument of Social Control", American Journal of Sociology, Vol. XLII, (Jan. 1937), pp. 484-492.

Heyman, E. "Charges of Short Weight Practices Unfounded", Chain Store Progress, Vol. III, (Mar. 1931), p. 4.

Hofer, R. M. "Something Different on Chain Stores", Industrial News Review, Vol. XLIV, (Oct. 1936), pp. 3, 4 ff.

Hollander, H. S. "Chain-Store Invasion Aids Independents", Barrons, Vol. IX, (Oct. 28, 1929), p. 21.

Hunter, M. H. "Shall We Tax Corporations or Business?" American Economic Review, Vol. XXVI, (Mar. 1936), pp. 84-89.

Johnson, R. W. "The Power to Tax Chain Stores", American Bankers Association, Journal, Vol. XXIV, (Nov. 1931), pp. 338 ff.

Jones, F. M. "Retail Sales in the United States, 1800-1860", Journal of Marketing, Vol. I, (Oct. 1936), pp. 134-142.

Klein, Julius. "The Outlook for the Chain Store", Chain Store Age, Vol. V, (Nov. 1929), pp. 55-56.

Krueger, L. B. "How Should Chain Stores Be Taxed?" Bulletin of the National Tax Association, Vol. XXI, (Dec. 1935), pp.75-80.

Krueger, L. B. "The Taxation of Chain Stores", Tax Magazine, Vol. XI, (Nov. 1933), pp. 412-415 ff.

LeBoutillier, P. "The Position of the Independent Store", Boston Conference on Retail Distribution, 1929, pp. 99-102.

Larsen, S. A. "Evolution in Retailing", Quarterly Journal, North Dakota University, Vol. XXI, (Spring, 1931), pp. 189-200.

_____. "Present Status of Chain Retailing", Quarterly Journal, North Dakota University, Vol. XXIII, (Winter, 1932), pp. 109-123.

Learned, E. P. "Quantity Buying From the Seller's Point of View", Harvard Business Review, Vol. VIII, (Oct. 1929), pp. 57-68.

_____ and Isaacs, N. "The Robinson-Patman Law", Harvard Business Review, Vol. XV, (Winter, 1937), pp. 137-155.

Lebhar, G. M. "As We See It", Chain Store Age, Vol. V, (May, 1929) p. 37.

_____. "Leaders, Loss Leaders, and Misleaders", Printer's Ink, Vol. CLVIII, (Feb. 11, 1932), pp. 17-20.

_____. "Sen. Copeland Calls Chain Stores Parasites", Chain Store Age, Vol. VI, (Aug. 13, 1930), p. 20.

_____. "The Chain Store and the Public", Chain Store Age, Vol. IV, (Mar. 1928), pp. 21-28.

_____. "The National Advertiser and the Chains", Chain Store Age, Vol. VII, (July 1931), pp. 27-28 ff.

_____. "What's Your Policy?" Chain Store Age, Vol. IV, (Mar. 1928), p. 101.

Lemon, Hal Y. "Chain Stores and Banks Get Together", Journal of the American Banker's Association, Vol. XXII, (Jan. 1930), pp. 665 ff.

Lewis. H. T. "Distribution", Annals of the American Academy of Political and Social Sciences, Vol. CXLIX, (May 1930), pp. 36-44.

Lowndes, C. L. B. "Rate and Measure in Jurisdiction to Tax", Harvard Law Review, Vol. XLIX, (Mar. 1936), pp. 756-783.

Lull, R. "The Case for the Chain Store", Industrial News Review, Vol. XLIII, (Aug. 1935), pp. 3, 4 ff.

Lyons, R. W. "Are Chains the Enemies of the Manufacturer", Nation's Business, Vol. XVIII, (May, 1930), pp. 24-26 ff.

_____. "Chain Association Backs Methods", Sales Management, Vol. XXII, (May 3, 1930), p. 222.

_____. "Chain Store Laws Valid--What Then?" Chain Store Progress, Vol. III, (July, 1931), pp. 1 ff.

_____. "Modern Merchandising", Proceedings of the National Association of Commercial Organization Secretaries, 1929, pp. 22-27.

_____. "Social Aspects of Chains Are Sound", Chain Store Progress, Vol. III, (April, 1931), p. 1.

_____. "The Chain Store Side", American Banker's Association Journal, Vol. XXII, (Sept. 1929), pp. 229 ff.

MacDonald, G. "Chain Tax Bills Now in Almost Every Legislature", Progressive Grocer, Vol. XI, (Sept. 1932), pp. 24-26 ff.

McGarry, E. D. "Mortality Among Stores", Boston Conference on Retail Distribution, 1930, pp. 43-48.

McNair, M. P. "Trends in Large-Scale Retailing", Harvard Business Review, Vol. X, (Oct. 1931), pp. 30-39.

Martin, B. F. "The Independent, et al., Versus the Chain", Harvard Business Review, Vol. IX, (Oct. 1930), pp. 47-56.

Mellen, J. M. "Weak Links in Chains of Stores", New Outlook, Vol. CLXI, (May, 1933), pp. 40-43.

Mitchell, C. G. "Handling the Chain Account", Banker's Magazine,
     Vol. CXXI, (Aug. 1930), pp. 205-207.
Morrill, A. H. "Development and Effect of Chain Stores", Journal
     of Accountancy, Vol. XLVIII, (Oct. 1929), pp. 260-268.
Mount, K. L. "Chain Store Taxation Before the Courts", George Wash-
     ington Law Review, Vol. IV, (Mar. 1936), pp. 335-347.
Mowry, D. E. "How Large-Scale Organizations View the Chamber of
     Commerce", Proceedings of the National Association of Com-
     mercial Organization Secretaries, 1932, pp. 166-174.
Mullen, W. H. "Some Aspects of Chain Store Development", Harvard
     Business Review, Vol. III, (Oct. 1924), pp. 69-80.
Murphy, J. A. "Can the Small Business Man Survive?" Harpers,
     Vol. CLXXV, (June 1937), pp. 1-7.
_____. "How the Small Bank Can Deal with the Chain Store",
     Journal of American Banker's Association, Vol. XXI, (Nov.
     1928), pp. 466 ff.
Nichols, J. P. "Shall the Chain Store Be Discriminatorily Taxed?"
     Illinois Journal of Commerce, (Apr. 1937), pp. 7-8 ff.
Nichols, W. B. "Chain Stores Fighting Unfair Taxes", Barrons, Vol.
     XI, (Aug. 3, 1931), pp. 18-19.
Nystrom, P. H. "Independent Store Grows", Printer's Ink, Vol. CLXXII,
     (Sept. 5, 1935), pp. 45-53.
_____. "Mars Over the Channels of Trade", Boston Conference
     on Retail Distribution, 1935, pp. 71-79.
_____. "Retail Trade", Encyclopedia of the Social Sciences,
     Vol. X, (1934), pp. 346-354.
Olsen, P. C. "Independent Mortality Unaffected By Chains", Chain
     Store Progress, Vol. III, (Feb. 1931), pp. 3 ff.
_____. "Louisville Blues?" Chain Store Progress, Vol. II,
     (Aug. 1930), p. 2.
Palmer, J. L. "Economic and Social Aspects of Chain Stores",
     Journal of Business, University of Chicago, Vol. II, (July
     1929), pp. 272-290.
Parsons, H. T. "Why Chain Stores Command Public Favor", Chain
     Store Age, Vol. IV, (Jan. 1928), pp. 21-22 ff.
Patch, P. W. "Taxation of Chain Stores", Editorial Research Re-
     ports, Vol. II, (Aug. 28, 1934), pp. 135-151.
Phelps, C. W. "Some Limitations and Disadvantages of the Chain
     Store System", Progressive Grocer, Vol. X, (March 1931),
     pp. 38-39 ff. and (April 1931), pp. 44-45 ff.
Phillips, C. F. "Chain, Voluntary Chain, and Independent Grocery
     Store Prices, 1930 and 1934," Journal of Business, University
     of Chicago, Vol. VIII, (1935), pp. 143-149.
_____. "Chain-Store Mortality", Journal of Business, Uni-
     versity of Chicago, Vol. VII, (1934), pp. 318-327.
_____. "State Discriminatory Chain Store Taxation", Har-
     vard Business Review, Vol. XIV, (Spring, 1936), pp. 349-359.
_____. "The Chain Store in the United States and Canada",
     American Economic Review, Vol. XXVII, (Mar. 1937), pp. 87-95.
_____. "The Robinson-Patman Anti-Price Discrimination Law
     and the Chain Store", Harvard Business Review, Vol. XV,
     (Aug. 1936), pp. 62-75.
Rabinovitz, S. "A Way to Lower Distribution Costs?" Printer's Ink,
     Vol. CXLI, (Nov. 3, 1927), pp. 89-92.
Rukeyser, M. S. "Chain Stores: The Revolution in Retailing",
     Nation, Vol. CXXVII, (Nov. 28, 1929), pp. 568-570.

Russell, F. A. (chairman). "Social and Economic Aspects of Chain
    Stores", American Economic Review, Vol. XXI (supplement),
    (Mar. 1931), pp. 27-36.

"W. J. S." "Robinson-Patman Bill", Georgetown Law Review, Vol.
    XXIV, (May 1936), pp. 951-961.

Sams, E. C. "Discriminatory Taxes and Distribution", Boston Con-
    ference on Retail Distribution, 1934, pp. 57-60.

Sams, E. C. "The Justification of the Chain Store in Our Present
    System of Distribution", Annals of the American Academy of
    Political and Social Sciences, Vol.CXV, (Sept. 1924), pp.
    226-235.

Schmalz, C. N. "Independent Stores vs. Chains in the Grocery
    Field," Harvard Business Review, Vol. IX, (July 1931),
    pp. 431-442.

Shepherd, W. G. "Local Boy Closes Gap", Colliers, Vol. LXXXIX,
    (Mar. 12, 1932), pp. 12-13 ff.

Smith, W. H. "A Billion From 'Cash and Carry'", Barrons, Vol.
    XI, (Jan. 19, 1931), pp. 22-23 ff.

Soule, Geo. "Farewell to the Shopkeeper", New Republic, Vol. LIX,
    (Apr. 4, 1928), pp. 210-212.

Sprague, J. R. "The Chain-Store Mind", Harpers, Vol. CLVIII,
    (Feb. 1929), pp. 356-366.

Steffler, C. W. "Chain Stores and the Public", Commerce and Fi-
    nance, Vol. XVII, (July 11, 1928), pp. 1487-1489.

_____. "Do Chain Methods Menace Free Competition?" Com-
    merce and Finance, Vol. XVII, (July 4, 1928), p. 144.

_____. "The Chain Store Era", World's Work, Vol. LVIII,
    (Jan. 1929), pp. 80-85.

Stevens, W.H.S. "A Comparison of Special Discounts and Allowances
    in the Grocery, Drug, and Tobacco Trades", Journal of Busi-
    ness, University of Chicago, (1934), pp. 95-105, 224-236.

_____. "Some Laws of Quantity Discounts", Journal of
    Business, University of Chicago, Vol. II, (1929), pp. 406-
    426 and Vol. III, (1930), pp. 51-71.

"E. E. T." "Discrimination Against Chain Stores", Southern
    California Law Review, Vol. IV, (Dec. 1930), pp. 140-145.

Taylor, M. D. "A Study of Weights in Chain and Independent Stores
    in Durham, North Carolina", Harvard Business Review, Vol. IX,
    (July, 1931), pp. 443-455.

_____. "Prices in Chain and Independent Grocery Stores in
    Durham, North Carolina", Harvard Business Review, Vol.VIII,
    (1930), pp. 413-424.

_____. "Prices of Branded Grocery Commodities During the
    Depression", Harvard Business Review, Vol. XII, (1934),
    pp. 437-449.

Thorp, W. L. "Chain Store Taxes", Dun and Bradstreet Review,
    (Mar. 1936), pp. 2-6.

Tolman, W. A. "Gross Sales Tax in Kentucky", Tax Magazine, Vol.X,
    (Mar. 1932), pp. 89-94, 109-114 and (Apr. 1932), pp. 127-
    128, 154.

Webbink, P. "Chain Store Problem in 1930", Editorial Research
    Reports, Vol. II, (1930), pp. 287-302.

Weld, L. D. H. "Do the Principles of Large-Scale Production Apply
    to Merchandising?" Amercian Economic Review, Vol. XIII,
    (supplement), (March 1923), pp. 185-197.

Westerfield, R. B. "The Rise of the Chain Store", Current History,
    Vol. XXXV, (1931), pp. 359-366.

Willis, H. E. "Chain Store Taxation", Indiana Law Journal, Vol.
     VII, (1931), pp. 179-187.
Zimmerman, C. F. "The Country Bank and the Chain Store Account",
     American Bankers Association Journal, Vol. XXII, (Nov. 1929),
     pp. 457 ff.

"A Chain Puts Its Links Under the Microscope", Business Week,
     (June 10, 1931), p. 14.
"A Chain Turns the X-Ray On Its Store Managers", Business Week,
     (Oct. 14, 1931), p. 10.
"Another Anti-chain Law Is Declared Void", Chain Store Age, Vol.
     IV, (June 1928), pp. 25-26 ff.
"Applicability of a Chain Store Tax to Filling Stations", Yale
     Law Journal, Vol. XLIII, (1934) pp. 1022-1026.
"Chain Store Taxation--Constitutional Questions", Columbia Law
     Review, Vol. XXXI, (Ja. 1931), pp. 145-154.
"Chain Stores Voted Down", Business Week, (Nov. 30, 1932), pp.11-12
"Chain Tax Snapped", Business Week, (Jan. 11, 1933), pp. 5, 6.
"Constitutionality of a State Chain Store Tax Based on Total Num-
     ber of Stores", Yale Law Journal, Vol. XLIV, (1935),
     pp. 619-638.
"Constitutionality of Statutes Discriminating Against Chain Stores",
     Iowa Law Review, Vol. XVI, (1931), pp. 427-430.
"Consumers Save Ten Percent in Albuquerque Stores", Chain Store
     Progress, Vol. III, (Nov. 1931), p. 4.
"E. Z. Palmer Finds Chains in Lexington 14.3% Below Independents",
     Chain Store Progress, Vol. II, (Sept. 1930), pp. 4, 5 ff.
"Henderson's Merchant's Minute Men Challenge the Chains", Print-
     er's Ink, Vol. CL, (Feb. 20, 1930), pp. 3, 4 ff.
"Louisiana Chain Store Tax Upheld in Last Appeal", Chicago Jour-
     nal of Commerce, (May 18, 1937), p. 1.
"Report of the Chain Store Committee", Proceedings of the National
     Association of Commercial Organization Secretaries, 1931,
     pp. 44-50.
"Report of the Chain Store Committee", Proceedings of the National
     Association of Commercial Organization Secretaries, 1932,
     pp. 49-67.
"Statutory Restraints on Chain Store Systems", Harvard Law Re-
     view, Vol. XLIV, (Jan. 1931), pp. 456-460.
"Taxation Directed Against the Chain Store", Yale Law Journal,
     Vol. XL, (1931), pp. 431-441.
"The Anti-Chain Store 'Racket'", Commerce and Finance, Vol. XIX,
     (Mar. 19, 1930), pp. 580-581.
"The Chain Store, Pro and Con", Congressional Digest, Vol. IX,
     (Aug., Sept. 1930), pp. 193-224.
"Validity of Chain Store License Law", Iowa Law Review, Vol.XVII,
     (1931), pp. 72-76.

Numerous short articles appear in the following magazines:
          Advertising and Selling
          Boston Conference on Retail Distribution
          Business Week
          Chain Store Age
          Chain Store Progress
          Commercial and Financial Chronicle

Interstate Grocer, St. Louis, Mo.
Magazine of Wall Street
Modern Merchant and Grocery World
National Petroleum News
Nation's Business
New York Times
Petroleum Age
Printer's Ink
Proceedings of the National Association of Commercial Organization Secretaries
Progressive Grocer
Retail Ledger
Sales Management

Government Publications
Federal Trade Commission.
Chain Store Inquiry,
"Chain-Store Advertising, 73d Congress, 2d Session, Sen. Doc. No. 84, 1934.
"Chain-Store Leaders and Loss Leaders", 72d Congress, 1st Session, Sen. Doc. No. 51, 1932.
"Chain-Store Manufacturing", 73d Congress, 1st Session, Sen. Doc. No. 13, 1933.
"Chain-Store Price Policies", 73d Congress, 2d Session, Sen. Doc. No. 85, 1934.
"Chain-Store Private Brands", 72d Congress, 2d Session, Sen. Doc. No. 142, 1933.
"Chain-Store Wages", 73d Congress, 2d Session, Sen. Doc. No. 82, 1933.
"Cooperative Drug and Hardware Chains", 72d Congress, 1st Session, Sen. Doc. No. 82, 1932.
"Cooperative Grocery Chains", 72d Congress, 1st Session, Sen. Doc. No. 12, 1932.
"Final Report on the Chain-Store Inquiry", 74th Congress, 1st Session, Sen. Doc. No. 4, 1935.
"Gross Profit and Average Sales Per Store of Retail Chains", 72d Congress, 2d Session, Sen. Doc. No. 178, 1933.
"Growth and Development of Chain Stores", 72d Congress, 1st Session, Sen. Doc. No. 100, 1932.
"Invested Capital and Rates of Return of Retail Chains", 73d Congress, 2d Session, Sen. Doc. No. 87, 1934.
"Miscellaneous Financial Results of Retail Chains", 73d Congress, 2d Session, Sen. Doc. No. 99, 1934.
"Quality of Canned Vegetables and Fruits", 72d Congress, 2d Session, Sen. Doc. No. 170, 1933.
"Prices and Margins of Chain and Independent Distributors", 73d Congress, 1st Session, Sen. Docs. Nos. 62, 69. 73d Congress, 2d Session, Sen. Docs. Nos. 81, 88, 95, 96, 97, 98, 1933 and 1934.
"Sales, Costs, and Profits of Retail Chains", 73d Congress, 1st Session, Sen. Doc. No. 40, 1933.
"Scope of the Chain-Store Inquiry", 72d Congress, 1st Session, Sen. Doc. No. 31, 1932.
"Service Features in Chain Stores", 73d Congress, 2d Session, Sen. Doc. No. 91, 1934.

"Short Weighing and Over Weighing in Chain and Independent Grocery Stores", 72d Congress, 2d Session, Sen. Doc. No. 153, 1933.

"Sizes of Stores of Retail Chains", 72d Congress, 2d Session, Sen. Doc. No. 156, 1933.

"Sources of Chain-Store Merchandise", 72d Congress, 1st Session, Sen. Doc. No. 30, 1932.

"Special Discounts and Allowances to Chain and Independent Distributors", 73d Congress, 2d Session, Sen. Docs. Nos. 86, 89, 94, 1934.

"State Distribution of Chain Stores, 1913-1928", 73d Congress, 2d Session, Sen. Doc. No. 130, 1934.

"The Chain Store in the Small Town", 73d Congress, 2d Session, Sen. Doc. No. 93, 1934.

"Wholesale Business of Retail Chains", 72d Congress, 1st Session, Sen. Doc. No. 29, 1932.

Hearings Before a Subcommittee of the Committee on Judiciary, House of Representatives, 74th Congress, 2d Session, On H. R. 4995, 8442, and 10,486, To Amend the Clayton Act Feb. 3, 4, 5, 7, 1936. 1936, Government Printing Office, Washington, D. C.

Hearings Before the Committee on Interstate and Foreign Commerce, House of Representatives, 63d Congress, 2d and 3d Sessions, On H. R. 13,315, To Prevent Discrimination in Prices, etc., Feb. 27, 1914 to Jan. 9, 1915. 1915, Government Printing Office, Washington, D. C.

Hearings Before the Committee on Interstate and Foreign Commerce, House of Representatives, 64th Congress, 2d Session, On H. R. 13,568, Regulation of Prices, Jan. 5-11, 1917. 1917, Government Printing Office, Washington, D.C.

Hearings Before the Committee on Interstate and Foreign Commerce, House of Representatives, 69th Congress, 1st Session, On H.R. 11, Price Regulation for Trade Marked Articles, Apr. 22, 23, 1926. 1926, Government Printing Office, Washington, D. C.

Hearings Before the Committee on Interstate Commerce, U. S. Senate, 72d Congress, 1st Session, On S. 97, Capper-Kelly Fair Trade Bill, Feb. 29, Mar. 1, 2, 1932. 1932 Government Printing Office, Washington, D. C.

Hearings Before the Committee on Judiciary, House of Representatives, 74th Congress, 1st Session, On H.R. 8442, H.R. 4995, H.R. 5062, To Amend the Clayton Act, July 10, 11, 17, 18, 19, 1935. 1935, Government Printing Office, Washington, D. C.

Hearings Before the Committee on Rules, House of Representatives, 71st Congress, 2d Session, on H.R. 11, Capper-Kelly Price-Fixing Bill, May 21, 1930. 1930, Government Printing Office, Washington, D. C.

Hearings Before the Special Committee to Investigate the American Retail Federation, House of Representatives, 74th Congress, 1stSession, Ju, Jl, Aug, 1935. 1935, Government Printing Office, Washington, D. C.

Recess Commission on Taxation for the State of Maine, The System of Taxation in Maine, 1934, State Document, Augusta, Maine.

United States Department of Commerce
  Bureau of Census
    <u>Fifteenth Census of the United States</u>, 1930, Distribution,
    1933, Government Printing Office, Washington, D. C.
    <u>Census of American Business</u>, 1933, 1935, Government Print-
    ing Office, Washington, D. C.
    <u>Census of Business</u>, 1935, 1937, Government Printing Office,
    Washington, D. C.
  Bureau of Foreign and Domestic Commerce
    <u>Distribution Cost Studies</u>, No. 1, Millard, J.W. "Analyzing
    Wholesale Distribution Costs", 1928, Government Printing
    Office, Washington, D. C.
    <u>Distribution Cost Studies</u>, No. 2, Bettner, G. E. "Analyzing
    Retail Selling Time", 1928, Government Printing Office,
    Washington, D. C.
    <u>Domestic Commerce Series</u>, No. 54, "Causes of Business Fail-
    ures and Bankruptcies of Individuals in New Jersey in 1929-
    1930", 1931, Government Printing Office, Washington, D. C.
    <u>Domestic Commerce Series</u>, No. 69, Sadd, V. and Williams,
    T. R. "Causes of Commercial Bankruptcies", 1932, Govern-
    ment Printing Office, Washington, D. C.
    <u>Trade Information Bulletin</u>, No. 575, Gerisn, E. F., "The
    Retailer and the Consumer in New England", 1928, Government
    Printing Office, Washington, D. C.
    <u>Trade Information Bulletin</u>, No. 627, Plummer, W. C., "Credit
    Extension and Business Failures", 1929, Government Printing
    Office, Washington, D. C.
  United States Department of Labor.
    <u>Bulletin of the Women's Bureau</u>, No. 76, M. E. Pidgeon, "Wo-
    men in 5-and-10-Cent Stores and Limited-Price Chains", 1930,
    Government Printing Office, Washington, D. C.

Cases

<u>Louis K. Liggett vs. Baldridge, et al</u>. 278 U.S. 105 (1929).
<u>State Board of Tax Commissioners vs. Jackson</u> 283 U.S. 527 (1931).
<u>Great Atlantic and Pacific Tea Company, vs. Maxwell</u>, 284 U.S. 575
  (1931), 199 N.C. 433 (1930).
<u>Great Atlantic and Pacific Tea Company vs. Morrissett et al</u>. 284
  U.S. 584 (1931)
<u>Louis K. Liggett et al. vs. Lee et al</u>. 288 U.S. 517 (1933).
<u>Fox vs. Standard Oil of New Jersey</u> 294 U.S. 87 (1935).
<u>Stewart Dry Goods vs. Lewis et al</u>. 294 U.S. 550 (1935).
<u>Valentine vs. Great Atlantic and Pacific Tea Company</u> 299 U.S. 32
  (1936)
<u>Great Atlantic and Pacific Tea Co. vs. Grosjean</u> 57 Sup. Ct. 772(1937)
<u>Great Atlantic and Pacific Tea Co. v. Doughton</u> 196 N.C. 145 (1928)
<u>Moore et al. vs. State Board of Charities and Corrections et al</u>.
  40 S.W. (2nd) 349 (1931)
<u>F. W. Woolworth Co. et al. vs. Harrison et al</u>. 42 Ga. 432 (1931)
<u>Louis K. Liggett et al. v. Amos et al</u>. 104 Fla. 609 (1932).
<u>Great Atlantic and Pacific Tea Co. vs. City of Spartanburg, S.C.</u>
  170 S.C. 262 (1933)
<u>J. C. Penney Co. v. Diefendorf</u>. 54 Idaho 374 (1934).
<u>C. F. Smith Co. vs. Fitzgerald et al</u>. 270 Mich. 259 (1935).

SMALL BUSINESS ENTERPRISE
IN AMERICA

An Arno Press Collection

Bruchey, Stuart Weems. **Robert Oliver, Merchant of Baltimore, 1783-1819.** 1956

Bunn, Verne A. **Buying and Selling A Small Business.** 1969

Bunzel, John H. **The American Small Businessman.** 1962

Carosso, Vincent P. and Stuart Bruchey, Eds. **The Survival of Small Business.** 1979

Carpenter, Walter H., Jr., and Edward Handler. **Small Business and Pattern Bargaining.** 1961

Christensen, C. Roland. **Management Succession in Small and Growing Enterprises.** 1953

Commerce Clearing House, Inc. **Small Business Investment Companies: Law, Regulations, Explanation; New Financing for Small Business.** 1959

Daughters, Charles G. **Wells of Discontent: A Study of the Economic, Social, and Political Aspects of the Chain Store.** 1937

Flink, Salomon J. **Equity Financing of Small Manufacturing Companies in New Jersey.** 1963

Glover, John Desmond. **Public Loans to Private Business** (Doctoral Dissertation, Harvard University, 1947). 1979

Haas, Harold M[ilburn]. **Social and Economic Aspects of the Chain Store Movement** (Doctoral Dissertation, University of Minnesota, 1939). 1979

Hollander, Edward D. and others. **The Future of Small Business.** 1967

Howard, Marshall Chapman. **The Marketing of Petroleum Products: A Study in the Relations Between Large and Small Business** (Doctoral Dissertation, Cornell University, 1951). 1979

Kaplan, A[braham] D.H. **Small Business: Its Place and Problems.** 1948

Konopa, Leonard Jesse. **The Methods of Operation and the Credit Accommodations of a Commercial Bank to Small Business in the Pittsburgh Area** (Doctoral Dissertation, University of Pittsburgh, 1954). 1979

Lumer, Wilfred. **Small Business at the Crossroads: A Study of the Small Business Retreat of 1953-1955.** 1956

McGee, John S[eneca]. **The Robinson-Patman Act and Effective Competition** (Doctoral Dissertation, Vanderbilt University, 1952). 1979

Merwin, Charles L. **Financing Small Corporations in Five Manufacturing Industries, 1926-36.** 1942

Morris, Bruce Robert. **The Economics of the Special Taxation of Chain Stores** (Doctoral Dissertation, University of Illinois, 1937). 1979

Neifeld, M[orris] R. **Cooperative Consumer Credit: With Special Reference to Credit Unions.** 1936

Pepper, Roger S. **Pressure Groups Among "Small Business Men"** (M.A. Thesis, Columbia University, 1940). 1979

Proxmire, William. **Can Small Business Survive?** 1964

Richards, Max Devoe. **Intermediate and Long-Term Credit for Small Corporations** (Doctoral Dissertation, University of Illinois, 1955). 1979

Schor, Stanley S. **The Capital Product Ratio and Size of Establishment for Manufacturing Industries** (Doctoral Dissertation, University of Pennsylvania, 1952). 1979

Still, Jack W. **A Guide to Managerial Accounting in Small Companies.** 1969

Tosiello, Rosario Joseph. **The Birth and Early Years of the Bell Telephone System, 1876-1880** (Doctoral Dissertation, Boston University, 1971). 1979

United States House of Representatives, Select Committee on Small Business. **Effects of Foreign Oil Imports on Independent Domestic Procedures: Hearings...Eighty-First Congress, Second Session Pursuant to H. Res. 22, a Resolution Creating a Select Committee to Conduct a Study and Investigation of Problems of Small Business, Part 3.** 1950

United States House of Representatives, Subcommittee No. 1 of the Select Committee on Small Business. **Monopolistic and Unfair Trade Practices: Hearings...Eightieth Congress, Second Session on the Matter of Problems of Small Business Resulting from Monopolistic and Unfair Trade Practices.** Two Volumes. 1949

United States House of Representatives, Subcommittee No. 1 of the Select Committee on Small Business. **Organization and Operation of the Small Business Administration: Hearings...Eighty-Sixth Congress, First Session Pursuant to H. Res. 51, a Resolution Creating a Select Committee to Conduct a Study and Investigation of the Problems of Small Business, Parts I & II.** 1959

United States House of Representatives, Subcommittee No. 1 of the Select Committee on Small Business. **The Organization and Procedures of the Federal Regulatory Commissions and Agencies and Their Effect on Small Business: Hearings...Eighty-Fourth Congress First and Second Sessions Pursuant to H. Res. 114, a Resolution Creating a Select Committee to Conduct a Study and Investigation of the Problems of Small Business, Parts 1-5, Federal Trade Commission.** 1956

United States House of Representatives, Select Committee on Small Business. **Problems of Small-Business Financing: A Report...Eighty-Fifth Congress, Second Session Pursuant to H. Res. 56, a Resolution Creating a Select Committee to Conduct a Study and Investigation of the Problems of Small Business.** 1958

United States House of Representatives, Select Committee on Small Business. **Problems of Small-Business Financing: Hearings...Eighty-Fifth Congress, First and Second Sessions Pursuant to H. Res. 56, a Resolution Creating a Select Committee to Conduct a Study and Investigation of the Problems of Small Business, Part I & II.** 1958

United States House of Representatives, Subcommittee No. 4 on Distribution Problems Affecting Small Business, Select Committee on Small Business. **Small Business Problems in Urban Areas: Hearings...Eighty-Eighth Congress, Second Session Pursuant to H. Res. 13, a Resolution Creating a Select Committee to Conduct Studies and Investigations of the Problems of Small Business.** 1965

United States House of Representatives, Select Committee on Small Business. **Status of Small Business in Retail Trade (1948-1958): Staff Report...Eighty-Sixth Congress, Second Session.** 1960

United States Senate, Subcommittee of the Committee on Banking and Currency. **Credit Needs of Small Business: Hearings...Eighty-Fifth Congress, First Session on Various Bills to Amend the Small Business Act of 1953, As Amended.** 1957

United States Senate, Subcommittee on Monopoly of the Select Committee on Small Business. **Foreign Legislation Concerning Monopoly and Cartel Practices: Report of the Department of State...Eighty-Second Congress, Second Session.** 1952

University of Pittsburgh, Bureau of Business Research. **Small Business Bibliography.** 1955

Vatter, Harold G. **Small Enterprise and Oliogopoly: A Study of the Butter, Flour, Automobile, and Glass Container Industries.** 1955

Vatter, Paul A. **The Structure of Retail Trade by Size of Store: An Analysis of 1948 Census Data** (Doctoral Dissertation, University of Pennsylvania, 1953). 1979

Weissman, Rudolph L. **Small Business and Venture Capital: An Economic Program.** 1945

Zeigler, Harmon. **The Politics of Small Business.** 1961